QUANTITATIVE LATIN AMERICAN STUDIES

UCLA Latin American Center Publications

Statistical Abstract of Latin America Supplement Series

JAMES W. WILKIE
Series editor

Teresa Joseph
Production editor

Colleen H. Trujillo
Production assistant

Advisory Board

Herbert S. Klein
Columbia University

Frank R. Safford
Northwestern University

John V. Lombardi
Indiana University

John J. TePaske
Duke University

Hans-Jürgen Puhle
Universität Münster

Joseph S. Tulchin
University of North Carolina

UCLA Latin American Center Statistical and Computer Support Committee

Bruce H. Herrick (*Economics*)

James Ward Keesling (*Education*)

Luis Laosa (*Education*)

Dwight Read (*Anthropology*)

Thomas S. Weisner (*Anthropology and Psychology*)

STATISTICAL ABSTRACT OF LATIN AMERICA SUPPLEMENT SERIES

Volume

1   **CUBA 1968.** C. Paul Roberts and Mukhtar Hamour, eds. 1970.
2   **LATIN AMERICAN POLITICAL STATISTICS.** Kenneth Ruddle and Philip Gillette, eds.
3   **STATISTICS AND NATIONAL POLICY.** James W. Wilkie. 1974.
4   **URBANIZATION IN 19th-CENTURY LATIN AMERICA.** Richard E. Boyer and Keith A. Davies. 1973.
5   **MEASURING LAND REFORM.** James W. Wilkie. 1974.
6   **QUANTITATIVE LATIN AMERICAN STUDIES: METHODS AND FINDINGS.** James W. Wilkie and Kenneth Ruddle, eds. 1977.
7   **MONEY AND POLITICS IN LATIN AMERICA.** James W. Wilkie, ed. Forthcoming, 1977.
8   **THE NARROWING SOCIAL GAP: LATIN AMERICAN AND THE UNITED STATES, 1940-1970.** James W. Wilkie. Forthcoming.
9   **LATIN AMERICA IN MAPS AND CARTOGRAMS.** Richard W. Wilkie. Forthcoming.

The purpose of the Statistical Abstract of Latin America Supplement Series is to offer longitudinal statistics, scholarly interpretation, and cartographic analysis of data published in the Statistical Abstract of Latin America Series published annually. There is no correlation between the volume numbers or years of the two series.

Volume 1, developed in cooperation with the Cuban government, presents detailed statistics for Cuba in the 1960s.

Volume 2 gives comprehensive Latin American presidential and congressional election data since about 1940, with a chronology of political events and an index of politicians.

Volume 3 offers the theoretical basis for UCLA's Statistical Abstract of Latin America Series and Constructs an analytical framework for investigating alternative sets of time-series data. It gives longitudinal data on the following topics for each of the twenty Latin American countries: population since 1900, educational enrollments since 1930, food and agricultural production since 1952, energy supplies since 1929, inflation since 1929, exchange rates since 1915, balance of payments since 1956, exports and imports since 1916, major trading partners since 1915, agricultural trade since 1935, U.S. investment since 1897, U.S. assistance since 1946, and national economic change since 1950. Case studies show use of data for Bolivia, Chile, Costa Rica, Mexico, Venezuela, and U.S. relations with Latin America.

Volume 4 deals with the growth of cities in Argentina, Brazil, Mexico, and Peru, presenting an exhaustive search of sources and critical comparison of population assessments from the nineteenth century.

Volume 5 gives the first "hard data" available for land reform in all Latin America, and specifically tests and applies concepts for assessment of the major cases of Bolivian and Venezuelan programs of land redistribution. Contains graphs, cartograms, and photos.

Volume 6 contains the following studies: "Employment and Lack of Employment in Mexico, 1900-70," by Donald B. Keesing; "Losers in Mexican Politics: A Comparative Study of Official Party Precandidates for Gubernatorial Elections, 1970-75," by Roderic Ai Camp; "An Index of Cuban Industrial Output, 1930-58; "Projecting the HEC (Health Education, and Communication) Index for Latin America Back to 1940," by James W. Wilkie and Maj-Britt Nilsson; and "Research Perspectives on the Revised Fitzgibbon-Johnson Index of the Image of Political Democracy in Latin America, 1945-75," by Kenneth F. Johnson.

Volume 7 treats the relationship of money and politics with two studies of explicit governmental budgeting and an analysis of implicit public budgeting involved in private corporate growth. Thus, Enrique A. Baloyra writes on "Democratic Versus Dictatorial Budgeting: The Case of Cuba with Reference to Venezuela and Mexico." James A. Hanson examines "Federal Expenditures and 'Personalism' in the Mexican 'Institutional' Revolution." And David K. Eiteman writes on "Financing Industrial Corporate Development in the Aftermath of the First Perón Period."

Volume 8 tests the idea of the "widening gap" between the underdeveloped and developed worlds. Wilkie's "HEC Index" shows that in social terms of health, education, and communication the gap between Latin America and the United States narrowed dramatically between 1940 and 1970. In showing the fallacy of logic in the widening gap theory, Wilkie argues that logically we should have hypothesized that the social gap would have to narrow rather than widen. The HEC Index also is used to rank the Latin American countries in social relation to each other in 1940, 1950, 1960, and 1970.

In Volume 9 Latin American population data are presented in maps and cartograms to show graphically size and space relationships for the Latin American region, with population clusters also set against the physical scene. A special case study of Mexican data reveals changing contours of rural life in 1910, 1930, 1950, and 1970, and includes cartograms of change of village and dispersed populations between 1960 and 1970.

QUANTITATIVE LATIN AMERICAN STUDIES
Methods and Findings

Statistical Abstract of Latin America Supplement 6

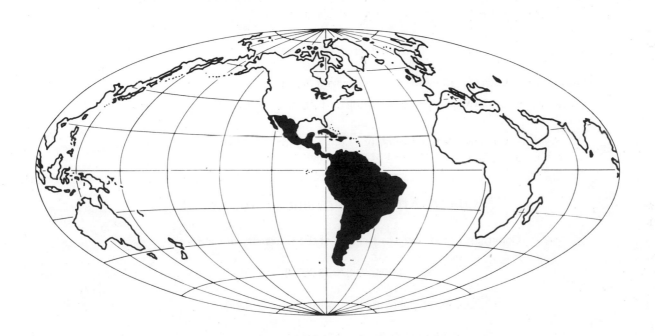

Edited by

JAMES W. WILKIE

KENNETH RUDDLE

UCLA Latin American Center Publications

UNIVERSITY OF CALIFORNIA   •   LOS ANGELES   •   1977

Note on volume numbers

There is no correlation between the volume number or year of the Statistical Abstract of Latin America Series and the Supplement Series.

Full citation

James W. Wilkie and Kenneth Ruddle, eds., *Quantitative Latin American Studies: Methods and Findings,* Statistical Abstract of Latin America Supplement 6 (Los Angeles, UCLA Latin American Center Publications, University of California, 1977).

Short citation

James W. Wilkie and Kenneth Ruddle, eds., *Quantitative Latin American Studies* (Los Angeles: UCLA Latin American Center Publications, 1977).

Library cross references

Statistical Abstract of Latin America, Supplement Series

University of California, Los Angeles. Statistical Abstract of Latin America, Supplement Series

UCLA Latin American Center (formerly "Committee on" and "Center of" Latin American Studies), Statistical Abstract of Latin America

---

QUANTITATIVE LATIN AMERICAN STUDIES

Copyright © 1977 by The Regents of the University of California

ISBN: 0-87903-227-8

Library of Congress Catalog Number: 77-620011

Printed in the United States of America

To

ROBERT N. BURR

Founder of the Statistical Abstract of Latin America

Contents

Tables   viii

Figures   x

Symbols Used in Tables   xi

Foreword by James W. Wilkie   xii

Part One   MEXICO

1   Employment and Lack of Employment in Mexico, 1900-70   3
     Donald B. Keesing
      World Bank

2   Losers in Mexican Politics: A Comparative Study of Official
Party Precandidates for Gubernatorial Elections, 1970-75   23
     Roderic Ai Camp
      Central College

Part Two   CUBA

3   An Index of Cuban Industrial Output, 1930-58   37
     Jorge F. Pérez-López
      U.S. Bureau of Labor Statistics

Part Three   LATIN AMERICA

4   Projecting the HEC (Health, Education, and Communication)
Index for Latin America Back to 1940   75
     James W. Wilkie and Maj-Britt Nilsson
      University of California, Los Angeles

5   Research Perspectives on the Revised Fitzgibbon-Johnson
Index of the Image of Political Democracy In Latin
America, 1945-75   87
     Kenneth F. Johnson
      University of Missouri, St. Louis

About the Contributors   92

Tables

1-1	Mexican Unemployment in the Years 1931 to 1940	5
1-2	Some Key Magnitude and Percentage Relationships for Mexican Population and Labor Force in Successive Censuses	11
1-3	Participation Rates in the Mexican Censuses from 1895 to 1970	12
1-4	Males and Females in the Mexican Labor Force Compared with the Male and Female Population 15 Years and Over in Censuses from 1895 to 1970	13
1-5	Economic Status of the Mexican Population 12 Years Old and Over in 1970 Compared with 1950	14
1-6	Mexican Labor Force by Sector Based on Census Data at Intervals from 1900 to 1969	14
1-7	Average Annual Growth Rates of Mexican Output per Worker by Sector in Four Periods	15
2-1	Career Path Percentages of Mexican Official Party Losers and Winners and Previous Governors, 1973-75	24
2-2	Six States Represented by a Winning Candidate without High-Level Political Experience in Mexico	25
2-3	Educational Backgrounds of Losing and Winning Candidates for Mexican Gubernatorial Nominations, 1973-75	26
2-4	Importance of Political Factors, Camarillas, and Previous Career Experience in Mexican Gubernatorial Candidate Selection, 1973-75	27
3-1	Time Interval Covered by Industrial Output Index for Selected Countries in the Current Literature	39
3-2	Summary of Cuban Products Covered in the Calculated Index	41
3-3	Product Coverage of the Calculated Index for Cuba	42
3-4	Participation of Product Sample in Total Cuban Industrial Production, 1953	44
3-5	Gross Value-Added Weights for Some Sectors and Subsectors of Cuban Industrial Production, 1953	49
3-6	Cuban Production, Prices, and Estimated Value of Raw Sugar, 1930-58	51
3-7	Calculated Indexes of Cuban Industrial Production, 1930-58	52
3-8	Rates of Growth of Calculated Indexes of Cuban Industrial Production, 1930-58	52
3-9	Calculated Indexes of Sectors of Cuban Nonsugar Industrial Production, 1930-58	53
3-10	Rates of Growth of Calculated Indexes of Sectors of Cuban Nonsugar Industrial Production, 1930-58	53
3-11	Growth Rate of the Calculated Index of Industrial Output in Cuba, 1930-58	54
3-12	Rate of Growth of the Industrial Sector in Selected Latin American Countries, 1948-58	55
3-13	Banco Nacional de Cuba Index and Calculated Industrial Output Index for the Cuban Economy, 1946-58	57

3-14   Banco Nacional de Cuba Index (1) and Calculated Industrial
        Output Index (2) for Some Sectors of the Cuban Economy,
        1946-58   57

4-1   Health, Education, and Communication (HEC) Index for Latin
        America, 1940-70   76
4-2   HEC Item 1: Life Expectancy at Birth in Latin America and the
        United States, 1930 and 1940   78
4-3   HEC Items 2, 3, and 4: Infant Mortality Rate, Persons per Hospital
        Bed, and Persons per Physician in Latin America and the United
        States, 1940   79
4-4   HEC Item 5: Persons per Dentist in Latin America and the United
        States, 1940   80
4-5   HEC Item 6: Literate Population Age 15 and Over in Latin America
        and the United States, 1940   81
4-6   HEC Items 7, 8, and 9: School-Age Population (7-14 and 13-18)
        Enrolled in School, and Higher School Enrollment as a Share
        of Primary Enrollment in Latin America and the United States,
        1940   82
4-7   Educational Enrollments in Latin America and the United States,
        1940   83
4-8   HEC Item 10: Newspaper Circulation in Latin America and the
        United States, 1930 and 1940   83
4-9   HEC Item 11: Number of Telephones per 100 Persons in Latin
        America and the United States, 1940   84
4-10   HEC Item 12: Number of Persons per Motor Vehicle in Use in
        Latin America and the United States, 1930 and 1940   84

5-1   Original Fitzgibbon-Johnson Index: U.S. View of Democracy in
        Latin America, 1945-75   88
5-2   Revised Fitzgibbon-Johnson Index: U.S. View of Democracy in
        Latin America, 1945-75: Five Key Criteria   89

Figures

3-1   Calculated Indexes of Cuban Industrial Production, 1930-58   51

3-2   Calculated Indexes of Sectors of Cuban Nonsugar Industrial Production, 1930-58   53

3-3   Banco Nacional de Cuba Index and Calculated Industrial Output Index for the Cuban Economy, 1946-58   57

3-4   Comparison of Banco Nacional de Cuba Index and Calculated Mining Production Index for the Cuban Economy, 1946-58   57

3-5   Comparison of Banco Nacional de Cuba Index and Calculated Electricity and Gas Production Index for the Cuban Economy, 1946-58   58

3-6   Comparison of Banco Nacional de Cuba Index and Calculated Nonsugar Manufacturing Production Index for the Cuban Economy, 1946-58   58

Symbols Used in Tables

~	Not available
#	0
*	Not applicable
**	Tie ranking
- - -	No production
C$	Cuban pesos
$	U.S. dollars

Foreword

James W. Wilkie

Although the studies in this volume are not directly related to one another in that they deal with diverse economic, political, and social aspects of Mexico, Cuba, and Latin America, they have a common denominator in that they expand our knowledge about methods and findings in quantitative Latin American Studies. We are concerned here with examining complexity in the meaning of data in order that it have deeper meaning in its *qualitative* as well as quantitative dimension. A predominant theme in the studies suggests that new interpretation in the social sciences involves assessment of qualities as they intermesh with quantities in time dimension. Thus, analysis that concentrates on only one of two dimensions of quality, quantity, and time may obscure our perspective on the affairs of mankind.

If we are now well past the stage where it was necessary to justify the need for quantitative analysis in the various scholarly disciplines, the increasing sophistication of quantitative practitioners and acceptance by nonpractitioners have led to a paradox. Statistical studies are used to "prove" revisionist interpretations or to suggest alternative hypotheses. Yet the suspicion exists among many scholars that quantitative analysis enables practitioners to play elegant games in their never ending search for a yet newer computer program to present the results with more sophistication. Nonpractitioners who formerly resisted quantitative study have come to recognize and support it, even if they admit that they do not understand it and remain skeptical of its methods and findings. Practitioners debate whether statistical treatments and weights assigned to data are "right" or "wrong."

Our paradox has been aggravated by the fact that recent publications about quantitative studies have tended to stress the ways data can be quantitatively manipulated instead of analyzing the quality of statistics under consideration.[1] An exception to this tendency is the analysis "Lies, Damn Lies, and Argentine GDP," by Laura Randall,[2] who shows how five different estimates of Argentine real gross domestic product yield different gauges of the success or failure of Perón's first government set in a time-series perspective ranging from the 1930s to the 1960s. Yet after an excellent summary of methodology in each of the time-series estimates, she wonders which estimate is "correct." Unfortunately her tongue-in-cheek answer may lead one to believe that one estimate (showing Perón to have been much more successful than previously thought) can be demonstrated to be "correct" also by a qualitative assessment (that Perón's support was based not upon "mindless and stomachless charisma" but upon his success in industrial policy translated into better living conditions). The problem here is that the quantitative estimates of Argentine manufacturing growth rate analyzed ably by Randall are not qualitatively (or quantitatively) related to production of food except in an indirect way — agricultural production actually suffered at the expense of industrial growth. Nevertheless, Randall helps us to understand how the estimates were made in order to analyze their meaning and to know how the choice of a base year affects the results. After assessing the limits of all estimates Randall implicitly suggests that the "truth" is not easily ascertainable: whereas it is desirable, for example, to use 1943 and not 1960 as a base year for calculations in order not to overassess the importance of branches of production that were virtually nonexistent between 1945 and 1958, neither the series based on 1943 nor the series based on 1960 is adjusted for changes in the quality of products.

To conclude that there is no "correct" answer seems to discourage an appreciation of statistics rather than to promote an appreciation of our enhanced understanding of the societal processes at work in all their glorious complexity. After all, where would scholars be if matters were simple and they had nothing to explain!

How can data be quantitatively analyzed for meaning? How can they be qualitatively assessed with observations directly appropriate to the case? How can we use partial or questionable data and still arrive at useful conclusions? These are problems addressed by the studies herein.

---

[1] E.g., Roberts S. Byars and Joseph L. Love, eds., *Quantitative Social Science Research on Latin America* (Urbana: University of Illinois Press, 1973); but see the article by Alejandro Portes on "Sociology and the Use of Secondary Data," in ibid., pp. 208-261.

[2] *Latin American Research Review* 11:1 (1976), pp. 137-158.

Donald B. Keesing tests reliability and meaning in the Mexican population censuses since 1900 in order to question a qualitative view that unemployment has been an extremely serious problem in that country. Moreover, he suggests that by keeping minimum wages relatively low in relation to other factors in economic production, Mexico has encouraged employment, in contrast with the situation in the United States where relatively high minimum wages have priced employees out of the labor market. Keesing stresses the high unemployment rates for women, which I explored in an earlier research (Wilkie, 1971). His study shows how, through an examination of internal consistency from census to census we can begin to understand the meaning of employment, unemployment, and underemployment in a developing country like Mexico. Implications for governmental policy are numerous and should be heeded if data collection on employment is to improve. By enmeshing us in the details of census materials, Keesing forces us to reshape our thinking on unemployment, a major problem in the social history of our time.

To shift the approach to Mexican politics, Roderic Camp asks us to consider losers as opposed to winners within the Mexican one-party system of government. Camp shows us that the official party of the Mexican Revolution (PRI) is not as monolithic as reputed. Implicit in his research is the conclusion that, given the growing number and increasingly high qualifications of members of the PRI who aspire to governorship, coupled with the relatively fixed number of high government posts, the official party will be hard-pressed to contain internal strife. Although we can see in Camp's case studies the logic of past PRI choices for governor, we cannot forecast events because, as Camp shows, circumstance dictates choice among equally qualified people. Camp's data compiled and scored quantitatively on a qualitative basis demonstrates that incomplete data can be organized to show that the policy was not irrational as so often suspected because of the secrecy in the PRI selection of each gubernatorial nominee from among many competing precandidates. His systematic organization of factors involved in personnel choice within the PRI would not be credible without time-series data, and it would not be understandable without juxtaposition of qualitative elements limiting "personalism" in Mexican politics.

Turning from Mexico to Cuba, we find in Jorge Pérez López's study a method for testing the rate of industrial growth in the pre-Castro era back to 1930. This study satisfies a need for a relatively nontechnical discussion of how indexes are prepared to acquaint the nonspecialist with the limits and uses of statistics. His findings dispel some of our doubts about the reliability of government economic statistics that may have suffered political tampering. Ostensibly the problem is simple: what was the real rate of economic growth before 1959? By calculating his own index of industrial output, Dr. Pérez-López offers an independent test of official figures, his data testing the traditional Bank of Cuba figures for which no methodology was ever published. His calculated index (based upon examination of methods, coverage, and limits of raw data developed and computed here) indicates an appreciably faster rate of growth for the industrial sector of the Cuban economy (particularly in nonsugar activities) during 1930-58 than has previously been suggested in the literature. The implications suggest that a reevaluation needs to be made of the factors involved in Castro's rise to power in 1959.

Two of the studies announced for publication in this volume have been rescheduled. Mine on the narrowing social gap between Latin America and the United States covering the years 1950 to 1970 will now appear as a separate publication in a much expanded form.[3] In its place Maj-Britt Nilsson and I have developed a technical study projecting the Health, Education, and Communication (HEC) Index back to 1940. Kenneth F. Johnson's data on democracy has been published in the Statistical Abstract of Latin America Series.[4] Professor Johnson here brings his date up through 1975 and separates out the Latin America view of democracy added in 1970 in order to maintain consistency of the Fitzgibbon-Johnson Index going back to 1945.

We do not seek definitive answers to the questions raised in the studies herein but argue that the methods of understanding of data presented offer possibilities for several types of investigation such as factor and regression analysis (e.g., see the "Methodological Appendix" in Chapter 4).

Although Pierre Chaunu has attempted to distinguish between "serial" statistics and what he calls true "quantitative" analysis apparently on the grounds that the preparation of descriptive serial statistics differs radically from applying inductive principles to descriptive data,[5] his distinction has not been generally accepted for several reasons. First, there is not always a clear line between descriptive and inductive statistics because the former may involve more than simply compiling data on a year-to-year basis; it may require conceptual adjustment, scoring, ranking, and other operations. Second, inductive methods may be used to predict missing data needed to fill in breaks in any given time series. Third, "quantitative analysis" requires more than application of classical mathematical techniques to search for substructural patterns otherwise not apparent, as is shown in the classic definition developed in the field of chemistry where the term means simply to determine the amounts and proportions of constituent parts of a whole.

In contrast with Chaunu, my own view has been to refine the definition of "quantitative studies" rather than to limit its meaning. In my view quantitative analysis encom-

[3] The Narrowing Social Gap: Latin America and the United States, 1940-1970, Statistical Abstract of Latin America Supplement 8 (Los Angeles: UCLA Latin America Center Publications, University of California, forthcoming.

[4] For Kenneth F. Johnson's study, see his "Measuring the Scholarly Image of Latin American Democracy, 1945-1970," in James W. Wilkie and Paul Turovsky, eds., Statistical Abstract of Latin America, Volume 17 (Los Angeles: UCLA Latin American Center Publications, University of California, 1976), pp. 347-365.

[5] See Pierre Chaunu "L'Histoire Sérielle . . ." Revue Historique (Paris) 243 (1970), pp. 297-320.

passes both classificatory (or descriptive) statistics and predictive (or inductive) statistics. To quote from my *Statistics and National Policy*:

> The relationship of classificatory to [predictive] statistics is not always clear-cut. On the one hand, the descriptive statistics provide the raw data necessary for inductive analysis. On the other hand, when, for example, there are problems or gaps in descriptive data, inductive statistics may be utilized to test meaning or fill the gaps. And either type of quantitative analysis may involve the study of historical data for one moment in time or for a time series.[6]

The studies in this volume are intended to illustrate this definition.

Berkeley, California
December 1976

[6] Statistical Abstract of Latin American Supplement 3 (Los Angeles: UCLA Latin American Center Publications, University of California, 1974), pp. 6-7.

Part One

MEXICO

Chapter 1

Employment and Lack of Employment in Mexico, 1900-70

Donald B. Keesing

World Bank

1. Introduction

In Mexico as in many developing countries there is now much public concern about the so-called employment problem. It is widely asserted that Mexico suffers from substantial rates of unemployment together with underemployment (or disguised unemployment) on an enormous scale. These assertions are often linked to suggestions that the problem worsens with time.

This study examines available evidence on the employment problem in Mexico up to 1970. Historical and recent data are explored in search of a clearer understanding of the nature and dimensions of the problem, underlying causes, and long-term trends, not only in employment and unemployment but also in participation rates, labor displacement and other related phenomena. Alternative interpretations of the same data, and questions of how to utilize the available evidence, raise a rich variety of methodological as well as substantive issues.

The principal data sources are the Mexican population censuses taken at roughly ten-year intervals from 1900 to 1970. Attention is also given to a statistical series on average monthly employment and unemployment from 1931 to 1940. Apart from this one series, relying on the population censuses is mandatory. The censuses are practically the only other source of data on employment and the labor force

prior to the 1960s. And for lack of other sources of information, the 1970 population census is the main source of statistical data on the employment problem in Mexico in recent years.[1] There is no unemployment compensation or registration scheme; no regular data have been collected on unemployment or underemployment since 1940; and new sample surveys aimed at shedding light on the employment problem were still in the planning and pilot-study stage when this study was completed.[2]

The population census evidence is far from ideal. Census figures on the census labor force are not always reliable, and until 1970 the censuses did not place much emphasis on unemployment. Data collected, concepts, categories, and statistics actually published have varied widely from one census

This study was written before the author joined the World Bank and does not necessarily reflect views of that organization. The research from which this study is distilled was financed by grants from the Social Science Research Council, the Committees on International Studies and Latin American Studies of Stanford University, and the Center for Development Economics of Williams College. Their support is gratefully acknowledged. The study benefited greatly from comments on an earlier version in faculty seminars at Williams College and the University of Western Ontario. It was originally prepared as Research Memorandum No. 64, Center for Development Economics, Williams College, Williamstown, Mass. March 1975.

[1] A small number of nationwide sample surveys have been made in Mexico since the late 1950s, focused on special subjects such as consumption patterns. Some of these surveys contain auxiliary evidence on such matters as participation rates and labor-force occupations, but none touches employment more than superficially. Labor force data in censuses other than the population census, such as the regular censuses of agriculture, industry, commerce, and services, appear extremely unreliable, largely as a result of the difficulties of sampling small establishments. By way of example, for the year 1960 the industrial census showed about half as many workers in manufacturing as the population census, while the censuses of agriculture and related activities showed two million more workers than the population census. Such biases are not consistent; the immediately preceding industrial and agricultural censuses erred in precisely opposite directions.

[2] These surveys were undertaken in the Dirección General de Estadística (then headed by Rubén Gleason Galicia) by a team initially under the direction of Clara Júsidman de Bialostozky. In 1975 and 1976 the first results, limited to the three largest cities, showed unemployment rates in the order of 6.5 to 7 percent with no clear time trend, according to information received verbally just before this study went to press. These rates appear to have been similar to those for Monterrey in 1963 and 1964 according to Universidad de Nuevo León (1964), which is discussed later below.

to the next. In consequence, the evidence must be pieced together in the manner of a detective solving a puzzle.

Increased concern over employment in Mexico in recent years reflects a sharp rise in worldwide concern over employment in developing countries. A chorus of alarm has been raised over this problem by international agencies such as the World Bank, International Labour Office, and Organization for Economic Cooperation and Development, major foundations including the Ford and Rockefeller Foundations, and scholarly conferences.

The evidence from Mexico is of interest not only to students of Mexico's economy and history but also to development specialists concerned with the worldwide problem. This study fills a gap since little research has been done to explore the historical origins of the employment problem in developing countries, and almost no information has been assembled on employment trends in these countries prior to World War II.

Mexico offers an illuminating case from the point of view of worldwide study of employment in developing countries for two special reasons. The first is that the country had until the 1970's a relatively undistorted price structure, compared with the highly distorted price incentives that may be contributing to unemployment in some other developing countries.[3] (To be sure, Mexico's prices have never been free of distortions caused by government intervention, but this is a relative matter.) The second reason is that Mexico has achieved a rather impressive growth record for several decades, and in the process has gone through major structural changes in employment so that by 1970 agriculture employed only about 40 percent of the labor force compared with nearly 70 percent in 1930. Both considerations could be taken to mean that Mexico's employment problem should not have been as severe as in some other developing countries.

This is not the place to discuss worldwide evidence on the employment problem in developing countries, which has been analyzed in detail elsewhere,[4] but in approaching the Mexican evidence it is important to point out that the evidence of a growing worldwide problem is not nearly as general or clearcut as the recent chorus of alarm might imply. True, one does find clear evidence of serious open unemployment in a considerable number of developing countries, especially in their urban centers; and in a number of places it can be shown that unemployment rates have climbed sharply over the last decade or two. But elsewhere, notably in East Asian countries, unemployment has unquestionably diminished. Meanwhile, in a majority of developing countries there is practically no direct evidence on the subject, and little indication that open unemployment has become a major problem.

There is strong reason, moreover, to suspect that throughout the developing countries the more fundamental problem is large masses of people with very low incomes. This is especially true since very poor people cannot afford to be unemployed in the absence of public assistance schemes. Foundations and international agencies prefer to regard the all-too-obvious problem of mass poverty as a challenge to create larger numbers of productive jobs, to limit population growth, and to increase food output. Such an approach sidesteps controversial issues surrounding the redistribution of income, wealth, property ownership, and social services.

In Mexico there has been a glaring problem of unequal income distribution for centuries; and this problem persists even after a succession of avowedly revolutionary governments. Mexicans and their governments have discussed for a long time the circumstance that masses of Mexicans still live in grinding poverty. Now that a new way of looking at these problems in terms of employment has become fashionable in influential circles abroad, it may become attractive to many people in Mexico to redefine the problem of persistent poverty in Mexico by discussing underemployment and low labor productivity in different sectors, thus drawing attention away from questions of ownership, income streams, and redistribution. Yet, anyone familiar with the vague and nearly circular definitions of "underemployment" that one finds in the literature of economics can readily imagine that much of the supposed employment problem in Mexico (and elsewhere) today is simply the old problem of low incomes and unequal income distribution dressed up in a new guise.

The present study concentrates on parts of the employment issue that are not simply the problems of poverty and income distribution in disguise. Only passing attention is given to evidence on "underemployment" or "disguised unemployment" based on income distribution and poverty; and the treatment emphasizes the ambiguity of this evidence. Attention is centered instead on evidence that jobs have been scarce, workers have been displaced in large numbers by technological change, and people have dropped out of the labor force in large numbers because they were unable to find acceptable jobs. At the same time, the limited evidence is scanned for clues as to the nature, causes and extent of open unemployment.

Clearly the problems of employment and income distribution overlap, even if low incomes are not considered an automatic sign of "underemployment." Unemployment affects income distribution directly. Perhaps even more important, superabundance of ordinary or unskilled labor in a market system leads to low wages and low incomes for large numbers of people. This shifts income toward the owners of

---

[3] For evidence on this point, see especially Little, Scitovsky and Scott (1970) and Balassa (1971): the point is discussed further in section 6 below.

[4] For surveys of the literature and evidence, see Turnham (1971), Morawetz (1974), Bruton (1974), and Edwards (1974). For a dissenting view on the problem in Latin America, see Ramos (1970), who argues that labor absorption there is proceeding as one would expect, and that rising real wages signal a healthy trend toward increasing labor scarcity. This interpretation is vulnerable, of course, to the extent that wage trends may be caused by changing power relationships or social *mores* rather than labor scarcity. For a more alarmist view on Latin America, see, for example, Prebisch (1970).

other, complementary factors or resources including property of various kinds. These common roots are explored here only in passing.

It is not expected that this study can yield a definitive history of the employment problem in Mexico. Some of the available evidence is ambiguous. Desirable information is missing, and some of the questions raised do not admit clear answers. But hopefully the findings give a reasonably objective picture of the true extent of the problem and the ambiguities of the evidence now available.

2. Direct Evidence on Open Unemployment

All Mexican figures on open unemployment, even those of the 1970 population census, must be taken with caution. Evidence from other countries — especially those in which censuses and employment surveys have been taken at times not far apart — suggests that national population censuses are not a reliable guide to the magnitude of open unemployment. Depending on the precise sequence of questions asked, a census may seriously underestimate unemployment that would stand revealed by alternative definitions and sequences of questions.[5] More generally, there may be no "true" rate of unemployment when people would work under some sets of conditions but not under others; the rate does literally depend on the questions asked.

Unemployment does not seem to have been perceived as a significant social problem in Mexico until the twentieth century, and there seems to be no statistical evidence of significant unemployment there before the 1930s. Yet if figures published several years later are reliable, one of the highest national unemployment rates ever recorded in Mexico — 5.5 percent — occurred during the Great Depression in 1931. This is the first year for which any unemployment figure is available. In light of this figure, one cannot reject the possibility that the country may have suffered significant unemployment in earlier years.

The population censuses contain little evidence on unemployment until 1940. Before 1921 there seems to be no evidence whatever. In the 1921 census the detailed occupational breakdown of the labor force includes a category, "persons temporarily without occupation," containing 10,886 people (.2 percent of the labor force), where the word "occupation" (*ocupación*) can as well be translated "employment"; but clearly this was merely unemployment that happened to be recorded as a byproduct of looking for people's regular occupations.[6]

The 1930 census included a residual category in the regular industry and occupational breakdown of the labor force, *personas sin ocupación,* "persons without occupation

or employment," equal to 1.2 percent of the labor force, but it is doubtful that this category can be fully equated with open unemployment.[7]

Then during the Depression the Mexican statistical authorities constructed a series of estimates of unemployed workers relative to economically active population, which were published in the 1938 and 1940 statistical yearbooks. The precise derivation of the estimates is not wholly clear.[8] Pending research on this subject, the statistics must be regarded with reservations, especially since it is not uncommon in Mexico to publish misleading retrospective data that magnify recent accomplishments.

As Table 1-1 shows, unemployment is supposed to have peaked at 6.5 percent in 1932 and then fallen to between 3 and 4 percent a year from 1935 to 1940, during the administration of President Lázaro Cárdenas. This series seems consistent with the sharp decline in output that took place in the early 1930s, followed by a recovery in the mid-30s. It is not clear, however, whether the statistical authorities had the capability to derive such a series by fully legitimate means, and it should be noted that the 1940 figure for the monthly average of the economically active

Table 1-1
MEXICAN UNEMPLOYMENT IN THE YEARS 1931 TO 1940

Year	Unemployed (monthly average)	Economically active population	Percent unemployed
1931	287,462	5,188,245	5.5
1932	339,378	5,238,124	6.5
1933	275,774	5,307,090	5.2
1934	234,538	5,386,192	4.4
1935	191,371	5,428,121	3.5
1936	186,904	5,482,307	3.4
1937	180,128	5,573,809	3.2
1938	209,332	5,649,142	3.7
1939	198,593	5,787,109	3.4
1940	184,247	5,858,116	3.1

SOURCE: Wilkie (1971, Table 4), based in turn on Dirección General de Estadística (1939, p. 158; 1941, p. 431).

---

[5] See, for example, Turnham (1971).

[6] These people included 9,120 men and 1,766 women. Larger numbers, 55,471 men and 102,969 women, were reported "without occupation, industry or profession" without being classed as invalids or engaged in studies or domestic tasks. Presumably most of these people were voluntarily inactive. See Departamento de la Estadística Nacional (1928, p. 99 and passim).

[7] The category comes next to last in a 98-category breakdown of the labor force, after "occupations insufficiently determined" and "persons with unproductive occupations," and before "persons whose occupation is unknown." Those "without occupation or employment" included 39,750 men and 25,908 women, a high proportion of women compared with unemployment in other years. See ibid. (1934*b*, p. 76). It should be added that the 1940 census retroactively for 1930 showed 89,690 people, all of them male, in a category "inhabitants unemployed completely for one month at the time of the census," suggesting that 1.7 percent of the labor force fell in this category in 1930; but this sort of retroactive classification in new categories is not reliable in Mexican censuses. See ibid. (1934*b*, p. 17).

[8] James Wilkie called my attention to these statistics after the research reported here was largely complete; and I have not had a chance to search in the statistical literature of the 1930s for further references and possible explanations.

population is exactly equal to the labor force found by the population census taken on March 6.

The 1940 census, in any case, included the first clear-cut evidence on unemployment in any Mexican population census. It contained a special category, "inhabitants unemployed (*desocupados*) completely for one month or more at the date of the census," separate from the industrial classification of the labor force. This category contained 59,238 people — 55,238 men and 3,993 women — equivalent to 1.0 percent of the labor force.[9] Presumably this figure is consistent with the estimate of 184,247 or 3.1 percent shown in Table 1-1 if the latter were to include persons unemployed for less than one month.

From then on it is necessary to rely on the population censuses, of which only those of 1950 and 1970 appear reliable in regard to labor-force data. The 1950 census found 105,177 workers unemployed including 32,030 who had been looking for work for 12 weeks or less, and 73,147 who had been looking for work for 13 weeks or more.[10] The total was equivalent to 1.3 percent of the labor force, or .9 percent, counting only those who had been looking for work for at least 13 weeks. A comparison with the figures for 1940 suggests that there had been no reduction in long-term open unemployment, but there may have been a fall in overall unemployment.

In 1970, census questions and procedures shifted once again. This time open unemployment in the week prior to the census was recorded as 485,187 workers, or 3.7 percent of the labor force. Of these people, however, only 148,516 (1.1 percent of the labor force) had been looking for work for 5 weeks or more, and only 64,843 (.5 percent of the labor force) had been looking 13 weeks or more, a smaller proportion than in 1950.[11] A comparison with the 1950 time structure suggests that short-term unemployment must have been underenumerated in terms of 1970 concepts in the earlier years.

It is not possible to be sure about trends in employment from 1950 to 1960 compared with the decade after 1960, because serious computational errors seem to have crept into the 1960 labor force data, which showed unemployment equal to 1.6 percent of the labor force.[12]

[9] The census also showed the sectors in which these people normally worked: 24,241 in agriculture, 17,015 in other clearly identified sectors, 4,084 in insufficiently identified activities, and 13,798 classed as "persons with antisocial occupations; without occupation, trade or profession, with unproductive occupations, or whose occupation is not known." Most of the latter were probably new additions to the labor force, but some may have been economically inactive by today's definitions. See ibid.

[10] Most of these people (28,373 in the first category and 62,722 in the second) were men. Occupationally, 40,382 were normally in agricultural activities and 19,196 in manufacturing; 16,405 were in insufficiently specified activities. About one-quarter were 12 to 19 years old. See ibid, (1952, pp. 58 and 245).

[11] Ibid., (1972*b*, pp. 184 and 298).

[12] The total number of unemployed was put at 182,633, including 79,370 from the agricultural sector. Supposedly no more than 29,736 (.3 percent of the labor force) had been unemployed for 13 weeks or more). See ibid. (1962, pp. 363 and 560). This census is discussed further in section 4.

The 1970 census found much higher rates of unemployment among women than among men. Fully 198,254 women or 7.5 percent of the female labor force were unemployed, compared with 2.8 percent of the males. Unemployment rates were highest among women who were married (10.9 percent) or living in "free union," a census term including common-law marriages (11.6 percent).[13] Women outnumbered men 34,935 to 29,110 among workers who had been unemployed and looking for work for periods of 13 weeks or more; of the people in this category, 16,585 women but only 3,663 men had never had a job before.[14] The incidence of economically active people out of work for over a month stood at 2.4 percent for women and .9 percent for men compared with .9 percent for women and 1.0 percent for men in the 1940 census.

A 1968 sample survey focused primarily on household incomes and expenditures casts some doubt on the finding that unemployment was highest among women. Researchers asked specifically about household members' main roles in March, 1968, the month before the survey. The responses showed unemployment rates of 4.2 percent overall including 4.7 percent among men but only 2.7 percent among women.[15]

The only sample surveys that seem to have been focused mainly on employment in Mexico from the 1940s up to the 1970s were made by university researchers in the city of Monterrey in October, 1963, and April, 1964. They found unemployment rates of 7.9 and 6.3 percent, respectively, but their questions were probably quite different from those in the census.[16] By comparison, in the 1970 census no territorial entity of Mexico reported rates higher than 6.6 percent or lower than 2.0 percent. The unemployment rate was 3.6 percent in the state of Nuevo León, where Monterrey is located, and close to 5 percent in the capital.

In other questions posed in the 1970 census, employed as well as unemployed persons were asked whether they had been looking for work. In response, fully 8.8 percent of the labor force including nearly 11 percent of all economically active women said that they had been looking for work, even though a majority of these people were already employed, at least in the census sense that they had worked at least one hour in the preceding week. Only one in ten of the work seekers said they had been looking for 13 weeks or more at the time of the census, while over three-fourths had been looking for less than four weeks.[17] The census also compiled considerable information on the characteristics of these work

[13] Ibid., (1972*a,* p. 745). Only 861,903 women were economically active in these two categories combined, according to this table. The unemployment rate was 5.5 percent for single women and ranged from 6 to 8 percent for women who were widowed, divorced or separated.

[14] Ibid. pp. 745 and 927.

[15] See Banco de México (1974, Table VIII-1).

[16] See Universidad de Nuevo León (1964).

[17] Dirección General de Estadística (1972*a*, p. 921) and (1972*b,* p. 298). Of those looking for 13 weeks or more, in turn, more than half had been looking for 27 weeks or more. But even counting people who were employed, the proportion looking for work for 13 weeks or more was no higher than in 1950.

seekers. Their distribution by industries in which they had worked in 1969 was very similar to that of the employed labor force, with over two-fifths in agriculture; and their average educational attainments were slightly below those of the adult population as a whole, 10 percent of them having had at least some exposure to postprimary education compared with 12 percent for the entire population of 12 and over.[18]

In summary, if the available statistics are taken at face value, open unemployment in Mexico rose to an all-time peak of 6.5 percent in 1932, declined to 3.1 percent by 1940, fell to less than half of this figure by 1950 (though this may be due to an underenumeration) and then climbed to 3.7 percent in 1970. This is still a modest rate by international standards, perhaps reflecting the fact that in Mexico with no unemployment insurance there may be no ready alternative except to work at whatever wage and job are available, or else join in the family division of labor.

The available census data also suggest that in census years from 1940 through 1970 less than 1 percent of the labor force has been unemployed for any substantial period such as 13 weeks or more. Among men only about 1 percent seem to have been unemployed for as long as one month, in 1940, 1950, and 1970 alike.

There is room to wonder if the trends and magnitudes suggested by these data are at all reliable. Most or all of the individual figures are suspect in one way or another. There are striking contrasts, too, between the 1970 census figures of 3.7 percent actually unemployed and 8.8 percent "looking for work"; and since unemployment was nearly three times as prevalent among women as among men in 1970, one wonders whether unemployed women were fully recorded in earlier statistics. The many doubts and questions that surround these unemployment figures provide all the more reason to look deeper, at trends in participation rates and assorted other evidence that could shed further light on the employment situation.

3. An Overview of Findings on Labor Force Participation, Labor Displacement, and Underemployment

Mexico seems to have had no shortage of jobs in 1895 or 1900 — certainly not for males in the peak agricultural seasons. Almost every male over the age of ten was recorded in the censuses as having a job, at least in the sense of an occupation. Compared with men, very few women were reported employed, especially in rural areas where their job titles classed them as domestic workers of various kinds, or corn-grinders (not counted as employed here), rather than field hands; but that must have been more a reflection of traditional role conceptions than of any shortage of work for women. To be sure, labor productivity and earnings were low in most traditional activities, including agriculture; and complaints in the subsequent Mexican Revolution suggest that many workers may have been poorly paid and poorly treated; but Mexico in 1900 with less than one-quarter of its

[18] Ibid., pp. 415, 569, 933, 973.

present population was hardly overpopulated, and there seems to have been work at least seasonally for everyone.

The evidence strongly suggests, however, that beginning in the decade from 1900 to 1910, the spread of new, labor-saving methods of production has led regularly to a displacement of labor and loss of jobs in nonagricultural sectors, especially manufacturing and handicrafts.[19] This process of labor displacement was slowed by the disruption of modern industrial production in the civil wars of the 1910s, but it resumed again after 1921. Until 1940, rises in labor productivity tended to occur faster than growth in the demand for industrial goods, so that manufacturing employment declined sharply relative to population.[20]

The shortage of jobs in urban areas of Mexico reached its height in the years 1930 to 1940. By 1940 the ratio of nonagricultural jobs to urban population had fallen to about five-eights (62.6 percent) of what it had been in 1900. Large numbers of workers were displaced from traditional activities such as handicrafts, so that the number of nonagricultural jobs fell relative to the total population. Many displaced workers had to join the agricultural labor force, which grew as a proportion of the total up to 1930. The burden of being displaced fell disporportionately on women. Their labor force participation rate (population divided by active labor force) was cut nearly in half compared with 1910. By 1940, even such roles as clerical office work were being performed mainly by men.

Admittedly, it is difficult in some census years to separate long-term trends in employment, as a result of modernization, from the shorter-run effects of worldwide economic fluctuations. From this perspective it is not entirely clear to what extent labor displacement from 1900 to 1910 should be attributed to the introduction of new technology or to slowdowns in industrial growth as a result of worldwide crises. The severe employment problem in 1930 partly reflected the Great Depression. But the trends just mentioned stand out clearly in relatively neutral comparisons, such as 1910 compared with 1940. From 1910 to 1940, for example, the overall labor force participation rate fell from 35.2 percent to 29.8 percent, and the labor force recorded in manufacturing, construction, mining, and utilities decreased by about 10 percent, while total population grew by nearly 30 percent.

World War II and the postwar boom period brought a huge increase in nonagricultural employment, not only because the demand for goods rose sharply, but also because the usual imports including new equipment became harder to get and the rise in industrial labor productivity slowed down temporarily. By the time of the 1950 census the employment situation had clearly eased, and the female participation rate had more than doubled compared with 1940.

From 1950 to 1970 the overall employment situation seems to have worsened once again. In these years the labor

[19] Evidence for this and other statements that are not supported by footnotes in this section may be found below in section 5 and the accompanying tables.

[20] See Keesing (1969) as well as the tables in section 5.

force participation rate fell from 32 percent to less than 27 percent, a low figure by international standards, suggesting that more people would have worked if jobs had been more numerous. By 1970, however, the number of students had grown so much as to fully explain the difference between the participation rates in 1940 (29.8 percent) and 1970 (26.9 percent). The participation rate for women expanded further from 1950 to 1970, but still remained less than one-quarter of the rate for men, a low rate compared with most other nations.

Another ominous trend in participation rates seems already to have begun in the years 1930 to 1940, when participation rates fell in rural areas. This trend was temporarily reversed from 1940 to 1950, but became pronounced in the two decades from 1950 to 1970. In these years there seems to have been a marked displacement of labor from agriculture, presumably as a result of mechanization and reorganization in commercial farming. The total agricultural labor force fell from the equivalent of 32.6 percent of the rural population in 1950 to only 25.5 percent in 1970.

A timing problem complicates the interpretation of these findings. The 1970 census was taken in January; and this feature may have biased downward the recorded participation rate compared with the 1950 census which was taken in early June, in a season of greater agricultural activity. The 1970 census did find 45,517 inactive in January who had been active the preceding year. Most of the labor force figures in the census (and in tables shown below) refer conceptually to 1969 to include these people; but in view of the sequence of questions the number 45,517 is probably an underestimate.[21] In turn, the agricultural labor force was probably underestimated within the total, to the extent that some workers in Mexico work in agriculture in seasons of peak farm activity, but switch into other sectors or go to school during the winter months.[22] There are also many workers who divide their time among two or more jobs; a sample survey in 1964-65 estimated their number at 1,276,969 or 12 percent of the labor force;[23] though the censuses have never investigated multiple economic roles.

In the 1970 census, besides the evidence already mentioned, it is possible to find further signs of seasonal and disguised unemployment. For example, the census reported that one economically active person in eight had worked less

than six months in the previous year, and 19 percent less than ten months; while fully 846,167 people worked without pay in family enterprises.[24] Low incomes remained common, presumably in part because of disguised unemployment and because of excess labor supply depressing earnings in the less regulated parts of the labor market. One person in six who had any earnings reported monthly incomes below 200 pesos (U.S. $16).[25] Thus, many employed workers could reasonably be classed as "underemployed" by one definition or another, though there is no simple way to untangle underemployment from low productivity or low wages. After all, output per worker in Mexican agriculture as a whole averaged not much more than 200 pesos per month in 1970 prices until around 1950;[26] and the incidence of very low incomes had been even higher in censuses and surveys made in earlier years. In the 1950 census, among people working for pay (rather than unpaid or self-employed), 63.9 percent or nearly two-thirds earned less than 200 pesos per month, then worth about U.S. $23.16.[27]

An able team of Mexican economists has attempted to measure underemployment in Mexico by a consistent definition using data from the 1970 census. Their research findings, which are discussed below, suggest underemployment, and/or very low incomes, involving about 40 percent of the labor force.[28] Unfortunately, there are insurmountable problems in trying to apply a consistent definition from one census to another — such an attempt becomes a study of low incomes rather than of underemployment. But there are indications of underemployment in earlier censuses as well. For example, the 1950 census found that 7.5 percent of the labor force worked four days or less in the week before the census.[29] And it is quite clear that seasonal underemployment had regularly existed in Mexican agriculture, along with huge numbers of families with extremely low incomes.

Further evidence on seasonal unemployment has been uncovered in an agricultural linear programming model by a World Bank team, suggesting that the cultivation of annual and other short-cycle crops in Mexico calls for nearly three times as much labor in man-hours in the peak months of July and August as it does in the slackest months.[30] February and September have the lowest labor requirements whereas December, January, March, and April also have less than half of the peak requirement. Yet the peak requirement as estimated using the technical coefficients in the model seems roughly

[21] See Dirección General de Estadística (1972b, pp. 184, 190, and Anexo 3). The census asked people 12 years old or over, first, whether they were going to school; next, their economic activity in the week before the census; after that, whether they had been looking for work and if so, for how long; and only after that, whether they worked in 1969 and if so, for how many months. This last question was probably not always asked or answered carefully when the earlier questions showed people to be economically inactive.

[22] For evidence on switching of jobs, see, for example, Nutini and Murphy (1970) and O'Mara (1971). The census has never focused on students who work; but about two-fifths of the students in the national university work at least part time. See UNAM (1964, pp. 14 and 312).

[23] Dirección General de Muestreo (1965, p. 25).

[24] Dirección General de Estadística (1972b pp. 277 and 285).

[25] Ibid., p. 288.

[26] Output per worker in agriculture in 1950 averaged about 1,800 pesos in prices of that year and around 3,100 pesos in prices of 1960, based on GDP figures in Banco de México (1969).

[27] Dirección General de Estadística (1955, Table 37). For assorted comparisons and references on income distribution, see, for example, Navarrete (1970), Solís (1970), and Reynolds (1974).

[28] Grupo de Estudio del Problema del Empleo (1974): see also Isbister (1969) and Organization of American States (1969).

[29] Dirección General de Estadística (1952, p. 240), adding in workers unemployed 13 weeks or more at the time of the census.

[30] See Goreux and Manne (1973, Part IV) and especially Duloy and Norton (1973, p. 380).

equal to the total year-round labor force in this type of agriculture.[31] These estimates come from applying the model to 1968 crop data, and do not take into account subsidiary rural production and investment activities. Like other programming models of Mexico in the same volume, which give a wide range of estimates of disguised unemployment from zero up, this one builds in its employment results through its underlying assumptions which should not be taken as a dependable reflection of reality. But it seems reasonable to suspect that in the past, seasonal fluctuations in labor requirements may have been even wider because there was less machinery available to reduce peak-season requirements, and less double cropping.

In summary, relatively low unemployment rates seem to have been achieved in Mexico at the cost of low participation rates for women, widespread seasonal underemployment, and low incomes for large numbers of workers. One finds indications that substantial numbers of workers have been displaced by mechanization. In addition to people searching for steadier and better jobs, there are probably many other people (most of them women) who would enter the labor force if more jobs were available.

Yet as in the case of open unemployment, these symptoms do not seem to be new. There is ample reason to believe that the situation in 1970 was no worse and was possibly significantly better than in the years 1930 through 1940. As in the case of open unemployment, there may have been a significant deterioration since 1950, but if so, the timing of the shift is far from clear.

4. Limitations of the Census Data

Mexico's first national population census took place in 1895, and the second in 1900. After that, censuses were undertaken at ten-year intervals, except that the census that would ordinarily have been taken in 1920 was delayed until 1921 by wars of the Mexican Revolution.

Census methods, classification, and questions relating to people's economic activities have changed sharply from one census to the next. The first three censuses (1895, 1900, and 1910) showed the most continuity in methods, but after that the people in charge of collecting statistics changed from census to census and so did the procedures. The last three censuses (1950, 1960, and 1970) show some continuities, having followed modified versions of approaches recom-

mended by the United Nations; but the three censuses in between (1921, 1930, and 1940) each differed sharply from all the rest in occupational and/or industrial classifications; and practically every census has involved experimental and unique features compared with the others. The extent to which results have been published and the format of the tables also varies greatly.

The reliability and accuracy of the census data have evidently varied as well, as one might expect in a developing country that started out backward, went through major political upheavals, and changed officials in charge of the census with practically every change in administration. The least-reliable censuses appear to be those of 1921 and 1960, the first because of disruptions of the countryside and administration by civil war, and the latter because computers were used but not mastered, so that the labor force data became distorted through computational errors. The 1921 census is believed to have missed many people; and the detailed census results which finally appeared in 1928 are suspect.

The problem in 1960 appears so serious that, in the tables included here, the findings of a sample from that census, made by the Centro de Estudios Económicos y Demográficos of El Colegio de México, are inflated and used instead of or along with the census, even though the sample was not designed for this purpose and some of its procedures, eliminating hard-to-read and clearly erroneous computer cards, probably bias the results for this purpose. [32] This careful census sample, using over half a million computer cards chosen at random from nearly 35 million made in the census, found a labor force participation rate of only 27.7 percent compared with 32.3 percent shown in the published census results. An unadjusted expansion or blow-up of these sample findings places the total labor force at less than 9.7 million in 1960, compared with more than 11.3 million reported in the census itself. This correction may be too large, especially since hard-to-read and erroneous cards eliminated in the sample may have included a disproportionate number of employed people; but there are numerous indications that the labor force figures in the original census are exaggerated. A recent study by Oscar Altimir of the United Nations estimates the 1960 labor force at 10,212,900 after comparing several different extrapolations from the El Colegio findings.[33]

Few labor force data were computed or published for 1960, but some that did appear proved an embarrassment. In several age groups, reported numbers of economically active males exceeded the total male population, a contradiction subsequently overcome by a census supplement that revised the age distribution of the labor force without changing the total.[34] The end result is that no reliable labor force data are available for 1960.

---

[31] The precise balance between supply and demand of agricultural labor in the model depends on a number of assumptions. Thus, for example, demand varies with the "reservation wage" assumed for farmers in each region. Supply in the original model should be reduced retroactively in light of the 1970 census showing fewer workers in agriculture than expected. Duloy and Norton's table on p. 380 shows that peak seasonal employment in a principal version of the model for 1968 was well over 4 million workers, rising in August to close to 4.2 million. By comparison, the 1970 population census found 4,641,593 people active in agriculture (narrowly defined) in 1969, of whom a few hundred thousand must have been primarily involved in permanent or long-cycle crops rather than the short-cycle crops included in the model.

[32] For details on methods and findings of this sample, see Bialostozky (1970).

[33] This estimate would place the participation rate at 29.2 percent, where other available estimates range from 27.4 to 30.4 percent. See Altimir (1974), pp. 62-71.

[34] Dirección General de Estadística (1964).

This lack is somewhat compensated by the availability of a few sample surveys that shed direct or indirect evidence on employment in the 1960s. One sample survey in 1963 implicitly found a labor force participation rate of 27.0 percent, and another in 1964-65 estimated a participation rate of 26.9 percent, the same as the rate found in the 1970 census; but a 1968 survey found a participation rate as high as 30.1 percent.[35] This survey found 39.3 percent of the employed labor force in agriculture, nearly the same proportion as the 1970 census. In 1969-70 another sample survey of family income and expenditures yielded, as a byproduct, estimates of sectoral employment that accord fairly well with the findings of the census itself: out of an estimated labor force of 12,970,808 (compared with 12,955,058 in the census itself), only 4,871,599 were in agriculture.[36]

Apart from the aberrations in 1921 and 1960, the other seven censuses seem to have followed a pattern of gradual improvement over time. At least, the 1970 census seems to have been the best yet, followed by 1950. The quality of the 1940 census appears uncertain; it may be reasonably good, except that the industry classification of the labor force is so unusual that major sectors that are now regularly distinguished from manufacturing overlap with it in several "industries." The 1930 census seems well done compared with its predecessors; and there may have been gains from learning in the first three censuses.

Here and there, I have seen scraps of evidence that cast serious doubt on the reliability of these earlier censuses. For example, glaring inconsistencies at the regional level between census data on numbers of students and official school statistics raise added questions about the accuracy of the 1895 and 1900 censuses;[37] while a special census of government functionaries in 1930 found far more of these workers than the regular census.[38] More generally, all the censuses have encountered large numbers of workers whose job titles were too vague to allow them to be classified; and concepts and procedures were so different in early censuses that the results of retrospectively trying to align the findings into more modern categories are inherently suspect. This is certainly true in regard to the participation of women and children in the labor force. Many young children were counted as employed in early censuses, while the 1950 and 1970 censuses, in some contrast, did not record anyone under twelve as economically active.

Even the 1970 census contains at least one significant internal contradiction. The tables show 2,466,257 women active in the labor force at any time in 1969, but 2,654,292 active the week before the census, which took place in January. Correspondingly, fewer men were active in January.[39]

Another example of a case in which bias may be present is the smallness of the agricultural labor force recorded in the 1940 census, relative to the rural population (i.e., in communities of less than 2,500 inhabitants). An underenumeration would help to account for the low overall participation rate in Mexico that year. One possibility is that following land reforms of the 1930s, census takers did not record many unpaid family workers as economically active; this in turn may be partly because the census took place in early March, a slack season. Out of 3,830,871 workers in agriculture, forestry, and fishing, all but 39,864 were males, not unlike earlier censuses in which most workers in these sectors were males. (In 1930 all but 25,633 were males.[40]) The workers in these sectors in 1940 included just 191,853 unpaid family workers, along with 1,726,262 persons operating their own enterprises and 1,907,199 manual wage workers.[41] In 1950, by comparison, the original census reported 857,154 unpaid family workers, though a later census supplement reduced this to 339,821.[42]

As already noted, census concepts and questions relating to open unemployment have shifted with each census. This is also true of other labor force categories. Prior to 1930, census questions focused on occupations more than on industries in which people were employed. Only in recent censuses have questions become sharply explicit — and census takers well trained — in asking about people's current economic activities rather than their habitual or expected economic roles.

In any case, people's answers to census questions on economic roles may not be reliable, and may depend on the exact wording, manner, and sequence in which questions are asked.

A sample survey could probably have found more unemployment, in 1970 or any earlier census year, by asking more probing questions on the subject, including "would you work if work were available?" A built-in problem here, however, is that the definition of unemployment is inherently unclear where people would work in some conditions but not in others.

Timing of the census has varied, as already noted, in terms of the calendar and consequently the rhythm of agricultural employment. The early censuses were taken in the fall (October or November). Subsequent censuses took place on May 15, 1930; March 6, 1940; June 6, 1950; June 8, 1960; and January 28, 1970.

In a slack agricultural season such as January, once people answered census takers that they had not worked the preceding week and were not looking for work, there may have been insufficient attempts to ascertain whether they were economically active the preceding year. This circum-

[35] See Banco de México (1963) and (1974), Dirección General de Muestreo (1965), and Altimir (1974, p. 63).

[36] Dirección General de Muestreo (n.d., Table 1.2); see also McFarland (1973, Table 2.3).

[37] The data can be found in El Colegio de México (1965) and in Dirección General de Estadística (1956).

[38] Ibid., (1934a) and (1934b, pp. 72 and 76).

[39] To be precise, 10,255,248 men were active in January compared

with 10,488,800 in 1969, a change that would be easier to believe. See ibid. (1972a, pp. 569-973). Unemployment rates and all other percentages for women have been computed in the present study on the basis of the lower (1969) figures.

[40] The highest number of females recorded in agriculture before 1950 was 62,600 in 1910.

[41] Ibid., (1943b, pp. 19-20).

[42] See ibid., (1952, pp. 59 and 66) and (1955, Table 35).

stance together with seasonal changes in people's economic roles may help to account for the smallness of the agricultural labor force relative to the rural population in the 1970 census.

As a result of these data limitations, it would not be wise to take literally or view as reliable the detailed statistics presented here. As we have seen, the 1960 data are particularly dubious because of the computer-card and computational problems associated with that census, and the unreliability of blowing up results from a sample that was not designed for this procedure. For other years, the census statistics are offered in the spirit that, for all their likely deficiencies, they are the best figures available.

5. Detailed Evidence on Participation and Related Issues

Table 1-2 is a useful point of departure for examining statistics that support the generalizations already made. The table includes for each of eight census years from 1900 to 1970 the absolute magnitudes (to the nearest thousand) of total population; urban population in towns of 2,500 or more; total labor force; and nonagricultural labor force, defined here to include workers in insufficiently specified activities. In addition, six key percentage relationships are shown: the percent of the population in urban areas; the overall labor force participation rate; the nonagricultural labor force as a percent of the *total* population; the nonagricultural labor force as a percent of the *urban* population; the proportion of the labor force outside agriculture; and the agricultural labor force as a percent of the rural population.[43] The results of a blow-up of the El Colegio de México

census sample are used in place of the published 1960 figures as estimates of the 1960 labor force, although this procedure may contain a downward bias.

Table 1-2 helps to illustrate the declining incidence of nonagricultural employment, and the falling participation rates up to 1930 and 1940 that have already been discussed. In looking at trends in the nonagricultural labor force from 1900 to 1930, it should be kept in mind that much of the nonagricultural employment in 1900 involved traditional activities — such as hand industries, mule transportation and domestic services — that were carried on in rural as well as urban areas, so that much of the labor displacement must have taken place in the countryside. Even in more recent decades, substantial numbers of nonagricultural workers have lived in rural areas and substantial numbers of agricultural workers have lived in urban areas, so that the apparent participation rates in categories 8 and 10 must be interpreted with caution. The figure in the table on rural participation in agriculture in 1921 should be viewed skeptically along with the rest of the data for that year and for 1960, in view of the unreliability of the two censuses.

In addition to falling nonagricultural and urban employment up to 1940, the statistics in Table 1-2 help to illustrate a number of the other trends discussed above: the apparent decline in rural participation from 1930 to 1940, and again more sharply from 1950 to 1970; the rapid expansion in the nonagricultural labor force since 1940; the overall jump in employment from 1940 to 1950; and the general worsening of the employment situation since 1950.

Concerning displacement of labor from agriculture, some further figures may be useful. Mexico's gross domestic

---

[43] Underlying magnitudes for this last computation can be derived from the data in the table by subtracting the nonagricultural labor force from the total labor force and the urban population from the total population.

Table 1-2
SOME KEY MAGNITUDE AND PERCENTAGE RELATIONSHIPS FOR MEXICAN POPULATION AND LABOR FORCE IN SUCCESSIVE CENSUSES

Category	1900	1910	1921	1930	1940	1950	1960	1970
(1) Total population (thousands)	13,607	15,160	14,335	16,553	19,654	25,791	34,923	48,225
(2) Urban population (thousands), over 2,500	3,849	4,348	4,461	5,541	6,897	10,983	17,705	28,309
(3) (2) as percent of (1)	28.3	28.7	31.1	33.5	35.1	42.6	50.7	58.7
(4) Total labor force (thousands)	4,985	5,404	5,111	5,352	5,858	8,272	9,691[b]	12,955
(5) (4) as percent of (1)	35.5	35.2	35.6	32.3	29.8	32.1	27.7[b]	26.9
(6) Nonagricultural labor force[a] (thousands)	1,807	1,820	1,621	1,679	2,027	3,448	4,641[b]	7,852
(7) (6) as percent of (1)	13.3	12.0	11.3	10.1	10.3	13.4	13.3[b]	16.2
(8) (6) as percent of (2)	46.9	41.9	36.3	30.3	29.4	31.4	26.2[b]	27.7
(9) (6) as percent of (4)	36.2	33.7	31.7	31.4	34.6	41.7	47.9[b]	60.6
(10) Agricultural labor force as percent of Rural Population	32.6	33.1	35.4	33.3	30.0	32.6	29.3[b]	25.5

a. Includes workers in insufficiently specified activities as well as those in particular nonagricultural sectors.

b. Based on a blow-up of the El Colegio de México census sample, a procedure that probably introduces a slight downward bias, except in category 9.

SOURCE: Underlying data are from Table 1-5, below; El Colegio de México (1965); Departamento de la Estadística Nacional (1928); and Dirección General de Estadística (1943a), (1952), (1962), (1972a), and (1973).

product in constant 1960 prices grew from 1950 to 1970 at an average annual rate of 6.3 percent, whereas agricultural output grew at 4.9 percent per year — both reasonably good performances by international standards.[44] In the same years, the nonagricultural labor force more than doubled, from 3.45 million to 7.85 million (when people in insufficiently specified activities are included); but the agricultural labor force only expanded from 4.82 million to 5.1 million. As a result, the agricultural labor force fell, as the table shows, from 32.6 percent of the rural population in 1950 to only 25.5 percent in 1970. (This is a slightly deceptive comparison under Mexican conditions, however, since the 1970 census showed that only 76 percent of the labor force in agriculture, forestry, and fishing lived in "rural" communities of less than 2,500 people, while 23 percent of the labor force in these communities worked in other or insufficiently specified activities.[45] The actual rural participation rate, however, was 25.4 percent, significantly below the national average.)

In contrast with most earlier periods when there was little growth in labor productivity in agriculture, from 1950 to 1970, labor productivity in the sense of output (value added) per worker in agriculture rose at a rate of nearly 4 percent per year, compared with about 2.5 percent in manufacturing and a little over 2 percent in the tertiary sectors (services, commerce, transport, and communications).[46] Thus, agricultural labor seems to have been displaced by technical progress not unlike the way nonagricultural labor had been displaced in an earlier era.

Table 1-3 shows total participation rates, and separate participation rates for males and females, in all nine censuses from 1895 to 1970, including the published results for 1960 (believed to be too high) as well as the rates in the El Colegio de México census sample for that year. The decline in the female participation rate from 1900 to 1940 and the jump in this rate from 1940 to 1950 are particularly striking.

The rates shown in Table 1-3 are not corrected for the changing age structure of the population, which became somewhat younger as population growth accelerated. Table 1-4 contains revealing further information, where the total male labor force of all ages is compared with the total male population 15 years old and over, while the female labor force is compared with the female population 15 and over. Up to 1930, the male labor force was considerably larger than the male population 15 and over, meaning that economically active boys under 15 years old significantly outnumbered economically inactive males above that age. Here again the 1921 figure is suspect. Tables 1-3 and 1-4 both show the low proportion of women working in Mexico compared with men throughout the twentieth century, as well as a very sharp decline in female participation from 1910 to 1930.

[44] See Grupo de Estudio del Problema del Empleo (1974, Table 12).
[45] These figures are based on Dirección General de Estadística (1972a, pp. 83 and 657).
[46] See Table 7 below. The precise rates depend on the sectoral assignment of workers in activities such as repair services, finance, and insufficiently specified activities, and the handling of the timing, since the 1970 labor force data refer conceptually to 1969.

Table 1-3
PARTICIPATION RATES IN THE MEXICAN CENSUSES FROM 1895 TO 1970
(Percent)

Census year	Rate for total population	Rate for male population	Rate for female population
1895	35.1	62.8	7.9
1900	35.5	63.0	8.4
1910	35.2	62.6	8.3
1921	35.6	65.2	7.3
1930	32.3	61.3	4.4
1940	29.8	56.0	4.3
1950	32.1	56.3	8.6
1960[a]	27.7[a]	47.3[a]	8.2[a]
1960[b]	32.4[b]	53.4[b]	11.6[b]
1970	26.9	43.6	10.2

a. Based on census sample by El Colegio de México.
b. Based on the 1960 census, which is believed to have exaggerated the labor force in that year.

SOURCE: Computed from data in the population censuses, Bialostozky (1970) and El Colegio de México (1965).

Evidently women served as a marginal category in the labor force. They tended to lose jobs and had to drop out of the labor force, as jobs became scarce, but were drawn once again into active roles as jobs became more plentiful. In 1900 and 1910, women constituted nearly one-third of the nonagricultural labor force, but by 1930 this proportion had fallen below one-fifth.

Even in traditional roles such as domestic service and the making of women's clothing, there seems to have been a substantial reduction in the number of jobs, cutting back employment for women.[47] This trend was more glaring in other activities. Thus, a contemporary classification scheme from the 1930 census showed 526,813 women under the heading "industries" in 1910, when they outnumbered male workers under this heading, but only 177,614 in 1921 and 104,641 (compared with 587,520 men) in 1930.[48] This category included not only craft and factory industries, but also laundry services and tortilla making, jobs that were largely displaced by electrification and new techniques.

By 1940, men outnumbered women workers in textiles by 71,891 to 13,660 and in food products by 61,543 to 5,448. Women were also displaced to a considerable extent in commerce and services. Out of 163,307 salaried clerical, sales and administrative workers (empleados y dependientes) in sectors other than public administration in 1940, only 34,069 or 21 percent were women. Men constituted 70 to 99 percent of these workers in every industry. Among 160,645 public employees and schoolteachers, only one-quarter (40,147) were women.[49]

[47] Total workers in domestic services fell from 324,748 in 1910 to 186,359 in 1930, of whom 54,389 were men and 131,970 were women; workers in clothing industries fell from 135,138 in 1910 to 69,438 in 1930, of whom 46,277 were women. See Thompson (1921, pp. 338-341) and Dirección General de Estadística (1934b, pp. 74-76).
[48] Ibid., p. 72.
[49] All the figures in this paragraph are computed or taken directly from ibid., pp. 19-29).

Table 1-4

MALES AND FEMALES IN THE MEXICAN LABOR FORCE COMPARED WITH THE MALE AND FEMALE POPULATION 15 YEARS AND OVER IN CENSUSES FROM 1895 TO 1970

Census year	Male labor force	Male population 15 years and over	(2) as percent of (3)	Female labor force	Female population 15 years and over	(5) as percent of (6)
(1)	(2)	(3)	(4)	(5)	(16)	(7)
1895	3,946,074	3,732,946	105.7	499,857	3,929,156	12.7
1910	4,699,726	4,404,167	106.7	638.113	4,697,109	13.6
1921	4,567,030	4,182,607	109.2	531,747	4,577,414	11.6
1930	4,979,520	4,796,192	103.8	372,242	5,263,587	7.1
1940	5,425,659	5,466,740	99.2	432,457	5,995,933	7.2
1950	7,207,594	7,210,935	99.9	1,137,646	7,779,274	14.6
1960	8,267,347[a]	9,473,863	87.3[a]	1,423,162[a]	9,883,606	14.4[a]
1970	10,488,800[b]	12,708,253	82.5[b]	2,466,257[b]	13,230,305	18.6[b]

a. Based on a blow-up of the El Colegio de México census sample.
b. Data on total size of the labor force actually relate to the previous year; 45,517 of these people were economically inactive in January when the census was taken.

SOURCE: Computed from data in the population censuses, El Colegio de México (1965, pp. 29-60) and Bialostozky (1970).

Conversely, when employment jumped from 1940 to 1950 as a result of the war and postwar booms, the number of women workers grew rapidly. Unfortunately, the 1950 census gives no sectoral breakdown of employment by sex, but by 1969 there were nearly 2.5 million women active in the labor force including 266,654 in agriculture, forestry, and fishing; from 447,526 to 454,770 in manufacturing, depending on the lines drawn around the sector;[50] and 488,344 in domestic service, about 20 percent of the total compared with around 35 percent in 1930 and 1940. Most of the rest were in services or commerce.

The fall in the male participation rates, shown in Tables 1-2 and 1-3, may reflect some displacement of very young males, another marginal employment category; but a larger influence has been a growth in the proportion of the population in school. The 1970 census, for example, found 2,075,414 students of both sexes above the primary level compared with 157,924 reported by the 1940 census.[51]

Table 1-5 compares the economic status of the population 12 years old and over in 1950 and 1970 based on data in the two censuses. This comparison shows that almost all of the decline in the participation rate can be explained by a rise in the number of students. In a comparison of 1940 and 1970, the growing number of students may be more than sufficient to explain the decline in the overall participation rate from 29.8 to 26.9 percent.[52]

Long-term trends in employment can be illustrated

further by Table 1-6, showing the approximate breakdown of the labor force into eight major sectors in census results from 1900 to 1969. (Data from the 1970 census refer, in this regard to 1969.) Data for 1921 have been omitted because of their problematical quality. The sectoral classification scheme is based on that for 1950 and 1960, with repair activities assigned to manufacturing.[53] Assignment of occupations to particular sectors in 1900 and 1910 represents a modification of well-known El Colegio de México calculations.[54] The number of workers in insufficiently specified activities in 1900 has been modified from their calculation by assuming that only one-fifth of the women in this category were really economically active.[55]

[50] The smaller figures is based on the census definition; the larger one is based on the 1950 definition used in Table 1-5. Data are from ibid. (1972, p. 205).

[51] Ibid. (1943b, pp. 17-19) and (1972, pp. 108-121).

[52] Information is not available on the ages of the students of 1940; but presumably students 12 years old and over constituted no more than 3 percent of the population in that age group compared with 12 percent in 1970. If three-fourths of the students in the latter year (i.e., 9 percent of the population 12 and over) had been freed from school to work, and three-fifths of these people had actually done so, this would have added more than 1.6 million workers to the labor force, raising the participation rate to about 30.2 percent.

[53] Compared with the census classifications for 1969, petroleum has been split between mining and manufacturing; finance, communications, and repair activities have been switched into commerce, transport, and manufacturing, respectively; and government has been assigned to services. The alignment is still far from perfect, however. For example, "electric power" includes gas and water utilities in some years (such as 1950 and 1960) but not in others (including 1970). The 1970 definition of agriculture, forestry, and fishing seems to have included a number of workers in forestry, beekeeping, and weaving of straw products who were not always classed in this sector; but in 1970 ejidatarios were not automatically assigned to agriculture as they were in most earlier censuses. Warehousing and storage have been classified sometimes in transport and communications (as in 1950), sometimes in services, or insufficiently specified.

[54] El Colegio de México (1965). Compared with the original scheme, architects and engineers have been reassigned from mining to services; smelter workers have been reassigned from mining to manufacturing; coal-men or colliers (carboneros) and electricians have been switched from electric power to insufficiently specified; private retainers are assigned to services; and three-fifths of all carpenters have been reassigned from manufacturing to construction, leaving the remainder in manufacturing. Data for 1900 used to modify the El Colegio figures were supplied to the author by Clara Júsidman de Bialostozky from her unpublished research on that census. Detailed occupational breakdowns for 1910 were taken from Thompson (1921) and Cleland (1922).

[55] According to El Colegio de México (1965) computations, this category contained 128,975 men and 182,849 women. Over half of these people were from the small state of Querétaro, suggesting that

Table 1-5
ECONOMIC STATUS OF THE MEXICAN POPULATION 12 YEARS OLD AND OVER IN 1970 COMPARED WITH 1950

Category	1950		1970	
	Number	Percent	Number	Percent
Economically active	8,329,240[a]	49.3	12,909,540[b]	43.5
Working for pay	3,831,143	22.7	8,054.822	27.1
Students	1,100,509	6.5	3,550,773	12.0
Other economically inactive	7,450,869	44.1	13,236,990	44.6
Doing housework	7,003,735	41.5	10,917,237	36.8
Total	16,896,618	100.0	29,697,303	100.0

a. This number is larger than in other tables because it includes persons unemployed 13 weeks or more.
b. This was the figure for the week before the census.

SOURCE: Based on Dirección General de Estadística (1952, pp.59 and 66), (1972a, pp. 569 and 637).

Table 1-6
MEXICAN LABOR FORCE BY SECTOR BASED ON CENSUS DATA AT INTERVALS FROM 1900 TO 1969

Sector	1900[a]	1910[a]	1930	1940[b]	1950	1960[c]	1969[d]
Agriculture, forestry, fishing	3,177,840	3,584,191	3,671,278	3,830,871	4,823,901	(5,049,219)	5,103,519
Mining	97,887	83,374	51,246	85,151	97,143	(123,865)	146,133
Manufacturing	593,666	582,998	503,651	530,106	972,542	(1,390,789)	2,439,242
Construction	99,634	115,111	93,515	95,168	224,512	(358,674)	571,006
Electric power	e	e	16,580	9,255	24,966	(34,040)	53,285
Transport, communications	59,666	55,091	107,052	149,470	210,592	(320,674)	390,911
Commerce, finance	261,455	293,753	267,558	509,836	684,092	(907,556)	1,302,549
Services including government	520,167	536,543	432,094	484,601	879,309	(1,313,469)	2,200,892
Insufficiently specified	174,455	82,828	209,188	163,658	354,966	(192,223)	747,525
Total	4,984,770	5,403,736	5,351,762	5,858,116	8,272,093	(9,690,509)	12,955,057

a. For an explanation of the adjustments to earlier computations by El Colegio de México researchers, see the text and textual footnotes, above.
b. Workers in four subindustries have been divided between manufacturing and other activities on the basis of proportions half way between those of 1930 and 1950.
c. Based on a blow up of the results of the El Colegio de México sample of the 1960 census.

d. Petroleum workers in 1969 have been assigned three fifths to mining and two fifths to manufacturing.

e. Included in insufficiently specified category.

SOURCE: Computation by the author based on data in the population census and related sources, including El Colegio de México (1965), Thompson (1921), and Bialostozky (1970).

In Table 1-6 the treatment of unemployed workers varies somewhat from one census year to the next; for example, in 1970 they are included, but in 1950 those out of work for 13 weeks or more (73,147 persons) are omitted. Workers in insufficiently specified activites were probably predominantly engaged in services and commerce, at least from 1930 on.[56]

authorities there did not complete this aspect of the census, so that a large majority of the women were really economically inactive.
[56] Many of these workers were recorded by nonspecific job titles, such as *empleado,* or worked in sectors that could not easily be classified, implying in almost all cases that they were not in agriculture. McFarland (1973) points out in regard to this category that 1969-70 labor force estimates, made in connection with a sample survey by Dirección General de Muestreo (n.d.), show fully 2,877,240 workers in services and 1,619,083 in commerce, as well as 514,442 in transport and communications, all significantly higher than the census figures shown in Table 1-5. In this survey only 42,058 out of 12.97 million workers were classified as engaged in insufficiently specified activities.

Table 1-6 shows what seems to have been an absolute decline in employment in manufacturing after 1900. In the years from 1900 to 1910, workers in mining and transportation also declined absolutely, presumably as a result of labor-saving technological change. Specific examples of this process could be cited in other sectors as well; for examples, employment in laundry and dry-cleaning services fell from 64,737 in 1910 to 33,172 in 1921 and 12,711 in 1930.[57]

After 1930 or 1940, numerous nonagricultural activities began to expand their employment quite rapidly around a more modern technology. This is just as true in tertiary sectors as in manufacturing. Medical services, for example, expanded their employment from 14,696 in 1930 to 47,810 in 1950, to 168,252 in 1969. Employment in finance grew from 769 in 1930 to 21,246 in 1950, and to 105,671 in

[57] Thompson (1921, p. 341), Departamento de la Estadística Nacional (1928, p. 89), Dirección General de Estadística (1934b, p. 75).

1969.[58] Thus, a large proportion of the growth in employment seems to have been propelled by structural changes caused by processes of economic development. Conversely, seemingly stationary or declining employment in particular sectors has often coincided with profound changes in the composition and technology of the activities involved.

Rapid growth in output per worker has occurred in one sector after another, with labor displacing effects. Usually the growth of labor productivity has then slowed, meaning that (other things being equal) employment growth has accelerated.

Table 1-7 shows average annual growth rates of output per worker for several sectors in four time periods, 1900 to 1910, 1910 to 1940, 1940 to 1950, and 1950 to 1969. In computing the growth rates shown in this table, the numbers in Table 1-6 have been used together with standard series on gross domestic product, which are probably less reliable for early years such as 1900 and 1910 than for later years.

The table helps to show that in manufacturing, and in a broad, residual nonagricultural sector including commerce, services, construction, and electric power, average labor productivity has tended to grow at rates in the order of 2 to 3 percent over long periods, except for a slowdown of productivity growth in manufacturing from 1940 to 1950. Other sectors have gone through periods in which output per worker has spurted forward, and other periods in which little increase has been made.

Table 1-7

AVERAGE ANNUAL GROWTH RATES OF MEXICAN OUTPUT PER WORKER BY SECTOR IN FOUR PERIODS

(In Percent based on Constant Prices)[a]

Sector	1900-10	1910-40	1940-50	1950-69
Agriculture, forestry, fishing	2.1	.5	1.1	3.8
Other sectors combined	3.5	2.4	1.3	2.2
Manufacturing	2.9	3.3	.8	2.3
Mining and petroleum	8.6	1.7	.6	4.1
Transport and communications	3.0	−.1	5.0	2.6
Other nonagricultural	3.6	2.5	2.8	2.2

a. In 1950 prices, except last column in 1960 prices.

SOURCE: Computed from labor force data in Table 1-5 and output data in Solís (1970, pp. 90-91); and Banco de México (1969, Table 87), and (1973, Table 3).

6. Interpretation and Apparent Causes of the Problem

A number of influences can be suggested as contributing to Mexico's employment problem, in light of both the

evidence reviewed here and the growing economic literature on employment in developing countries.[59] Listed briefly, the chief contributing influences are probably the following:

1. Most important has been the spread to Mexico of mechanization, new equipment, and labor-saving techniques originating in advanced industrial countries, and designed for factor-supply conditions in which unskilled labor is relatively expensive.

2. Another influence has been the rapid growth of the potential labor force, especially since the 1940s, as a result of accelerating population growth.

3. Discrimination against women almost certainly plays a major role in making women the marginal category in the labor force and the group that suffers most from open unemployment.

4. Commercial, capitalist enterprises that hire wage labor in pursuit of profits have tended to displace family enterprises and preindustrial systems of mutual obligations that provided greater employment.

5. The shift in the structure of employment from primarily agricultural to primarily nonagricultural has led to a growth in frictional unemployment, since in an urban setting with its complex division of labor, long job searches and hiring searches are more often rational, in the sense that they repay the costs to the individuals and firms involved.

6. Inappropriate choices of technique have almost certainly been caused in some activities by price-distorting policies making imported equipment cheap and unskilled labor artificially expensive, so that less labor is used in particular tasks than would otherwise be so. This effect appears milder in Mexico, however, than in many other developing countries because price distortions have been somewhat smaller in Mexico.

7. There is excessive migration of labor to the cities, caused by the lure of high wages paid for ordinary labor in many urban jobs (though here again, Mexican wage and price distortions are mild in comparison with many other developing countries) and by greater public attention to the needs of the cities than of the countryside. As a result, some of the migrants end up unemployed.

8. The growth of real income, particularly in urban areas, allows more people — especially in families in which some members are already employed — to afford to search for really good jobs and to bear the costs of being unemployed, rather than settle for unattractive jobs.

9. In the period under study, Mexico's economic policies, while promoting output growth, generally avoided creating excess aggregate demand in an effort to avoid inflation, financial crises, exchange rate depreciation, shortages, and associated ill effects such as deteriorating product quality and efficiency. Instead, economic policies generally take advantage of the abundance and low supply price of unskilled labor and prevented any artificial growth of labor shortages.

10. Changes have almost certainly taken place in cultural values and attitudes in relation to unemployment, so

---

[58] Ibid. (1934b, p. 76), (1955, Table 36), and (1972, p. 205).

[59] For guides to the literature, see the surveys by Morawetz (1974), Bruton (1974), Edwards (1974), and Turnham (1971).

that governments are now ready to investigate the problem, and people may be more willing to be seen as unemployed and looking for work.

11. Last but not least, Mexico has a factor proportion problem in the sense that by standards of industrial countries, unskilled labor has been abundant all along compared to skilled and educated manpower, technical knowledge, savings, man-made means of production, foreign exchange, well-watered land, and other resources needed in development. By 1970, more of Mexico's unskilled labor pool had been absorbed into the technically advanced sectors of the economy than in earlier years, but not enough had been absorbed to alter the fundamental relationship.

This last problem may have meant that the country has had practically no alternative but low incomes, disguised unemployment, or open unemployment for the bulk of the labor force.

Most of the influences need not be elaborated in the present context, but more must be said about (1) population growth, (2) the relative influence of distorted prices as against labor displacement inherent in borrowed techniques, (3) the labor-displacing nature of capitalist as against family enterprises, (4) Mexican attitudes toward acceptance of manual and low-paid work, and (5) the evidence provided by the incidence of unemployment among different age groups and regions in 1970.

Labor force growth as a delayed effect of population growth can hardly be blamed for Mexico's employment problem until after 1950. Mexico's population expanded at a rather moderate rate from 13.6 million in 1900 to nearly 20 million in 1940 (a growth rate no faster than in the last half of the nineteenth century), then grew rapidly from 25 million in 1950 to over 48 million in early 1970.[60] During much of the latter period the growth rate of population exceeded 3 percent a year, and as a result, the potential labor force will now grow rapidly for years to come. But it is worth recalling that Mexico began to show signs of serious job shortages in 1930 and 1940, even before labor-force growth accelerated, despite the face that the Mexican Revolution caused significant losses in the working-age male population.[61]

It is also important that from 1940 to 1970, Mexico's gross domestic product per capita expanded at average rates around 3 percent per year.[62] This means that added employment would have been created, relative to population, if labor productivity had grown at annual rates any lower than 3 percent. Thus, even in recent years of more rapid labor force growth, the employment problem must be attributed in large part to efficiency gains and new techniques that have raised labor productivity.

In regard to the spread of new techniques and new equipment, the evidence from Mexico suggests that this has been a major cause of jobs being eliminated and labor being displaced, starting at an early stage in development when techniques were first modernized on a large scale. The spread of labor-saving techniques centered initially in industry and transportation, but more recently is has spread to other sectors, most importantly to agriculture.

In Mexico this spread of labor-saving techniques can be attributed mainly to realistic economic calculations, given the limited range of relevant techniques available. Only secondarily can labor displacement be attributed to employment-reducing choices caused by distorted price signals. After all, until the mid-1970s, Mexico's prices were not severely distorted. The currency remained convertible and no black market exchange rate existed through most of this seventy-year period; and although protection favored import substitution in manufacturing throughout this period, and most imported capital equipment has paid low duties, there have never been high rates of effective protection. Price distortions attributable to government policies were generally smaller throughout the twentieth century, in fact, than in the previous century. To illustrate this point, Mexico's tariff revenues from import duties, expressed as a percentage of the officially recorded value of imports, equaled 52 percent as early as the fiscal year 1826-27, 56 percent in fiscal 1873-74, 59 percent in 1884-85, and 53 percent in 1895-96, compared with 18 percent in 1901-02, 24 percent in 1910-11, and 23 percent in 1967.[63] In 1960 rates of *effective* protection in Mexican manufacturing industries are estimated to have averaged about 27 percent, based on comparisons of Mexican and U.S. prices — a low figure compared with other developing countries where rates of over 100 percent are common.[64] Meanwhile, wages of ordinary workers have been raised in the larger industrial enterprises by social security measures, after payroll taxes, and collective bargaining, especially since 1930; but realistically low wages have continued to be paid in agriculture and in small urban enterprises. In 1968-69, official minimum wages, which were little enforced, varied in agriculture from the equivalent of US$.94 per day in the lowest-wage areas of Mexico to US$2.72 per day in the highest-wage areas, while minimum wages in urban jobs started as low as US$1.10.[65]

On balance, then, the evidence from Mexico confirms that mechnization and reorganization, using labor-saving

---

[60] For a summary table of past population figures see Dirección General de Estadística (1973, p. 29). See also Table 1-1. One other demographic influence deserves attention: increasing temporary migration (including illegal migration) to work in the United States. This presumably serves to ease the employment situation in Mexico, but it probably reduces the labor participation rate there since most migrants would otherwise be in the active labor force.

[61] These losses are discussed, for example, in Reynolds (1970).

[62] Time series in constant prices can be found, for example, in Solís (1970, pp. 90-91 and 104-105) and Banco de México (1969) and (1973).

[63] This computation is based on data from Butterfield (1860), Romero (1898), El Colegio de México (1965), and Dirección General de Estadística (1969).

[64] See Bueno (1971), Balassa (1971), and Little, Scitovsky, and Scott (1970).i,

[65] Dirección General de Estadística (1969, pp. 338-340). These wages are so little enforced that, as King (1970, p. 114) points out (citing a sample survey by J. Puente Leyva in 1964), almost 40 percent of the people employed in Monterrey were receiving less than the legal minimum wage.

techniques, have afforded a strong impetus toward unemployment in developing countries.

At the same time, there is nothing in Mexico's experience to contradict a view that distorted price signals greatly aggravate the employment problem in many developing countries, both by distorting techniques of production and by causing excessive migration to urban areas. After all, by international comparative standards, the rate of open unemployment has not been high in Mexico, perhaps because price distortions have been relatively mild.

It may also be significant that employment in Mexico's manufacturing sector reached its historical low point relative to population in the 1940 census, at a time when social policies made industrial labor artificially expensive. Conversely, manufacturing employment expanded rapidly in the following decade while real industrial wage rates were allowed to fall to more realistic levels.

The third subject to be discussed further is the labor-displacing effect of a spread of capitalist, wage-labor organization in place of family enterprises and other older institutions such as haciendas based on traditional mutual obligations.

In an organization that hires labor in pursuit of profits, it only makes economic sense to hire labor up to the point where the marginal revenue product of labor is at least equal to the wage. Further application of labor would be unprofitable. In a family enterprise, by contrast, family members know ahead of time that they will receive fair shares of the average product, and they feel obliged to contribute in return. As a result, they tend to lavish labor on tasks within the family up to the point where there is still some net addition to the well-being and total output of the family. Thus, the application of labor is pushed further and more employment is generated than under a capitalist, wage-profit system of organization.[66]

The contrast is not so clear-cut between capitalist enterprises and institutions such as haciendas that combined capitalist and "feudal" features. After all, acting as a local monopsonist and/or monopolist, many old rural estates in Mexico may have offered not only lower wages but also less work than a competitive market would have offered. (Of course, modern commercial farmers and other enterprises in Mexico may also act as exploitative monopsonists in the market for labor, when they have sufficient market power.) But rural estate owners and other bosses before 1910 held their labor forces not only by unsavory means such as debt-servitude and local law-enforcing powers, but also in many areas by undertaking mutual obligations that helped to provide a measure of security to their workers, including giving them land to cultivate within the estate.

As these older forms of tenure disappeared during and after the Revolution, they were largely replaced by the ejido (communal land-ownership) created by land reforms. The ejidos presumably became an influence keeping Mexican peasants employed, albeit at low living standards, since communal ownership rights would be lost if villagers moved away. In more recent years, however, even ejido holdings seem to have been transformed to a large extent into capitalistically operated enterprises (many are illegally leased and farmed for profit), and concentration of farm ownership has made a comeback through the growth of irrigated commercial farms in new agricultural zones.

To illustrate this trend, from 1950 to 1970 the number of self-employed workers in agriculture declined by nearly three-quarters of a million while wage workers in agriculture increased by about one million.[67] Meanwhile, increasing labor mobility and the cumulative effects of economic and cultural change have broken down paternalistic and family relationships in other sectors of the economy as well. Thus, persons working for wages composed 63 percent of the total labor force in 1970 compared to 46 percent in 1950.[68]

Turning to attitudes toward acceptance of manual and low-paid jobs, I share a widespread impression that prejudices against accepting manual jobs are not so great in Mexico as in many other developing countries, and that people with relatively advanced education are fairly flexible in accepting low-paid jobs, especially since there is an enormous variance in wages and salaries paid to people in professional, technical, and other skilled occupations. (In this respect as in many others, the price system appears to have been flexible and realistic.) Moreover, up to 1970 the market for educated people was so strong in Mexico — where as late as 1960, only 122,901 people had university-level education[69] — that there cannot have been much educated unemployment. No such problem was ever mentioned to me when I was doing research on education in Mexico beginning in 1967-1968.[70]

A final source of evidence on the causes of open unemployment is the age and regional patterns of this unemployment. In 1970 the highest unemployment rate was found, as is usually the case, among people 15 to 19 years of age; but that rate was only 6.1 percent — 5.2 percent for males and 8.0 percent for females.[71] Thus, it is hardly possible to attribute more than a fraction of the observed

---

[66] For a rigorous exposition see Sen (1966).

[67] The original census showed within agriculture, forestry, and fishing fully 2,535,852 people working in their own enterprises or ejido holdings, and another 857,154 who were unpaid family workers, compared with 1,430,895 wage workers. See Dirección General de Estadística (1952, pp. 59 and 66). These figures were later modified in a census supplement, which showed 339,821 "persons who helped their families without remuneration in agricultural activities of a nonmanagerial character"; 1,566,741 "laborers, *peones* and other wage workers in agriculture and stockraising"; and 2,855,869 "proprietors, ejidatarios, administrators, foremen, and others in occupations of a managerial character in agriculture," plus small numbers in forestry and fishing. See Dirección General de Estadística (1955, Table 35). By comparison, the 1970 census found 2,075,872 working in their own enterprises or ejido holdings; 528,193 unpaid family workers; and 2,499,454 wage workers. See ibid. (1972, p. 285).

[68] See Table 1-4.

[69] Dirección General de Estadística (1962, p. 3).

[70] Urquidi (1974), however, argues plausibly that inadequacies of the educational system, by reducing the quality of training and aggravating shortages of skilled manpower, effectively contribute to unemployment and underemployment.

[71] Computed from Dirección General de Estadística (1972a, p. 569).

unemployment to either excessive job expectations based on education or prolonged job searches by young dependents. Unemployment rates of slightly over 3 percent characterize older age groups such as 25-29, 30-34, 35-39, 40-44, and 45-49; and over one-quarter of the unemployed were over 40 years old.[72] The fact that three-fourths of the unemployed had been looking for work for 4 weeks or less confirms that few people engage in long job searches, and suggests that much of the observed open unemployment is frictional.

The relatively even geographical pattern of open unemployment, ranging regionally from 2.4 to 4.8 percent when the country is divided into nine regions,[73] would seem to support a view that there has been technological displacement throughout Mexico in agriculture as well as in industry. The relative evenness of unemployment by ages and regions makes it unlikely that much of it is a luxury associated with dependent status and higher incomes. Yet the fact that unemployment rates are higher in the more urbanized and wealthy regions means that this could be a contributing factor, along with frictional unemployment in a complex division of labor and the lure of the cities with their chance for relatively high incomes for people fortunate enough to find steady jobs.

To sum up, the principal cause of Mexico's employment problem over the last 50 years seems to be the displacement of labor and loss of jobs through technological change, in combination with the ever-present factor proportion problem, causing unskilled labor to become redundant as techniques have been modernized. The low incidence of prolonged open unemployment in the face of these influences may be a credit to the flexibility of the price system and the social and family system. But something has had to give under these conditions; and the results have been low incomes, underemployment, and job shortages for women.

A number of other causes are also apparently at work in causing unemployment. Perhaps most notably, much of the open unemployment that surfaced in the 1970 census may have been frictional as a result of an increasingly complex economy, in which aggregate economic policy avoided serious shortages in order to give buyers with money, including people hiring labor, the usual advantages (at least for them) of a successfully growing market economy.

7. Evidence on "Underemployment"

One final subject that deserves attention is evidence on "underemployment." Recently a team of Mexican economists attempted a careful study of the 1970 census data as part of an examination of the employment problem. These researchers estimate, based on the census data, that in 1969 from 4.8 million to 5.8 million people, or from 37.6 to 44.8 percent of the labor force, were "underemployed" in addition to those who were unemployed.[74] The study group's definition of underemployment is complex, but essentially it includes almost all unpaid family workers, others with incomes below official minimum wage guidelines which vary from one region to another, and people working much less than the full year.

Clearly there are pitfalls in all three dimensions of this definition, so that these estimates are suspect and vulnerable to criticism. This is also true of the accompanying estimate that total underemployment was equivalent, in full-time unemployment, to as much as 23 percent of the economically active population. Note that these numbers do not include people such as housewives who were economically inactive but would have worked if more and better-paying jobs had been available.

Perhaps the chief inherent shortcoming in this estimate is that the numbers probably include many people who were physically productive and working hard in socially necessary tasks, but received low wages (and thus produced low output measured at factor costs) because there was so much unskilled labor hanging over the less regulated parts of the labor market. This is probably the chief explanation of low incomes and low output per worker in many small-scale and service industries (for example, laundries and dry cleaning, repair services, barber and beauty shops, cafes and restaurants, and small-scale industrial establishments making clothing or processing foods) and probably also in agricultural tasks on modern commercial farms (casual empiricism suggests that in most of the activities named, equipment, organization, and physical performance are really the same in Mexico as in leading industrial countries). It is hardly reasonable to call such Mexican workers underemployed, especially when in many of these activities one finds fewer workers relative to population in Mexico than in richer countries. The low-opportunity costs of people's time, due to low wages in sectors such as these, in turn help to hold down costs, profit margins, and selling prices (and consequently output as it is usually measured) in activities such as agriculture and retail trade, whether or not small-scale and old-fashioned techniques are used. Thus, it is somewhat circular to say that these people are underemployed because their marginal productivity is low — a labor shortage would create a different price structure, changing the whole picture. It is also worth noting that low productivity in many of these activities would simply represent lags, such as farmers who in 1970 still settled for incomes that a generation before were above the rural average.

From these remarks it is evident that abundance of unskilled labor has had a profound effect on the entire structure of the Mexican economy, through prices and wages, through income and substitution effects on the structure of demand, and through choices of technique. Under these conditions it is practically impossible to separate employment effects in any reliable way from these other effects, especially in regard to what are usually called "underemployment" or "disguised unemployment." It is fairly clear, however, that in recent decades, despite the labor-displacing effects of technical progress, a growing proportion of the

---

[72] Computed from data in ibid. (1972b, p. 184).

[73] Grupo de Estudio del Problema del Empleo (1974, Table 2).

[74] Ibid.

labor force is being drawn into activities producing modern-style goods and services using reasonably up-to-date techniques and equipment. If it went far enough this process could hardly fail to raise the earnings of unskilled labor relative to skilled labor. There is much room for concern, however, because this process is moving slowly and has a long way to go. Whether this process of job creation can get ahead and stay ahead of the growth of the potential labor force will of course depend on special policies that are devised to meet the employment problem, as well as trends in population, advances (and falling costs) of automation, and the country's economic growth performance.

8. Concluding Comments

Major conclusions of this study regarding the causes and character of the employment problem have already been summarized in section 3 and toward the end of sections 2, 6, and 7. Only brief further remarks need be made here.

The employment problem in Mexico does not seem to be quite so serious as has often been alleged. Massive underemployment can only be identified by redefining the problem of low incomes as an employment problem in a manner that does not appear fully legitimate.[75]

Mexico does seem to have a chronic problem in the area of employment and job shortages, as distinct from low incomes. Abundant indications can be found of workers searching for steadier or better jobs, seasonal and frictional unemployment, and women who would like to work but cannot find jobs.

A particularly striking feature of the employment situation — and a point scarcely mentioned in Mexico — is that open and hidden unemployment are both concentrated among women. In 1970 the open unemployment rate among women was more than double the rate for both sexes combined and was nearly three times the rate for men. More generally, it may be only a mild exaggeration to suggest that nearly full employment of the male labor force has been achieved by encouraging men to take any job that is available; by allowing wages and incomes to stay low in many activities so that more people become employed; and by discriminating against women who would like jobs. Almost certainly a further contributing factor has been continuing

[75] Among other shortcomings, such a redefinition would disguise the possibility of overcoming low incomes through direct redistributive measures, by implying that the problem must be overcome by creating more jobs.

cultural pressures for women to stay out of the labor force. Despite these pressures, increasing numbers of women have joined the labor force since 1940.

Comparisons of successive censuses yield strong indications that Mexico's overall employment or job shortage problem made its appearance in the years from 1900 to 1930, starting in urban areas where workers (especially women workers) were displaced in large numbers by technical progress. More recently the technological displacement process has spread to agriculture.

Perhaps the most tantalizing finding is that Mexico's employment problem seems to have been in many ways at least as serious by the 1930s as it was in 1970. The problem seems to have been alleviated somewhat from 1940 to 1950, and then worsened somewhat from 1950 to 1970.

Of course, it is not easy to compare the situation in years thirty or forty years apart, not only for lack of sufficient data, but also because so many changes had taken place in between. For example, by 1970 Mexico's labor force had practically doubled, compared with the 1930s, and contained a larger proportion of women; employment included a much larger proportion of paid jobs relative to self- and family-employment; relatively fewer jobs were in agriculture, and more involved complex "modern" activities; a larger percentage of young people were in school; people's job expectations may have changed; and so on. Deficiencies in the data raise great uncertainties regarding employment trends over shorter periods such as 1960-70. Indeed, one might conceivably argue that any seeming deterioration in the employment situation from 1950 to 1970 is illusory, reflecting structural changes that have reduced hidden and seasonal unemployment, without significantly increasing open unemployment. Then again, one might argue in a contrary vein that people's residential locations and expectations have shifted so that today's underemployment is more serious, or at least qualitatively different.

This study is not definitive partly for lack of better data. The methodology has been in places experimental, in others eclectic. Perhaps inevitably, the research has raised many unresolved questions; some of these involve facts and others conceptual issues. By their nature, some of these questions may never be resolved. But hopefully, the overall result is to shed considerable light on an employment situation that turns out to be neither as bad as it is often painted, nor as reassuring as it looks from a quick summary of the figures on open unemployment.

References

Altimir, O.
1974   "La Medición de la Población Económicamente Activa de México, 1950-1970." *Demografía y Economía* 8:50-83.

Balassa, B., ed.
1971   *The Structure of Protection in Developing Countries.* Baltimore: Johns Hopkins University Press.

Banco de México, México, D.F.
1966   *Encuesta sobre Ingresos y Gastos Familiares.*
1969   *Cuentas Nacionales y Acervos de Capital, Consolidadas y por Tipo de Actividad Económica, 1950-1967.*
1973   *Informe Anual, 1972.*
1974   La Distribución del Ingreso en México; Encuesta sobre los Ingresos y Gastos de las Familias, 1968. México, D.F.: Fondo de Cultura Económica.

Bialostozky, C. J. de
1970   *Recursos humanos: Tabulaciones con Base en una Muestra del Censo de Población de 1960.* 2 vols. México, D.F.: Centro de Estudios Económicos y Demográficos, El Colegio de México.

Bruton, H. J.
1974   "Economic Development and Labor Use: A Review." *World Development* 1(12):1-22

Bueno, G.
1971   "The Structure of Protection in Mexico." In Balassa, ed., *The Structure of Protection in Developing Countries.*

Butterfield, C.
1860   *United States and Mexican Mail Steamship Line and Statistics on Mexico.* New York: Hasbrouck.

Cleland, R. G., ed.
1922   *Mexican Year Book, 1920-21.* Los Angeles: Mexican Year Book Publishing Co.

Departamento de la Estadística Nacional, México, D.F.
1928   *Resumen del Censo General de Habitantes, 30 de Noviembre de 1921.*

Dirección General de Estadística, México, D.F.
1898   *Resumen del Censo General de la República Mexicana, Verificado el 20 de Octubre de 1895.*
1905   *Resumen General del Censo de la República Mexicana, Verificado el 28 de Octubre de 1900.*
1934a   *Censo de Funcionarios y Empleados Públicos, 30 de Noviembre de 1930.*
1934b   *Quinto Censo de Población, 15 de Mayo de 1930: Resumen General.*
1939   *Anuario Estadístico de los Estados Unidos Mexicanos, 1938.*
1941   *Anuario Estadístico de los Estados Unidos Mexicanos, 1940.*
1943a   *Anuario Estadístico de los Estados Unidos Mexicanos, 1942.*
1943b   *6º Censo de Población, 1940: Resumen General.*
1952   *Séptimo Censo General de Población, 6 de Junio de 1950: Resumen General.*
1955   *Séptimo Censo General de Población, 6 de Junio de 1950: Parte Especial.*
1956   *Estadísticas Sociales del Porfiriato, 1877-1910.*
1962   *VIII Censo General de Población, 8 de Junio de 1960: Resumen General.*
1964   *VIII Censo General de Población, 8 de Junio de 1960: Rectificación a los Cuadros 25, 26 y 27 del Resumen General ya Publicado.*
1969   *Anuario Estadístico de los Estados Unidos Mexicanos, 1966-67.*

1972a   *IX Censo General de Población, 1970, 28 de Enero de 1970: Resumen General.*
1972b   *IX Censo General de Población, 1970, 28 de Enero de 1970: Resumen General Abreviado.*
1973   *Anuario Estadístico de los Estados Unidos Mexicanos, 1970-1971.*

Dirección General de Muestreo, México, D.F.
1965   *La Población Económicamente Activa de México, 1964-65: Resumen General de la República Mexicana.*
n.d.   *Ingresos y Egresos de las Familias en la República Mexicana, 1969.*

Duloy. J. H., and R. D. Norton.
1973   "CHAC Results: Economic Alternatives for Mexican Agriculture." In L. M. Goreux and A. S. Manne, eds., *Multi-Level Planning: Case Studies in Mexico.*

Edwards, E. O., ed.
1974   *Employment in Developing Nations: Report on a Ford Foundation Study.* New York: Columbia University Press.

El Colegio de México
1965   *Estadísticas Económicas del Porfiriato: Fuerza de Trabajo y Actividad Económica por Sectores.* México, D.F.

Goreux, L. M., and A. S. Manne
1973   *Multi-Level planning: Case Studies in Mexico.* Amsterdam: North-Holland Publishing Co.

Grupo de Estudio del Problema del Empleo
1974   *El Problema Ocupacional en México: Magnitud y Recomendaciones, Versión Preliminar.* México, D.F. Fondo de Cultura Económica.

Isbister, J.
1969   "The Growth of Employment in Mexico." Ph.D. dissertation, Princeton University.

Keesing, D. B.
1969   "Structural Change Early in Development: Mexico's Changing Industrial and Occupational Structure from 1895 to 1950." *Journal of Economic History,* 5:716-738.

King, T.
1970   *Mexico: Industrialization and Trade Policies Since 1940.* London: Oxford University Press.

Little I., T. Scitovsky, and M. Scott
1970   *Industry and Trade in Some Developing Countries: A Comparative Study.* London: Oxford University Press.

McFarland, E.
1973   "Service Employment: Mexico, 1950-1969." Ph.D. Dissertation, Columbia University, New York.

Morawetz, D.
1974   "Employment Implications of Industrialization in Developing Countries: A Survey." *Economic Journal,* 84:491-542.

Morelos, J. B.
1968   "Entradas a la Actividad, Salidas y Vida Media Activa en México, 1960-1965." *Demografía y Economía,* 2:19-43.

Navarrete, I. M. de
1970   "La Distribución del Ingreso en México." In D. Ibarra et al., *El Perfil de México en 1980.* México, D.F.: Siglo XXI, 1:15-71.

Nutini, H. G. and T. D. Murphy
1970   "Labor Migration and Family Structures in the Tlaxcala-Puebla Area." In W. Goldschmidt and H. Hoijer, eds., *The Social Anthropology of Latin America: Essays in Honor of Ralph Leon Beals.* Los Angeles: Latin American Center Publications, University of California.

O'Mara, G. T.
1971   "A Decision-Theoretic View of the Micro-Economics of Technique Diffusion in a Developing Country." Ph.D. Dissertation, Stanford University.

Organization of American States, Washington, D.C.
1969   *The Unemployment Problem in Latin America.*

Prebisch, R.
1970   *Transformación y Desarrollo: La Gran Tarea de la América Latina.* México, D.F.: Fondo de Cultura Económica. Trans. as *Change and Development: Latin America's Great Task.* New York: Praeger, 1971.

Ramos, J. R.
1970   *Labor and Development in Latin America.* New York: Columbia University Press.

Reynolds, C. W.
1970   *The Mexican Economy: Twentieth-Century Structure and Growth.* New Haven: Yale University Press.
1974   "The Recent Evolution of Savings and the Financial System in Mexico in Relation to the Distribution of Income and Wealth," paper presented to the U.S.-Mexico Financial Relations Conference, Stanford University.

Romero, M.
1898   *Mexico and the United States.* New York: G. P. Putnam.

Sen, A. K.
1966   "Peasants and Dualism with or without Surplus Labor. *Journal of Political Economy,* 74:425-450.

Solis, L.
1970   *La Realidad Económica Mexicana: Retrovisión y Perspectivas.* México, D.F.: Siglo Veintiuno.

Thompson, W.
1921   *The People of Mexico.* New York: Harper Brothers.

Trejo Reyes, S.
1974   "El Desempleo en México: Características Generales," *Comercio Exterior,* 24:730-738.

Trejo Reyes, S.
1971   "Industrialization and Employment Growth: Mexico, 1950-1965." New Haven: Ph.D. dissertation, Yale University.

Turnham, D.
1971   *The Employment Problem in Less Developed Countries: A Review of Evidence.* Paris: OECD Development Centre.

Universidad Nacional Autónoma de México (UNAM), México, D.F.
1964   *Anuario Estadístico, 1963*

Unikel, L.
1970   "Urbanización," in *Dinámica de la problación de México.* México, D.F.: El Colegio de México, Pp. 115-147.

Universidad de Nuevo León, Centro de Investigaciones Económicas, Monterrey.
1964   *Ocupación y Salarios en Monterrey Metropolitano, 1963-64.*

Urquidi, V.L.
1974   "Empleo y Explosión Demográfica. *Demografía y Economía,* 8:141-153.

Wilkie, J. W.
1970   "La Ciudad de México como Imán de la Población Economicamente Activa, 1930-1965." In Bernardo García et al., eds. *Historia y Sociedad en el Mundo de Habla Española; Homenaje a José Miranda.* México, D.F.: El Colegio de México, pp. Reprinted in Wilkie (1974, pp. 41-51), translated as "Mexico City as a Magnet for Mexico's Economically Active Population."
1971   "New Hypotheses for Statistical Research in Recent Mexican History," *Latin American Research Review,* 6:3-17. Reprinted in Wilkie (1974, pp. 27-37).
1974   *Statistics and National Policy.* Statistical Abstract of Latin America Supplement 3. Los Angeles: UCLA Latin American Center Publications, University of California, 1974.

Chapter 2

Losers in Mexican Politics:
A Comparative Study of Official
Party Precandidates for
Gubernatorial Elections,
1970-75

Roderic Ai Camp

Central College, Pella, Iowa

In an attempt to determine how the official political system operates, recent studies of Mexican politics have examined the careers of those who hold top-level political positions.[1] Although elite studies that concentrate on "winners" have provided and will continue to provide valuable insights into the Mexican political system, "losers" should not be neglected. Thus my purpose here is to develop a comparative analysis of those persons who lose with those who win in order to reveal much about the victorious politicians, the selection process, and political trends in Mexico.

This essay examines contestants for the official party nomination in each of the twenty gubernatorial elections that took place in Mexico during the term of office of President Luis Echeverría. (For victories and dates of office, see Appendix A.) Where possible, I attempt to evaluate the political situation in each state that held an election between December 1970 and December 1975, and I use case examples from several states to describe the career qualifications for the official party's "precandidates" for governor in order to suggest why one candidate emerged victorious. (The term "precandidate" is used in the official Mexican party system where contestants for the nomination do not compete in primary elections but are in effect designated by national leaders of the official party; the victorious precandidate never loses a gubernatorial election to opponents of the

official party.) Further, I compare the losing precandidates with successful contenders to determine if these individuals lacked some qualifications apparent in successful precandidates as well as to weigh the importance of certain variables in the selection process. Lastly, I analyze political trends reflected by the nomination process.

Students of the Mexican political system have identified several variables which appear to be significant in the process of candidate selection in Mexico. Three such variables are important for gubernatorial candidates: career experience, political friendships, and qualifications peculiarly suited to the political-economic situation of the state in question. Roger C. Anderson, for example, concludes that Mexican governors are college-educated, come from urban backgrounds, and rise in increasing numbers via careers in the federal government.[2] William Tuohy, Kenneth Johnson, Richard Fagen, and Octavio Paz suggest that political friendships may be the determining factor for successful politicians in Mexico.[3] My own research, results which agree with these authors, indicates that political experience is significant in enabling the candidate to solve the unique set of political and economic problems of the state at the time of the election.

---

[1] See Peter H. Smith, "Making It in Mexico: Aspects of Political Mobility since 1946," paper delivered at the 1974 American Political Science Association Annual Meeting, Chicago, Illinois; Donald Mabry, "Mexico's Party Deputy System: The First Decade," *Journal of Interamerican Studies and World Affairs* (1974), pp. 221-233; and Roderic Ai Camp, "Mexican Governors since Cárdenas: Education and Career Contacts," *Journal of Interamerican Studies and World Affairs* 16 (1974), pp. 454-481.

[2] Roger C. Anderson, "The Functional Role of Governors and Their States in the Political Development of Mexico, 1940-64," Ph.D. dissertation, Department of Political Science, University of Wisconsin, Madison, 1971.

[3] William S. Tuohy, "Centralism and Political Elite Behavior in Mexico," in Clarence E. Thurber and Lawrence S. Graham, eds., *Development Administration in Latin America* (Durham: Duke University Press, 1973); Kenneth F. Johnson, *Mexican Democracy: A Critical View* (Boston: Allyn and Bacon, 1971); Richard Fagen and William Tuohy, *Politics and Privilege in a Mexican City* (Stanford: Stanford University Press, 1972) and Octavio Paz, *The Other Mexico: Critique of the Pyramid* (New York: Grove Press, 1972).

In order to understand the Mexican political process, at least in the selection of gubernatorial candidates, we need to examine the interplay among these variables in relation to the political situation of a state. It is argued here that neither special qualifications of the candidate, national political experience, nor political contacts as separate variables can explain which candidates win or lose, but when looked at together with the situation in the state itself, they explain most selections which have taken place for governors in Mexico from 1971 to 1975.

An examination of the seventy-two losing precandidates for governor reveals some interesting comparisons with the twenty winning candidates and past governors in Mexico. In general, Table 2-1 reveals that losers and winners tend to have very similar career patterns. For some career positions, no conclusions can be reached because we have incomplete information for losing candidates. But winning candidates tend to have career experiences in the following four positions: federal deputy, mayor, state party leader, and cabinet or subcabinet secretary. Also, an extremely high proportion

of recent governors have been student leaders, indicating early political recruitment and activity. Losing precandidates have been federal deputies, and to a lesser extent mayors, but they have seldom been state party leaders or members of the federal cabinet. In general, governors in the period before 1973 also had career experiences as federal deputies or senators and state or national party leaders. The key experience which appears to be missing from losers' careers is a high-level position in the federal government or the party.

The significance of this missing career experience becomes more apparent if we examine each of the contests to determine if the winning candidate held a high-level political office before his selection by the official party.[4] In only six states, San Luis Potosí, Hidalgo, Guerrero, Sinaloa, Querétaro, and Puebla, did a candidate win the nomination without having held important national positions (Table 2-2).

[4] A position qualifies as high-level if it is among the following: Oficial Mayor or above in cabinet agencies, Subdirector General or above in major federal banks or decentralized agencies, or a member of the National Executive Committee (CEN) of the official party (PRI).

Table 2-1
CAREER PATH PERCENTAGES OF MEXICAN OFFICIAL PARTY LOSERS AND WINNERS AND PREVIOUS GOVERNORS, 1973-75

Position	Losers[a]			Winners[a]		Previous Governors[a]	
	Held Position	Did Not Hold Position	(Absolute Number Not Included)	Held Position	Did Not Hold Position	Held Position	Did Not Hold Position
Student Leader	12.5	20.8	(48)	55.0	45.0	6.4	93.2
Federal Deputy	45.8	54.2	(*)	70.0	30.0	44.4	55.6
Federal Senator	18.0	82.0	(*)	30.0	70.0	32.0	68.0
Local Deputy	5.5	58.3	(26)	15.0	85.0	16.0	84.0
City Councilman	#	59.7	(29)	10.0	90.0	1.0	~
Mayor	13.9	69.4	(12)	30.0	70.0	11.2	88.8
Secretary General of Government	5.6	94.4	(*)	10.0	90.0	15.2	84.8
Oficial Mayor (National Level)	9.7	92.3	(*)	15.0	85.0	11.2	88.8
National Party Position	5.6	94.4	(*)	15.0	85.0	37.5[b]	64.3[b]
State Party Position	8.3	50.0	(30)	35.0	65.0	~	~
National Union and Professional Leader Affiliated with PRI	2.7	97.3	(*)	20.0	80.0	11.7	88.3
Private Secretary to National Leader	8.3	34.7	(41)	20.0	80.0	9.8	90.2
State Judge	4.2	83.3	(9)	10.0	90.0	13.0	87.0
State Bureaucracy	9.7	52.8	(27)	10.0	90.0	17.0	83.0
Cabinet Subsecretary or Secretary	18.0	82.0	(*)	35.0	65.0	12.6[c]	87.4[c]
Decentralized Agency Director or Subdirector	8.3	91.7	(*)	5.0	95.0	~	~
Military	6.9	93.1	(*)	5.0	95.0	30.0	70.0

a. Figures for losers are based on a sample of 72; for winners, 20; for previous governors, the figures are adapted from Camp, "Mexican Governors since Cárdenas" and from Anderson, "The Functional Role of Governors." The Camp data are for all three groups, and the Anderson data are for the winners only. The Camp data include a nearly complete population of 286 governors from 1935 to 1973.

b. These figures combine data for both national and state party positions.

c. These figures combine data for both cabinet and decentralized agency positions.

Table 2-2

SIX STATES REPRESENTED BY A WINNING CANDIDATE WITHOUT HIGH-LEVEL POLITICAL EXPERIENCE IN MEXICO

State	Number of losing candidates without high-level experience	Number of losing candidates with high-level experience
San Luis Potosí[a]	~	~
Hidalgo	5	1
Guerrero	6	#
Sinaloa	6	1
Querétaro	1	~
Puebla	2	2

a. Insufficient information available on San Luis Potosí.

Of twenty winners, 70 percent held such positions, while of 72 losers, this was true of only 25 percent. A closer examination indicates that of the six winning candidates without national office only three defeated candidates with national experience. Therefore, in 85 percent of the contests, the precandidate with national political experience emerged victorious.

The recent trend toward national political experience is important because it differs remarkably from that among governors who held office prior to 1973. If we look at the comparable figures in Table 2-1 for governors before 1973 holding cabinet, subcabinet, and decentralized agency positions, we can see that eight, or 40 percent, of our recent winners had such experience as contrasted with only thirty-six or 12.6 percent of all governors from 1935 to 1973. We can only speculate on the reasons for this recent change. Most students of political history in Mexico seem to agree that the number of powerful regional or state bosses in Mexico has been on the decline as the political and economic power of the federal government has increased. As a result, except in the states of Hidalgo, Tamaulipas, and Oaxaca, the national political leadership has had to make fewer concessions to powerful regional leaders. The lack of national political experience has been characteristic of men receiving regional boss support; thus, a decline in this type of governor is probably a reflection of the decline of regional bossism itself.[5]

It is suggested here that national experience has been extremely significant in *recent* gubernatorial choices. National officeholding at high levels is indicative of several qualities in the Mexican political system. First, by virtue of

having held such a position, a politician is personally acquainted with or his abilities are known to the president of Mexico or to a political leader of national prominence. Second, such a precandidate tends to have more access to national political leaders who appear to make these decisions. Lastly, his ability to gain access to decision makers in the federal government who control federal monies is considered a favorable asset by many state supporters.

The only other career factor which might be of some importance to gubernatorial candidates is type and level of education. In Table 2-3, we see that losers and winners are remarkably similar in this respect. Both precandidates and governors are professionally educated, the largest single field being law. The governorship is not readily accessible to representatives of the two largest groups which support the official party in Mexico — the labor and agrarian sectors. True representatives from these groups would not have a professional education. Statistics for the winning candidates indicate (there are insufficient data on losers) that only one successful contender, Alfonso Calderón Velarde of Sinaloa, had a labor background, and he had no preparatory or college education. The high level of education among precandidates is supported by figures on the sectoral membership of winning candidates in the official party. Of nineteen winning candidates for whom data are available, one was from the labor sector and two from the agrarian sector, while the popular or professional sector had sixteen winners, hardly an equitable distribution. The two representatives of the agrarian sector were not from farming backgrounds, and both had professional degrees. The educational and sectoral backgrounds of winning candidates are indicative of the dominance of professional, middle-class persons in the most important state positions in Mexico, similar to office holders at the federal level.[6]

In addition to career background, primarily high-level national experience, political friendships, or membership in a national political camarilla were important in candidate selection. This is so because the camarilla system is an integral part of the Mexican political process.[7] Briefly, the camarilla system is a network of personal political alliances or cliques which operate within the governing elite in Mexico. I have described it as follows:

> This personal clique, like the official system itself, tends to form a pyramidal structure within the larger pyramid of the official system. It should not be assumed, however, that *all* men in a particular camarilla

[5] For support, both analytically and statistically, see Anderson, p. 8ff. Cf. John F. H. Purcell and Susan Kaufman Purcell, "Machine politics and Socioeconomic Change in Mexico," in James W. Wilkie, Michael C. Meyer, Edna Monzón de Wilkie, eds., *Contemporary Mexico; Papers of the IV International Congress of Mexican History* (Berkeley and Mexico City: University of California Press and El Colegio de México, 1976), pp. 348-366. See also the Purcells "Community Power and Benefits from the Nation: The Case of Mexico," *Latin American Urban Research*, III:49-76.

[6] See Roderic Ai Camp, "The Cabinet and the Técnico in Mexico and the United States," *Journal of Comparative Administration* (1971), pp. 188-214; James Cochrane, "Mexico's New Científicos: the Díaz Ordaz Cabinet," *Inter-American Economic Affairs* 21 (1967), pp. 61-72; Donald Mabry, *Mexico's Acción National: A Catholic Alternative to Revolution* (Syracuse: Syracuse University Press, 1973); and Julio A. Fernández, *Political Administration in Mexico* (Boulder: University of Colorado, 1969).

[7] Roderic Ai Camp, "El Sistema Mexicano y las Decisiones Sobre el Personal Político," *Foro Internacional* 17:1 (1976), pp. 51-83. pp. 51-83.

Table 2-3
EDUCATIONAL BACKGROUNDS OF LOSING AND WINNING CANDIDATES FOR MEXICAN GUBERNATORIAL NOMINATIONS, 1973-75

Type of Degree	Winners		Previous Governors 1935-73		Losers	
	Number	Percent	Number	Percent	Number	Percent
Law	9	45.0	87	30.5	33	45.8
Architecture	1	5.0	#	#	#	#
Medicine	2	10.0	24	8.4	8	11.1
Economics	2	10.0	37[a]	13.0	7	9.7
Engineering	2	10.0	d	d	10	13.9
Teaching[b]	2	10.0	28	9.8[b]	2	2.8
Military[c]	1	5.0	~	~	2	2.8
None	1	5.0	109	38.2	4	5.6
No data	*	*	1	#	6	8.3
	20	100.0	286	99.9	72	100.0

a. This is a combined figure for economics and engineering degrees.
b. Teaching certificate from a normal school, including urban, rural, primary, and secondary certification. This is not equivalent to a professional degree.

c. Graduate of the National Military College or the National War College. Military equivalent to a professional degree.
d. Included in category for economics.

are loyal to the man at the top, but that there are many camarillas within the original camarilla headed by men who command their loyalties. To give a realistic explanation of this process, one needs to look at the political system at a given time to determine who is the leader of the Revolutionary Family, or for our purposes, the primary camarilla. Normally, except when a weak president succeeds a strong president, the head of the primary camarilla will be the president of Mexico. The secondary camarillas will often be headed by his closest associates, normally in the cabinet or major decentralized agencies, the National Executive Committee (CEN) of the official party, and occasionally the unions or sectoral organizations. The tertiary camarillas are headed by men who are in turn loyal to the men closest to the leader of the Revolutionary Family. . . . Symbolically, then, the camarilla becomes a small pyramidal group of men which in turn is engulfed by a larger and then a still larger pyramidal structure, until the official system or pyramid itself emerges.[8]

If we examine each of our contenders for the governorship in Mexico, we can see the significance of membership in various camarillas.

Of the winning candidates examined in Table 2-4, eleven of nineteen could be identified with a presidential or influential national camarilla leader. In four additional contests, the winner, who was not a member of a significant national camarilla, had no competition from other precandidates who were known members of such a group. Therefore, in only four cases do we have winning candidates who defeated members of such camarillas. Two of the losing

precandidates have something in common: both were sons of former governors of their states. In Oaxaca, Pedro Vázquez Colmenares, a member of the camarilla of Hugo Cervantes del Río, a precandidate for president in 1976, lost because his father had made numerous, influential enemies in his state.[9] The winner, while not having membership in such an important camarilla, did have the support of a cabinet member and former governor of Oaxaca. In Colima, we cannot make a complete analysis because we do not know the political ties of the winner. We do know, however, that despite the loser's membership in Echeverría's camarilla, he too was the son of a former governor, which may have worked to his disadvantage. While camarilla memberships can be shifted, blood ties cannot, and they often restrict the maneuverability of Mexican politicians.[10] The case of Durango is somewhat less clear. One of the losers, although not a favorite, was Echeverría's personal physician during the presidential campaign. The winning candidate had considerably more experience, however, and was also a member of the same national group as the winner in Oaxaca. Although the contest in Puebla is analyzed in some detail below as a case

[8] Ibid.

[9] Excélsior, March 14, 1974. p. 11A.
[10] Excélsior, June 1, 1974, p. 16A, gives a very good example of the interplay of such a relationship in the political history of the state of Tlaxcala. In 1969 the two strongest contestants for the governorship were Ignacio Bonilla and Luciano Huerta Sánchez. Bonilla's father, while governor of the same state, had shot and killed Huerta Sánchez's older brother. The elder Bonilla was forced to leave political life, but his son had the good fortune to join a camarilla including Echeverría in the 1940s. Later when Echeverría was Secretary of Government, Bonilla won the gubernatorial nomination from Huerta Sánchez. Just fourteen months later, he died of a heart attack, and in the new election, Huerta Sánchez, with his rival now dead, became the new candidate.

Table 2-4

IMPORTANCE OF POLITICAL FACTORS, CAMARILLAS, AND PREVIOUS CAREER EXPERIENCE IN MEXICAN GUBERNATORIAL CANDIDATE SELECTION, 1973-75

State and candidate	Score				State and candidate	Score			
	Political factors	National camarilla	National office	Total		Political factors	National camarilla	National office	Total
AGUASCALIENTES	slight				NUEVO LEON	moderate			
Esparza Reyes	3	3	2	8	Zorrilla Martínez	2	3	3	8
Barrientos	1	0	3	4	Martínez Domínguez	2	1	3	6
Landeros	1	2	0	3					
Díaz de León	2	0	0	2	OAXACA	slight			
					Zarate Aquino	1	2	1	4
CAMPECHE	slight				Suárez Torres	1	2	3	6
Rodríguez Barrera	3	3	3	9	Vázquez Colmenares	1	3[a]	3	7
Pérez Camara	2	0	1	3	Pérez y Pérez	1	0	1	2
CHIHUAHUA	slight				PUEBLA	heavy			
Aguirre Samaniego	3	3	3	9	Toxqui Fernández	2	2	1	5
González Herrera	1	0	1	2	Langle Martínez	1	2	3	6
González Soto	3	0	1	4	González Sosa	1	3	3	7
Caballero	1	2	0	3	Sánchez Cruz	1	2[a]	1	4
					Fabre del Rivero	2	3	2	7
COLIMA	slight								
Barbosa Heldt	2	0	2	4	QUERETARO	slight			
Rivas Guzmán	1	0	1	2	Calzada	1	3	0	4
Noriega Pisano[b]	2	2	0	4	Bonfil	2	3[a]	3	8
Santa Ana	2	3[a]	3	8					
Ruvalcaba	1	0	1	2	SAN LUIS POTOSI	slight			
					Fonseca Alvarez	3	2	1	6
DURANGO	slight								
Mayagoitia Domínguez	2	2	3	7	SINALOA	heavy			
González	1	0	3	4	Calderón Velarde	3	2	1	6
López Faudoa	1	3	3	7	Robles Quintero	1	2	1	4
Soto Ruiz	2	0	1	3	Vega Amador	1	2	2	5
Terrones Langone	1	0	2	3	Ortegón	2	2	0	4
Gámiz Fernández	2	0	1	3	Alvarez Nolasco	2	0	3	5
					Carlón	2	2	0	4
GUANAJUATO	moderate				Ruiz Almada	2	3	2	7
Ducong Gamba	3	3	3	9	Vega Alvarado	2	3	2	7
Rodríguez	3	2[a]	1	6	SONORA	moderate			
GUERRERO	heavy				Biebrich Torres	3	3	3	9
Figueroa Figueroa	3	2	2	7	Bernal Miranda	1	0	1	2
Cervantes Delgado	2	0	1	3	Vízcaino Murray	1	2	3	6
Osorio Marban	2	0	1	3	Carrillo Marcor	1	2	2	5
Soberón	1	2	0	3					
Fernández	1	0	0	1	TAMAULIPAS	slight			
Aguilera	1	0	0	1	Cárdenas González	3	3	3	9
					Ibarra Herrera	2	3	2	7
HIDALGO	moderate				Bermúdez Limón	2	3	2	7
Miranda Andrade	1	2	0	3					
Corona del Rosal	1	2[a]	1	4	TLAXCALA	heavy			
Bravo Santos	2	0	1	3	Sánchez Piedras	3	2	1	6
Lugo Gil	2	0	1	3	Juárez Carro	2	0	1	3
Lozano Ramírez	2	2	1	5					
Rojo Lugo	2	2[a]	2	6	VERACRUZ	heavy			
Bonfil	2	0	3	5	Hernández Ochoa	2	3	3	8
					Méndez Docurro	1	3	3	7
MICHOACAN	slight				Carbonell de la Hoz	1	2	0	3
Torres Manzo	3	3	3	9	Llorente González	3	2	3	8
Cárdenas	1	2[a]	0	3	Vargas Saldana	2	0	0	2
Pena	2	2	1	5	Cubría Palma	1	0	2	3
Pliego	1	0	0	1	Aguirre Beltrán	2	0	3	5
Díaz Rubio	2	0	0	2	Cházaro Lara	1	2	3	6
Bravo Valencia	2	0	1	3	Senties	1	3	3	7
Mora Plancarte	1	0	1	2	Patiño	1	0	0	1

Table 2-4 (Continued)

IMPORTANCE OF POLITICAL FACTORS, CAMARILLAS,
AND PREVIOUS CAREER EXPERIENCE IN MEXICAN
GUBERNATORIAL CANDIDATE SELECTION,
1973-75

State and candidate	Score			
	Political factors	National camarilla	National office	Total
ZACATECAS	slight			
Pámanes Escobedo	2	2	3	7
Cervantes Corona	2	1	1	4
Rodríguez Santoyo	2	2	1	5
Contreras Serrano	1	0	1	2
Salinas Iniguez	1	0	0	1
García Cervantes	1	0	0	1

a. Indicates father was governor of the same state or a national political leader.
b. Noriega Pisano became the new official candidate of the PRI when special elections were held to replace the deceased governor-elect.

Key

POLITICAL FACTORS

Score for the state:

Slight: No major conflicts with opposition groups, with interest groups with the national party organization, or within the state party organization.

Moderate: Some recent difficulties with an identifiable group, such as students, businessmen, etc.; traditionally organized opposition which has produced some instability; or considerable infighting among factional groups within the state organization.

Heavy: Recent difficulties with groups has resulted in violence involving police action; opposition from organized parties has resulted in immediate victories for that party on the municipal or national levels or consistent charges of fraud in individual municipalities and electoral districts

Score for the candidate:
0   Not related to the following scale
1   Career experience slightly helpful to state problems
2   Career experience helpful to state problems
3   Career experience ideal for state problems

NATIONAL CAMARILLA

Score for the candidate:
0   Not related to the following scale
1   "Burned" camarilla or not nationally important
2   Influential camarilla, but not one of the major groups since 1971; or preceding governor's group
3   Presidential or major camarilla

Camarilla identification has been determined by the following criteria: published information about political mentors; identification with an immediate superior if a person has served as his private secretary, secretary general of government, campaign aide, personal physician, or in two or more positions as a direct subordinate to the same individual. While such criteria cannot account for complete accuracy in identifying camarillas, past research, when compared with published sources, indicates it is a generally accurate measure. See my study "El Sistema Mexicano y las Decisiones sobre el Personal Político," *Foro Internacional,* 17:1 (1976), pp. 51-83.

NATIONAL OFFICE

Score for the candidate:
0   Not related to the following scale
1   Federal deputy or senator
2   Oficial Mayor, subdirector of a decentralized agency, or director general of smaller federal agencies
3   Secretary, subsecretary of cabinet level agency, member of the CEN or the PRI, or a congressional leader or national labor secretary

study, suffice it to say here that, like Durango, it reflects the political influence of persons outside the presidential camarilla.

Our figures and examples indicate a complex conclusion about national camarilla membership. On the one hand, such membership is an asset to the winning candidate, but it is not necessarily a prerequisite. On the other hand, while the camarilla system is the critical organization within the Mexican political process, it does not seem to be the only factor necessary for success. Presidents of Mexico have to deal with competing interests represented by other national camarillas and by regional political bosses, thus they cannot always select the men closest to them for important political offices.

The Selection Process in the States:
Some Case Histories

While both national office and camarilla membership are obviously important to the winning candidates in gubernatorial selections, the political situation of the state itself also explains, in part, the success and failure of precandidates. If we examine several case histories of preelection contests, and consider all three variables (national office, national camarilla membership, and state political difficulties), we can see the significance of these variables in varied situations.

Sonora (1972)

Before the election in 1973, the political situation in Sonora, where there had been considerable opposition to the most recent governor, was rather fragile for the official party.[11] Furthermore, there was a strongly organized opposition movement from the National Action Party (PAN), which competed successfully in Sonora on the municipal level in 1967.[12] The official party was split in the 1967 campaign for governor, and many members of the PRI supported the PAN candidate for governor that year.[13] Given this immediate political background of the state, in 1973 the PRI needed a candidate who could unify the political factions within the state party organization, improve relations between the national and state representatives of the official

[11] Robert R. Bezdek, "Electoral Oppositions in Mexico: Emergence, Suppression, and Impact on Political Processes," Ph.D. dissertation, Department of Political Science, Ohio State University, 1973, p. 57.
[12] Mabry, *Mexico's Acción Nacional,* p. 77.
[13] Ibid., p. 78; Johnson *Mexican Democracy*, pp. 133-134.

party, and present himself to the Sonoran populace as a young, aggressive, innovative candidate.[14]

Four precandidates were particularly strong in the competition for the nomination: Benito Bernal Miranda, Alejandro Carrillo Marcor, Carlos A. Biebrich Torres, and Francisco Vizcaíno Murray. The weakest candidate, the late Senator Bernal Miranda, former Chief of Staff to General Obregón and a career military man, was too old and in the wrong profession.[15] Furthermore, he did not meet any of the needs in Sonora, even as the PRI seemed to perceive them. Of the remaining three candidates, Senator Carrillo Marcor was atypical of precandidates and their career patterns. First, he was a *cardenista* who was closely tied to the national labor leader Vicente Lombardo Toledano and was prominent in national politics during the 1940s. Second, he was in his sixties, and his political experience from 1930 to 1970 had been confined to the Federal District. Therefore, his lack of recent national experience and unfamiliarity with Sonoran politics made him a losing candidate.

The other two precandidates were more competitive. Francisco Vizcaíno Murray was only thirty-seven years old, held a Ph.D. degree in administration, and had considerable financial and administrative experience culminating in his selection as Subsecretary of the Environment. It is probable that he would have aroused little opposition, but he lacked several essential ingredients: he had never held a party, electoral, or administrative position in Sonora, and his positions, mostly at the national level, were appointive.[16] On the other hand, his opponent, Carlos A. Biebrich Torres, who was Subsecretary of Government, the most politically oriented secretariat of the federal government, had nearly perfect credentials for the Sonoran situation. First, he had held positions at both the city and state levels in Sonora. Second, he was the state director of the PRI for Sonora. Third, as governor he would have to deal with the Secretariat of Government in federal-state political relations, making his former position invaluable. Unlike all of the other precandidates with an education, Biebrich was educated entirely in the state university and was director of the Federation of University Students of Sonora in 1958. Furthermore, in contrast to Vizcaíno Murray, his electoral skills were considerable, and he had won the national PRI oratory contest, a very competitive event. Biebrich was the ultimate choice of the national leadership. His base within the state organization

was strong because he had worked closely with the current governor when that individual was a mayor, and he had served as private secretary to the previous governor. Since both were dominant forces in the local PRI organization, he would have strong contacts needed for conciliation, and Biebrich himself was responsible for the political training of many of the local PRI leaders and members. His experience as a student leader and professor enabled him to deal with the most troublesome and vocal group in Sonora, the university students. Lastly, he had the confidence of the president himself, having served as his campaign aide in 1970. With his varied state and national experience, with his ties to national and state leaders, and his specific qualifications for dealing with the Sonoran situation at that time, he was a winning candidate.

Puebla (1974)

Puebla, the state with the most political disruptions under the Echeverría administration, did not provide enviable conditions for any politician seeking to win the gubernatorial election in 1974. Five persons had served as governor during the last two gubernatorial periods. In 1963, General Antonio Nava Castillo resigned under duress after violence erupted in response to student strikes.[17] His successor took over the state government "with tanks in the streets and with a private sector which believed that communist groups were on the increase."[18] Dr. Rafael Moreno Valle, with considerable national political experience as Majority Leader of the Senate, Political Action Secretary of the National Executive Committee of the PRI, and as Secretary of Health, became the third governor in February 1969. He too resigned, in April 1972, after being unable to solve the political problems. He was replaced by Mayor of Puebla, Gonzalo Bautista O'Farrill, the son of a former governor. Bautista O'Farrill failed to cope with a situation which saw increased violence, conflicts between students and police, and dissatisfaction on the part of the private sector.[19] He too resigned after a year in office and was replaced by one of the federal senators from Puebla. Economically, the state was comparatively underdeveloped, and politically, bossism was still widespread.[20] As a result of this political-economic situation, PAN stood to benefit considerably. What the official party needed in the state was a knowledgeable Puebla politician with considerable skills at conciliation, but someone who could also stimulate economic progress. Although the political situation in Puebla was disrupted, there were numerous precandidates for the nomination: Eduardo Langle Martínez, Rodolfo Sánchez Cruz, Rubén González Sosa, Carlos Fabre del Rivero, and Alfredo Toxqui Fernández.

Langle Martínez had served as the Secretary General of

[14] Students, because of their education and middle-class background, tend to be perennial troublemakers for governors. Sonora had been the site of much recent student political violence. Any candidate would find good relations with students an asset in stabilizing political affairs in Sonora.

[15] *Hispano Americano*, October 28, 1974, p. 14 and *Excélsior*, October 22, 1974.

[16] The author maintains that it is essential to separate the Mexican political leadership into two broad groups: those with appointive-administrative experience and those with party-electoral experience. While some persons have experience in both categories, the vast majority are easily identified with one career or the other. Each career emphasizes different skills necessary to succeed within the official system. See Camp, "The Cabinet," pp. 189-190.

[17] Marvin Alisky, "The Governors of Mexico," *Southwestern Studies* 3 (1965), p. 31.

[18] *Excélsior*, July 6, 1974, p. 11.

[19] *Excélsior*, November 26, 1974, p. 4.

[20] For a background on state politics, see David Ronfeldt, *Atencingo, The Politics of Agrarian Struggle in a Mexican Ejido* (Stanford: Stanford University Press, 1973).

Government under the interim governor, which might associate him with the failures of that administration. His most noticeable lack of career experience, however, was in the field of party political positions and electoral positions on either the state or national level. With the exception of his most recent position, his career centered on national appointive posts.

In contrast to Langle Martínez, Rodolfo Sánchez Cruz had considerable state political experience, but in Chihuahua, not Puebla, where he served a close friend of his father, General Sánchez Taboada, the former President of the National Executive Committee of the PRI. Most helpful to his chances for the governorship was the fact that President Echeverría, like a number of other successful Mexican politicians, was a young protégé of his father. His lack of experience with Puebla and its problems, however, probably prevented his successful candidacy.

The third candidate, Rubén González Sosa, had been a career foreign service officer since 1946, and became Subsecretary of Foreign Relations in 1970. He had know Echeverría since his student days and was a prominent leader at the National Law School in 1942. He had never served in an elective or party post at the state or national level, nor had he held any administrative post in Puebla; he was therefore not likely to appeal to the Puebla state organization.

As nomination time approached, the two strongest precandidates appeared to be Fabre del Rivero and Toxqui Fernández. Both men had similarities: they were educated in Puebla, they served in student leadership positions at the University of Puebla, they were state oratory champions, they held state administrative positions, and they were both known as men with conciliatory abilities. Here the similarities ended. They were men of different generations since Fabre del Rivero was thirty-six years old and Toxqui Fernández was sixty-one. Furthermore, Fabre del Rivero's experience was primarily appointive. Although he had served as a substitute mayor of Puebla in 1969, his two most recent positions were Director of Industrial Development in Puebla and Oficial Mayor of the Secretariat of Industry and Commerce. His advantages were two: he had access to persons who controlled federal funds, which gave him support among entrepreneurs in Puebla,[21] one of the key disgruntled groups; and he was known personally to the president, having served as a campaign aide in 1970.

On the other hand, Toxqui Fernández had much greater depth of experience in state politics and in electoral positions, and while he did not have contact with Echeverría, he was known to a number of recent governors in Puebla. His distinct disadvantage was that as the state director of the PRI in 1971, he was held responsible for the loss of fifteen municipal presidents (mayors) to opposition party or independent candidates; in 1973, the PRI, under his leadership, lost two federal deputy elections and a third was annulled because of electoral irregularities.[22] Toxqui Fernández became the PRI choice despite his reputed failures as state

director of the PRI. Although he had neither national political experience nor specific economic contacts in the federal government, he may have had the edge in the final analysis because of his numerous contacts within the state organization, and because "above all, he is a man who does not arouse passions."[23]

Michoacán (1973)

Unlike the other two states discussed above, on the eve of a recent election in late 1973, Michoacán had not been characterized by political upsets in recent years. But like Sonora and Puebla, Michoacán was the home state of a recent Mexican president (Cárdenas), and any candidate would have to deal with his factions going back into the 1930s.[24] The state was also a stronghold for the PAN, primarily because of its widespread regionalism, catholicism, and participation against the federal government in the Cristero rebellion of the 1920s as well as the Sinarquista movement of the 1930s. As of 1974, however, political skills were not at a premium and the more long-range problems of economic development were of greater significance. In fact, what would have been most useful against the organized opposition in Michoacán was an administrator who could achieve economic and industrial growth for the state.

There was no shortage of candidates for the office of governor. Among the four strongest precandidates were Cuauhtémoc Cárdenas, Enrique Bravo Valencia, Melchor Díaz Rubio, and Carlos Torres Manzo.

For Cuauhtémoc Cárdenas, both a strength and a weakness was the fact that he was the son of former President Lázaro Cárdenas, a man with more than his share of political enemies as well as friends. Cuauhtémoc Cárdenas had not been a strong supporter of the official party in the past, and he had associated with outgroups led by such imprisoned leaders as Herberto Castillo and Demetrio Vallejo.[25] Further, although he had considerable support from old-line *cardenistas* in Michoacán, he did not have good relations with the business community nor ready access to the purse-strings of the federal government.

The second precandidate, Enrique Bravo Valencia, was similar to the successful precandidate in Puebla, Senator Toxqui Fernández. His career was almost entirely in the political-electoral sphere of Michoacán politics. He was a career politician of the older generation, having served as federal deputy and senator in the 1940s and 1950s. Although he was a moderate within Michoacán political circles, he suffered from overexposure, having tried for the governorship on three previous occasions. In short, his skills were not economic, and his political skills were meager.

[21] *Excélsior*, June 1, 1975, p. 16A.
[22] *Excélsior*, July 4, 1974, p. 15A.

[23] *Excélsior*, July 6, 1974, p. 11A.
[24] For background on state politics see: Alberto Bremauntz, *Setenta años de mi vida* (México: Ediciones Jurídico Sociales, 1968); Lázaro Cárdenas, *Obras, apuntes 1913-1940* (México: Universidad Nacional Autónoma de México, 1972); Eduardo Villaseñor, *Memorias-Testimonio* (México: Fondo de Cultura Económica, 1974); and Armando María y Campos, *Múgica crónica biográfica* (México: Ediciones Populares, 1939).
[25] *Excélsior*, December 20, 1973, p. 9A.

A stronger precandidate was Melchor Díaz Rubio, a doctor and rector of the University of Michoacán. He had served as a federal deputy and as mayor of the capital city. While he was seen as a competent, experienced candidate, he had one fatal weakness: his Protestant religion. As the reporter Angel Trinidad Ferreira pointed out, a protestant candidate would be at a decisive disadvantage in a state which has produced eight bishops, the cardinal of Guadalajara, and the archbishops of Mérida and Hermosillo.[26]

This left Carlos Torres Manzo as the only really strong precandidate. His career strengths corresponded with the needs of Michoacán: through his position as Secretary of Industry and Commerce he had access to and contacts with leaders in the federal government and private enterprise. He had no experience in state politics or in electoral positions, but he did have widespread support among a group of Michoacán economists and public men who had recently been influential in state politics.[27] Of the precandidates, Torres Manzo had the professional qualifications which, at that particular time in Michoacán, appeared to be more important than political affiliations of the other precandidates on either the state or national levels.

These three cases add some information to our knowledge about the variables discussed above. No single variable is consistently important. In combination with recent state political histories, we see that national political experience need not be relevant, as in the case of Puebla; further, membership in a national camarilla, especially one in which the candidate is tied by blood, as in the case of Cárdenas, often works to the disadvantage of the precandidate. In fact, as Table 2-4 illustrates, none of the eight precandidates who were relatives of well-known national or regional political leaders were a winning candidate.

If we summarize the contents of Table 2-4 by groups of states, we can discern several clear patterns. In one group of states including Sonora, Campeche, Guanajuato, Michoacán, Chihuahua, and Tamaulipas the successful candidates all maximized the three variables discussed above: their qualifications, experiences, and political contacts were ample and well suited to their states. They defeated other precandidates who did not have equal strengths in all three areas. Further, none of these states, in comparison with others, had major political problems at the time of the selection process. A second group of states including Nuevo León, Durango, Zacatecas, and Aguascalientes also had no major political problems, and the winning candidates, while not having the best scores in Table 2-4, defeated men with equal or even lower scores. Only the winning candidates in a third group of states including Querétaro, Colima, Sinaloa, Hidalgo, Puebla, and Oaxaca defeated other precandidates with better composite scores.

Can we explain the reasons for these exceptions? In each case, there are additional factors. In Querétaro, the

strongest competitor against Antonio Calzada was Alfredo Bonfil. Newspaper reporters pointed out that Bonfil did not want to be governor, which was understandable since he was Secretary General of the National Farmers Federation, a position more influential than the governorship of one of the smaller and politically less influential states.[28] In the case of Colima, we lack complete information about the winning candidate, but one of the strong contenders, Cuauhtémoc Santa Ana, had only national experience and was the son of a former governor, which may have caused him some difficulty. In the case of Puebla the winner appears to have succeeded because of his local camarilla ties and political experience, although the latter was considerably tainted. Local political interests, whose influences are unknown, may have predominated in that decision.

Sinaloa, one of the major "problem states" in the Mexico of recent years, was faced with a political history of internal dissension and a drug issue of immense proportions.[29] The governor at the time was unpopular and his efforts favored the privileged class in Sinaloa. While the winning candidate, Alfonso Calderón Velarde, was a surprise, prompting *Excélsior* to refer to his selection as *tapadismo de nuevo* (secretism again), the editor conceded that despite his lack of national experience his selection was plausible as a representative of those groups ignored by past governors. Unlike his two strongest rivals, he was very experienced in state political and administrative activities, had earned a favorable image as an efficient mayor of one of the larger Sinaloan communities, and was not associated with the past two governors, both unpopular. Seen in this light, Calderón's selection was not an example of true *tapadismo* in Mexican politics.

True tapadismo may be seen in Hidalgo, a case that fits readily into the old mode of secret imposition influenced by a local political boss.[30] The "winner" in the Hidalgo selection, Dr. Otoniel Miranda Andrade, had all the qualities of locally imposed candidates: personal friendship with and political dependence on the person responsible for impositions,[31] a lack of national political experience or membership in a national camarilla, and state political experience only in fringe positions. The local strong man in Hidalgo was Manuel Sánchez Vite, who left the governorship in 1970 to become president of the Central Executive Committee of the PRI; he became governor once again in 1972 after one of the most lengthy and unusual leaves of absence granted a governor in recent political history. Instead of supporting other well-qualified friends, Sánchez Vite supported a man dependent upon his political power. This attempt at *continuismo* was pointed out publicly by none other than the Secretary

---

[26] *Excélsior*, December 27, 1973, pp. 10A-11A.

[27] Economists and graduates of the National School of Economics have been particularly influential in Michoacán politics. Among his supporters were several former costudents and professors.

[28] For evidence of the levels of political power in Mexico, see my *Mexican Political Biographies, 1935-1975* (Tucson: University of Arizona Press, 1976).

[29] *Excélsior*, October 17, 1974, p. 1A.

[30] *Excélsior*, October 12, 1974, p. 4A and October 15, p. 7A.

[31] The Secretary General of the National Action Party accused Dr. Miranda Andrade of helping his patron in sequestering a number of injured *panistas* after violence erupted in Tulancingo in 1972. For details of this affair, see *Excélsior*, October 13, 1974, p. 12A.

General of the National Federation of Popular Organizations (CNOP), who told the press that Sánchez Vite was a man who "had mental gaps and was lacking in political tact" and "wanted to continue running the state through the imposition of his successor." [32] Erroneously, he predicted that such an imposition would not be allowed and that Sánchez Vite's political career would end. But thirteen days later, on October 12, he publicly gave CNOP support to Miranda Andrade's candidacy. Miranda Andrade's precandidacy was further opposed by both federal senators, themselves early precandidates from Hidalgo, one of whom was a friend of Sánchez Vite. [33] Another precandidate, federal deputy Oscar Bravo Santos, opposed him because he had violated Article 48 of the Hidalgo constitution by not relinquishing his public post six months before the election. [34] Miranda Andrade was selected from among a group of close local cohorts because the other possible precandidates were too politically independent. [35]

In a category by themselves are the cases of Veracruz, Guerrero, and Tlaxcala. In Guerrero and Tlaxcala we find that the composite score of a successful was superior to that of his competitors, but that these states had serious political problems. On the other hand, *PRI decision makers* felt that Rubén Figueroa had the qualifications to reconcile some of the political problems in Guerrero. [36] He did not, however, have a popular following in Guerrero. In the Tlaxcalan case the state was split by political feuding and disagreements between state and municipal authorities. This was precisely the reason for selecting a man from the past, and someone with political skills.

Veracruz stands as an unusual case during the years from 1973 to 1975. When the imposition of Manuel Carbonell de la Hoz was announced, [37] the president of the National Executive Committee of the PRI, Jesús Reyes Heroles, said, "I, as a *veracruzano*, have not voted for him." [38] The result of this statement was nothing short of spectacular because in less than 72 hours, his assured candidacy was withdrawn. The statement by Reyes Heroles had pointed up an important fact: the "local support" claimed for precandidate Carbonell did not exist, such "localism" serving in this case as in so many others as a pretext for control by "the most sinister bossism." [39] The withdrawal of the boss's candidate opened the contest to a number of strong precandidates with national reputations, one of whom eventually won. The difference between the Hidalgo case and that of Veracruz which changed the course of events, was the personal interest of a native veracruzano in a position of sufficient influence to change the decision. [40]

Conclusions

Initially, we made three assumptions in our study of losing precandidates in Mexico. We suggested that our examination would reveal characteristics of victorious gubernatorial candidates of the official party, of the selection process itself, and possibly of some of the political trends in Mexico.

Victorious gubernatorial candidates nominated by the PRI do not have fixed and therefore predictable career patterns. The majority of them do, however, have certain characteristics which typify all potential precandidates in this process — professional education. While not necessarily suggesting a requirement, a candidate who has held office at the highest levels in the national governmental or party structure is much more likely to succeed in competition than candidates who have not had such experience. [41] In general, the largest number of victorious precandidates, as contrasted with the losers, have had a balance between state or local and national experience.

As for the way in which the PRI selects the winning precandidate, much remains a mystery, a mystery that only national leaders could help solve by revealing the intricacies of that process. We have, however, expanded our perceptions

[32] *Excélsior*, September 30, 1974, p. 1A.

[33] *Excélsior*, October 18, 1974, p. 1A. After Miranda Andrade took office on April 1, 1975, his political enemies, gaining in strength, were able to have him deposed by the Permanent Commission of the Congress on April 29. Both he and his political mentor, Sánchez Vite, fled Hidalgo to avoid prosecution for various charges. To my knowledge, this is the shortest elective term served by a Mexican governor since 1935. In removing his man from office, political enemies of Sánchez Vite seem to have permanently destroyed Sánchez Vite's influence in Hidalgo. For additional details, see *Hispano Americano*, May 5, 1975, p. 42, and *Latin America*, May 9, 1975, p. 141.

[34] *Excélsior*, October 17, 1974, p. 4A.

[35] *Excélsior*, October 10, 1974, p. 1A.

[36] This is reflected by his willingness to deal personally with the guerrilla leader Lucio Cabañas, who later kidnapped him. Despite some uncomplimentary comments about Cabañas after his rescue, Figueroa was still willing to interview him, alone. His consistent willingness to face his opponents was clearly useful to him as a precandidate.

[37] Manuel Carbonell de la Hoz was not only a close confidant of the governor, but he was closely tied to a previous governor and well-known political boss of Veracruz, Fernando López Arias. Carbonell had a reputation as a state official who frequently resorted to violence to achieve his goals.

[38] *Excélsior*, April 19, 1974, p. 1A.

[39] *Excélsior*, April 24, 1974, p. 4A. Carbonell was also strongly opposed by Popular Socialist Party leaders and by the mayor of Veracruz.

[40] For a short comparative analysis of the selection process in Hidalgo and Veracruz, see the editorial by Miguel Angel Granados Chapa, "Relección en Hidalgo, Imposición Inevitable?," *Excélsior*, October 15, 1974, p. 7A.

[41] This is supported by the makeup of gubernatorial nominations since January, 1975. These include Jorge Jiménez Cantu, who resigned as Secretary of Health to become the candidate for Mexico; Oscar Flores Tapia, who left the directorship of CNOP to become the candidate for Coahuila; Rogelio Flores Curiel, a federal senator and former police chief of the Federal District, who became the party's candidate for Nayarit; and Jorge de la Vega Domínguez, who resigned as head of CONASUPO to become the candidate for Chiapas. In the case of Morelos and Yucatán, candidates with more important national positions lost to other precandidates, but those also had national experience.

of some factors involved in the selection of winners — and losers. Let us look back again and list the states we ranked as heavy in political conflicts — Puebla, Tlaxcala, Guerrero, Veracruz, and Sinaloa. If we had Veracruz without the intervention of PRI President Reyes Heroles, an interesting pattern emerges. In three states, known friends of the President were defeated for the candidacy: under Echeverría, a state having major political problems was more likely to emerge with a candidate outside the President's camarilla, one who was a sop to powerful interests in the state or to a national leader retaining considerable interest in his state. This type of candidate usually had local political experience and was identified with old-style politics, in which precandidacy is handled in a very secretive style.

The more secretive the selection process, the more controversial the candidate. It cannot be proved that the president has to compromise with powerful competing interests, but our analysis definitely suggests that he does this more frequently than might be suspected. Further, sufficient agitation by appropriate individuals and interests can alter the selection of a "strong" precandidate.

While computation of a simple score for precandidates in Table 2-4 offers a tenuous means of determining the importance of certain variables in a selection process so closed to the outside observer, a general overview of all the variables together with qualitative analysis of specific individual cases provides some insight into the reasons for each official party choice. All of our variables are relevant, and a candidate who has membership in a national camarilla, has held or is holding a high-level party or administrative position, and has the best qualifications to cope with the state's economic-political problems will usually win.

What does our examination of these governors tell us about recent political trends in Mexico? A recent article suggests that the seven state governors selected in 1973 were part of Echeverría's experimental politics and reforms, while the twelve selected in 1974 are tried and trusted party stalwarts, who will put the PRI into "smooth running order for the selections of its presidential candidate next year, and the elections of 1976."[42] This analysis is at once too simple and full of exceptions. Most of the 1974 choices had not held major party positions, and several of them, as we have seen, were candidates of local interest groups in politically less important states. It seems clear that Echeverría, like most recent presidents before him, has refrained from imposing his personal friends on many governorships and has attempted to achieve a balance between various political interests within the official structure in Mexico. It would be a fruitless effort to try to predict future selections because each president and each state confronts the system with different choices. It appears, however, that precandidates with national political experience will become increasingly prevalent, an indication of the growing centralization of political and economic power in Mexico.

[42] *Latin America*, August 30, 1974, p. 271.

APPENDIX A
WINNING GUBERNATORIAL CANDIDATES UNDER ECHEVERRIA

State	Date term began	Candidate
Chiapas	Dec. 1, 1970[a]	Manuel Velasco Suárez
Tabasco	Jan. 1, 1971[a]	Mario Trujillo García
Jalisco	Mar. 1, 1971[a]	Alberto Orozco Romero
Sonora	Sept. 1, 1973	Carlos A. Biebrich Torres[c]
Campeche	Sept. 16, 1973	Rafael Rodríguez Barrera
Guanajuato	Sept. 26, 1973	Louis Ducoing Gamba
San Luis Potosí	Sept. 26, 1973	Guillermo Fonseca Alvarez
Querétaro	Oct. 1, 1973	Antonio Calzada
Nuevo León	Oct. 4, 1973	Pedro Zorrilla Martínez
Colima	Nov. 1, 1973	Antonio Barbosa Heldt[b]
Durango	Sept. 15, 1974	Héctor Mayagoitia Domínguez
Michoacán	Sept. 16, 1974	Carlos Torres Manzo
Zacatecas	Sept. 16, 1974	Fernando Pámanes Escobedo
Chihuahua	Oct. 4, 1974	Manuel Aguirre Samaniego
Aguascalientes	Dec. 1, 1974	J. Rufugio Esparza Reyes
Veracruz	Dec. 1, 1974	Rafael Hernández Ochoa
Oaxaca	Dec. 1, 1974	Manuel Zárate Aquino
Sinaloa	Jan. 1, 1975	Alfonso Calderón Velarde
Tlaxcala	Jan. 15, 1975	Emilio Sánchez Piedras
Puebla	Feb. 1, 1975	Alfredo Toxqui Fernández
Tamaulipas	Feb. 5, 1975	Enrique Cárdenas González
Hidalgo	April 1, 1975	Otoniel Miranda Andrade[c]
Guerrero	April 1, 1975	Rubén Figueroa Figueroa

a. These governors took office with or after President Echeverría, but their selection and election took place under a previous president, and they will not be considered in the analysis here.

b. Antonio Barbosa Heldt committed suicide before taking office. He will be considered here since he was the original official party precandidate and governor-elect.

c. Carlos Biebrich Torres was forced to resign October 25, 1975, and was replaced by Alejandro Carrillo Marcor. His downfall can be attributed in part to his inability to deal skillfully with agrarian problems which became more pronounced after his selection in 1973. Otoniel Miranda Andrade was removed April 1, 1975. See note 33 for details.

Part Two

CUBA

Chapter 3

An Index of Cuban Industrial
Output, 1930-58

Jorge F. Pérez-López

Introduction

Cuba has been the subject of much interest in the United States and abroad since Castro's revolutionary government took power in 1959. More publications about Cuba have been produced over this period than during any other comparable period of Cuban history. Serious studies of the Cuban economy, however, have been scarce. Economists, hindered by the lack of economic data originating from Cuba and by the difficulty in entering the island to conduct fieldwork, have, until recently, lagged behind researchers in other disciplines in analyzing the Cuban phenomenon.

Late in 1965, the Cuban Junta Central de Planificación (JUCEPLAN), broke the silence that had persisted since 1959 with the publication of a modest statistical abstract, *Compendio Estadístico de Cuba, 1965.*[1] This was followed by more comprehensive compendia.[2] In 1968, JUCEPLAN made available within government circles a yearbook, *Boletín Estadístico 1966,*[3] containing statistical data primarily from the period 1963-1966. Despite circulation restrictions, a number of copies eventually found their way abroad. Finally, in 1970, the UCLA Latin American Center published the data in the United States. The resulting volume entitled *Cuba*

1968[4] provided, for the first time in almost a decade, official Cuban statistics on many social, vital, and economic areas heretofore available to researchers only through such spurious sources as speeches and addresses by Cuban revolutionary leaders.[5] The publication of *Cuba 1968* kindled the interest of researchers in studying the economic aspects of the Cuban revolutionary process.

In the late 1960s, the Cuban government indicated a willingness to make materials and data available to scholars from the United States, and to participate in exchange publications programs with United States libraries. During April, 1970, the Library of Congress, in cooperation with Yale University, organized and hosted an International Conference on Cuban Acquisitions and Bibliography.[6] The acquisition of official Cuban materials by the Library of Congress and University libraries in the United States has filled a data gap that had existed for almost a decade and has partly satisfied

[Special thanks for assistance are due Elizabeth Salzer and Charity Roth (Inter-Library Loans Staff at the University Library, State University of New York at Albany), Ana Rosa Núñez and Rosa Abella (University of Miami Library), Roberto Hernández Morales, Juan Vizcaino and Ulises Prieto. I am indebted to Guillermo Pérez-López for assistance in the calculations; to James A. Gregory, Melanie Pérez-López, and Edythe Sweet for editorial and typing assistance; and to Carmelo Mesa-Lago, René Pérez-López, the late Carlos M. Raggi, Marvin Sternberg, and especially to Pong S. Lee, for criticism and encouragement.

[1] Cuba, Junta Central de Planificación, Dirección Central de Estadística, *Compendio Estadístico de Cuba, 1965.*

[2] *Ibid., 1966, 1967, 1968.* Cf. *Cuban Studies Newsletter*, 1:2 (May, 1971), p. 10, for annotations.

[3] Cuba, Junta Central de Planificación, Dirección Central de Estadística, *Boletín Estadístico 1968.* See also annotation in *Cuban Studies Newsletter*, 2:1 (November, 1971), pp. 22-23.

[4] C. Paul Roberts and Mukhtar Hamour, eds., *Cuba 1968*, Statistical Abstract of Latin America Supplement 1 (Los Angeles: UCLA Latin American Center Publications, University of California, 1970). The Economic Commission for Latin America in its *Economic Survey of Latin America, 1963*, published a report entitled "The Cuban Economy in the Period 1959-1963." It was pointed out that most of the statistics in the the report came from exclusively official sources (p. 259). An abridged version of the study was published in the December, 1964, issue of *Noticias de la CEPAL* and reprinted under the title "La Economía Cubana en el Período 1959-1963" in *Economía y Agricultura* (Lima, Peru), 2:6 (1965) and in *Comercio Exterior* (Banco Nacional de Comercio Exterior, México),15:2 (February, 1965). For the original and full text, see, United Nations, Economic Commission for Latin America, *Economic Survey of Latin America, 1963*, pp. 259-289. Shortly after, however, the Economic Commission for Latin America acknowledged the inaccuracy of some of the data previously reported and attempted to make adjustments since some of the reported data were target rather than actual data. See United Nations, Economic Commission for Latin America, *Economic Survey of Latin America, 1965*, e.g., Table 224, p. 284; Table 225, p. 285.

[5] For limitations of the data see Carmelo Mesa-Lago, "Availability and Reliability of Statistics in Socialist Cuba," *Latin American Research Review*, 4:1 (Spring, 1969) and *ibid* 4:2 (Summer, 1969).

[6] See Earl J. Pariseau, ed. *Cuban Acquisitions and Bibliography* (Washington: Library of Congress, 1970).

scholars involved in investigations of Cuban culture and society.

In addition, the largely unsuccessful revolutionary economic offensive,[7] which began in 1968, spearheaded by the "Zafra de los Diez Millones," sparked renewed interest in the study of the Cuban economy and indicated the primary importance of examining economic variables in the Cuban experience.

Most recent studies of the Cuban economy carried out in the United States or abroad through the end of 1973 can be classified in three general categories: those that deal with the organization of the economy and its operation under a socialist system; those that deal with the issue of income distribution, and specifically the controversy of moral versus material incentives; and those that attempt to compare the Cuban economy, or some sectors of the Cuban economy, before and after the revolutionary take-over on January 1, 1959.[8]

An examination of the last category, comparative studies of the Cuban economy, indicates the preponderance of studies geared to the agricultural or the foreign commerce sectors. These have not been matched by studies of the industrial sector of the economy or by assessments of the rate and extent of industrialization in Cuba.[9] The lack of published materials on these topics has not prevented writers who either sympathize with or oppose the Cuban revolution from attempting to evaluate and interpret the industrialization process to their own best advantage.

In this essay I contend that comparisons of the extent and rate of growth of the industrial sector of the Cuban economy before and after the revolution are not feasible given the relative unavailability of statistical data and of comprehensive long-run industrial production figures for the prerevolutionary period. Although fragmented data of the production volumes of some industrial commodities are available, there is no single study that compiles and combines all the available information into an instrument which can be used for comparative purposes.[10] A creditable attempt, in the form of an industrial output index for the period 1946-57, was first published by the Banco Nacional de Cuba starting with its 1954-55 *Memoria* and updated in subsequent editions. That index, however, covers a relatively short time period and its methodology of aggregation and coverage is not clearly explained. These factors, which are analyzed in detail below, raise serious doubts about the validity of analysis based on the Banco Nacional de Cuba index.

It is my purpose to calculate an industrial output index for Cuba for the period 1930-58 using published data on physical output volumes in the industrial sector. The methodology involved in the calculation of the index as well as the data used in the computations are clearly described in order to indicate the limitations of the index and its usefulness as an indicator of industrial activity. The calculated index is compared with the Banco Nacional de Cuba's index in an effort to estimate the rate of growth of the industrial sector for the period under consideration.

The study is not intended to incriminate or justify the political regimes that governed Cuba. Its aim is to clarify the historical record concerning the process of industrialization in Cuba before 1959 and to calculate an industrial output index that may validly be used as a point of departure in comparisons of the Cuban prerevolutionary experience with that of other countries or with the revolutionary period.

Time Period

My original intention was to study industrial production in Cuba since independence in 1902 and to include

[7] The "revolutionary offensive" is thoroughly treated in Carmelo Mesa-Lago, "Ideological Radicalization and Economic Policy in Cuba," *Studies in Comparative International Development*, 5:10 (1969-1970). See also his "The Revolutionary Offensive," *Trans-Action*, 6:6 (April, 1969).

[8] The categories are not mutually exclusive. Examples of works in the different categories (the list is not exhaustive):

Group 1. Michel Gutelman, *La Agricultura Socializada en Cuba* (México: Ediciones Era, 1970); René Dumont, *Cuba: Socialism and Development* (New York: Grove Press, 1970); idem, *Cuba ¿Es Socialista?* (Caracas: Editorial Tiempo Nuevo, 1970); Edward Boorstein, *The Economic Transformation of Cuba* (New York: Monthly Review Press, 1968); Sergio Aranda, *La Revolución Agraria en Cuba* (México: Siglo XXI Editores, 1968); James O'Connor, *The Origins of Socialism in Cuba* (Ithaca: Cornell University Press, 1970); Leo Huberman and Paul Sweezy, *Cuba: Anatomy of a Revolution* (New York: Monthly Review Press, 1960).

Group 2. Roberto M. Bernardo, *The Theory of Moral Incentives in Cuba* (University: University of Alabama Press, 1971); Bertram Silverman, *Man and Socialism in Cuba: The Great Economic Debate* (New York: Atheneum, 1971); Arch R. M. Ritter, "Human Resource Mobilization Strategies in Revolutionary Cuba," *Carleton Economic Papers*, 72-13, (May, 1973); Carmelo Mesa-Lago, "La Posición de Cuba en la Polémica Socialista de los Incentivos Morales y Materiales," *Revista Cubana*, 1:2 (July-December, 1968), *The Labor Sector and Socialist Distribution in Cuba* (New York: Praeger, 1968) and "Cuba: Teoría y Práctica de los Incentivos," *Aportes*, 20 (April, 1971).

Group 3. Alberto Arredondo, *Reforma Agraria: La Experiencia Cubana* (San Juan, Puerto Rico: Editorial San Juan, 1969); Aranda, *La Revolución Agraria en Cuba;* Cuban Economic Research Project, *Cuba: Agriculture and Planning* (Miami: Editorial AIP, 1965); Gutelman, *La Agricultura Socializada en Cuba;* Oscar Echeverría Salvat, *La Agricultura Cubana, 1934-1966* (Miami: Ediciones Universal, 1971).

[9] An exception is the work by the Cuban Economic Research Project, "Stages and Problems of Industrial Development in Cuba" (Miami: mimeographed, 1965?). Cf. Max Nolff, "Industry," in Dudley Seers,
ed., *Cuba: The Economic and Social Revolution* (Chapel Hill: University of North Carolina Press, 1964); "El Desarrollo Industrial de Cuba," *Panorama Económico* (Santiago de Chile), Part I, 16 (November, 1963), and Part II, 17 (May, 1964); and "El Desarrollo Industrial de Cuba," *Cuba Socialista*, Part I (April, 1966) and Part II (May, 1966).

[10] Yearbooks of International Organizations (United Nations, Economic Commission for Latin America, Food and Agriculture Organization, etc.) supply little information on Cuban industrial production. Cuba is missing entirely from three well-known international studies: United Nations, *Patterns of Industrial Growth, 1938-1958* (New York: 1960); idem, *The Growth of World Industry 1938-1961* (New York: 1963); and idem, *The Growth of World Industry, 1953-1966* (New York: 1969).

current developments. That time span was drastically short-ened to the period 1930-58 for two reasons.

First and foremost, reliable industrial statistical data are almost nonexistent for Cuba for the years before 1930. For the more recent period since the revolutionary take-over, there exists a statistical gap spanning 1959-63. In practical terms, the period 1930-58 is the only period for which reasonably accurate and complete production data are available.

Second, the industrial production index is a measure for comparison over time. The period selected for analysis must be long enough so that trends and cyclical fluctuations may be discerned, yet not so extended that a fixed-base fixed-weight index number series would not have economic meaning. An implicit assumption in fixed-weight quantity index numbers is that the relative importance of sectors and subsectors in the economy remains the same throughout the period. Given deep structural changes in the Cuban economic system and in the property relations that began in 1959, this assumption was not tenable for the period beyond 1958.

As a result of these two constraints, the period 1930-58 was the period analyzed here. This time span of 28 years compares with the time periods chosen by researchers in similar analyses of other economies. Industrial output indexes for China, Romania, Czechoslovakia, Russia, and North Korea (Table 3-1), use a period averaging about 24 years in length, the longest being 37 years, and the shortest being 11. In addition, the time period 1930-58 is interesting in the light of Cuban economic history since it coincides with that period of economic development when agricultural and industrial diversification commenced in earnest.

Historical Background

The interval 1902-1927 saw a vigorous expansion of the Cuban sugar industry which led to a continuation and acceleration of the fusion of the domestic economy with that of the United States. The Reciprocity Agreement with the United States signed in 1902 assured Cuba a large market for its sugar, tobacco, minerals, and other products, but, at the same time, it facilitated the entrance of U.S. agricultural and industrial products into Cuba, thus deterring domestic concerns. Modern productive techniques were introduced in the sugar sector, and Cuba, by embracing monoculture, became a very specialized export economy.[11]

During the first quarter of the twentieth century prosperity reigned in Cuba. Population doubled, monetary national income quadrupled, and real per capita income rose from 176 pesos in 1903 to 239 pesos in 1924.[12] The labor force was so fully employed that between 1902 and 1931, the country permanently absorbed 1,259,864 immigrant

[11] Julio Le Riverend, *Historia Económica de Cuba*, 2d ed. (La Habana: Editorial Nacional de Cuba, 1965), p. 235.

[12] Cuban Economic Research Project, *A Study on Cuba* (Miami: University of Miami Press, 1965), pp. 290-291. While these figures are in pesos, they can be treated as dollars here and throughout this study.

Table 3-1

TIME INTERVAL COVERED BY INDUSTRIAL OUTPUT INDEX FOR SELECTED COUNTRIES IN THE CURRENT LITERATURE

Author	Country	Period	Number of years
Kaplan and Moorsteen	Russia	1928-58	30
Staller	Czechoslovakia	1948-59	11
Lee and Montias	Romania	1938-63	25
Chang	China	1912-49	37
Lee	North Korea	1946-63	17
Hodgman	Russia	1928-51	23

SOURCE:

John K. Chang, *Industrial Development in Pre-Communist China* (Chicago: Aldine, 1969).

Donald R. Hodgman, *Soviet Industrial Production, 1928-1951* (Cambridge: Harvard University Press, 1954).

Norman N. Kaplan and Richard H. Moorsteen, "An Index of Soviet Industrial Output," *American Economic Review*, 50:3 (June, 1960), pp. 295-318.

Pong S. Lee, "An Index of North Korean Industrial Output, 1946-1963," unpublished manuscript, 1971.

Pong S. Lee and John Michael Montias, "Indices of Rumanian Industrial Production," in Montias, *Economic Development in Communist Romania* (Cambridge; MIT Press, 1967).

George J. Staller, "Czechoslovak Industrial Growth: 1948-1959," *American Economic Review*, 52:3 (June, 1962), pp. 385-407.

laborers from Spain, the United States, Haiti, Jamaica, the British Antilles, and China.[13] The income generated by exports greatly increased the capacity to import and created an economic boom.

With the outbreak of World War I in 1914, and the threat that the war posed to the European sugar industry, U.S. capital flowed in great volume into the sugar sector. Entrepreneurs expected the resultant expansion to continue in the post-World War I period with the advantageous profit margin that they enjoyed: although sugar could be produced at an average cost of less than US$.05 per pound, it reached a price of US$.225 per pound in the World Market in May, 1920.[14] The country was experiencing a time of high prosperity, "La Danza de los Millones."

It was a short-lived dance. Soon after the end of the war, European beet production revived and the United States output of sugar was placed in the domestic market. By November, 1920, the price of sugar had plunged to US$.055 per pound.[15] By May, 1921, it had fallen further to US$.018 per pound,[16] and chaos swept Cuba. National banking institutions, which had been founded during the boom primarily to provide funds for the sugar industry, became insolvent when many of the sugar enterprises could not meet their

[13] Carmelo Mesa-Lago, *The Labor Force, Employment, Unemployment and Underemployment in Cuba: 1899-1970* (Beverly Hills: Sage Publications, 1972), pp. 9-10.

[14] Cuban Economic Research Project, *Cuba: Geopolítica y Pensamiento Económico* (Miami, Duplex, 1964), p. 178.

[15] *Ibid.*, p. 179.

[16] Cuban Economic Research Project, *A Study on Cuba*, p. 230.

obligations. Depositors ran on the banks, many of which did not have enough cash to meet the demand. Branches of foreign banks, backed by their principal offices, were able to meet the rush of their depositors, but also required fulfillment of the obligations of their debtors.

Fearing a total banking collapse, the government took action in the form of a moratorium covering credit documents, mortgages, pledges, security contracts, and other types of obligations that would fall due before December 1, 1920. A limit of 10 percent on withdrawals of individual deposits was set.[17] The end result was that most of the Cuban banks were forced to close, leaving the foreign banks (controlled mainly by United States and Canadian capital) in control of the financial sector and in possession of substantial property interests, primarily in the sugar industry.[18] At the same time foreigners strengthened their control on other productive resources. The value of United States private investments in Cuba, which in 1903 had amounted to US$98 million, had attained a figure of US$1,505 million by 1928.[19]

The tariff reform of 1927 was nationalistic and attempted to break away from the dominance of sugar in the economy while achieving a more developed internal system. It offered protection to numerous industrial and agricultural producers who prospered despite the adverse economic conditions that existed among some sectors of the population. The tariff also signaled that the Cuban government had broken away from the traditional laissez-faire doctrine and had actively intervened in favor of industrialization and diversification of the economy. But the tariff was doomed to failure. The economic crisis that engulfed the country as a result of the Great Depression, political unrest, and Cuba's agreement to the Chadbourne plan[20] were serious obstacles to the fulfillment of its aims.

In 1930, the Hawley-Smoot Tariff, enacted by the United States Congress, increased to US$.02 the duty of Cuban raw sugar, forcing Cuban producers to further reduce the price of sugar to the point that they were selling sugar below the cost of production. Production and prices of sugar suffered abysmally low values during 1932 and 1933. United States and world demand for sugar decreased. While the economic front was in crisis, political unrest ran rampant. The Machado government was violently overthrown and a nationalistic revolutionary government established.

The new government was quick to institute social and economic reforms. Significant pieces of legislation were passed in the areas of minimum wages, length of the work day, and the nationalization of employment.

A new Reciprocity agreement signed with the United States in 1934, shortly after Machado's overthrow, granted that country numerous tariff reductions on items previously protected under the 1927 tariff. It was a step backward along the road toward industrial and agricultural diversification and political and economic independence from the United States.[21] However detrimental to the diversification of agriculture and industry, the Reciprocity agreement of 1934 reduced the duties on Cuban raw sugar exported to the United States and established a system of quotas which helped to resuscitate the sugar industry and with it the economy of Cuba.

Political stability, the reduction of sugar duties, the establishment of sugar export quotas, and the social legislation passed by the revolutionary government did much to improve economic conditions. In 1940, a new progressive constitution was enacted to take the place of that of 1901. The Constitution of 1940 incorporated labor legislation that had been passed earlier as well as stipulations for the creation of a merchant marine, a national bank, and a host of institutional reforms which, in time, would play a leading role in the economic development of the country. The new constitution gave Cuba, in principle, an institutional base capable of supporting democratic life and achieving political stability. Favorable world-market conditions for sugar after 1940 would provide the climate for the expansion of industrial and agricultural enterprises established under the protection of the 1927 tariff as well as for the creation of new productive units.

The outbreak of World War II had a favorable effect upon the production and price of sugar. The war paralyzed European sugar production and aided Cuba in the slow recovery of its sugar industry, dormant since the 1920s. The decline in international trade caused by war increased Cuba's foreign exchange and promoted both the establishment of new industries and the expansion of existing ones to meet domestically the demand for commodities that were formerly imported. International trade concessions gained within the framework of the General Agreement on Tariff and Trade gave advantages to domestic products without jeopardizing Cuba's export position. Monetary income, which amounted to 1,062 million pesos in 1945, rose to 1,946 pesos in 1952. Over the same period of time, per capita income rose from 206 pesos per year to 344 pesos per year, a 67 percent increase in six years, or almost 9 percent per year.[22] The price level remained stable after the end of the war; inflation was not a source of economic concern.

Government policies were deliberately geared at the stimulation of the nonsugar industrial sector and the diversification of agricultural production. Government institutions were created in order to implement new directions in the economy. The first Cuban central bank, the Banco Nacional

[17] Henry C. Wallich, *Monetary Problems of an Export Economy: The Cuban Experience 1914-1947* (Cambridge: Harvard University Press, 1960), p. 55, 58.

[18] *Ibid.*, pp. 67-68.

[19] Oscar Pino Santos, *El Imperialismo Norteamericano en la Economía de Cuba* (La Habana: Editorial Lex, 1960), p. 21.

[20] The International Sugar Agreement, signed in Bussels on May 9, 1931, is generally known as the Chadbourne Plan. For a detailed description of the developments leading to the Chadbourne Stabilization Agreement see Robert F. Smith, *The United States and Cuba: Business and Diplomacy, 1917-1960* (New Haven: College and University Press, 1960), Chapter 4, especially pp. 69-71.

[21] Julio Le Riverend, *Historia Económica de Cuba*, p. 257.

[22] Cuban Economic Research Project, *A Study on Cuba*, p. 620.

de Cuba, established in 1948, began operations in 1950. Swiftly following were the Banco de Fomento Agrícola e Industrial de Cuba,[23] an institution created in 1951 to provide credit for the promotion of agricultural diversification and new industries; the Fondo de Seguro de Depósito, funded in 1952 to promote the expansion of personal savings and to insure time deposits against the risk of bankruptcy of commercial banks; Financiera Nacional de Cuba, established in 1953 to finance self-liquidating public and semipublic works; the Banco Cubano del Comercio Exterior (BANCEX), 1954, whose role was to coordinate and promote Cuban exports either by aiding private exporters or by its own efforts; the Banco de Desarrollo Económico y Social (BANDES), established in 1954 to provide credit for the promotion of economic development in general; as well as some institutions of lesser importance such as the Instituto Cubano de Investigaciones Tecnológicas (ICIT) and the Corporación de Fomento de Hipotecas Aseguradas (FHA). [24] Commercial banking institutions, still recuperating from the crash of twenty years earlier, expanded and intensified their credit. The new government lending institutions, combined with the commercial banks, established a credit system capable of financing the development of agricultural, industrial, and social activities. The government further stimulated the creation of new industrial enterprises by passing Law-Decree No. 1038 on August 15, 1953. This "Law-Decree on Industrial Stimulation" offered fiscal and import tax incentives to new industries established in the country.[25]

The process of "Cubanization" of the economy, and in particular of the sugar industry, was accelerated during that period. In 1939, Cuban nationals owned 54 sugar mills that produced 22 percent of the total sugar production of the island. By 1952, the number had increased to 113, producing 55 percent of total sugar production; in 1958 Cubans owned outright 221 sugar mills (which produced 62 percent of total sugar production) and held controlling interest in others. [26]

A brief economic downturn was smoothed out by the expansion of exports brought forth by the Korean War. Deliberate government anticyclical economic policy (emphasizing expenditures in public works and infrastructure which nearly completely depleted substantial foreign currency reserves amassed during World War II and the period immediately following) served the purpose of stimulating the economy. In general, prosperous economic conditions prevailed in the country. The political front, however, was undergoing a deep transformation. Batista's coup d'etat in 1952 marked

the end of constitutional government and the establishment of a strong-man regime. Political life in the country, which had already suffered from corruption during the presidential terms of Grau and Prio, deteriorated quickly from this point on, despite continued economic prosperity and economic gains by some segments of the population.

The economic bonanza, however, apparently could not make up for the political malady that had overtaken the country. The revolutionary victory of January 1, 1959, toppled the Republican era and brought the country into a Socialist period which exists to this day.

Industrial Product Coverage, 1930-58

The industrial products that I have used to calculate my index of Cuban Industrial production are listed in Tables 3-2 and 3-3. Table 3-2 lists the products that originated from each of four industrial sectors, whereas Table 3-3 arranges the individual products within the divisions, groups, and subgroups of the industrial classification system used here.

Table 3-2

SUMMARY OF CUBAN PRODUCTS COVERED IN THE CALCULATED INDEX

Industrial sector and subsectors		Number of products
Fishing		1
Electricity and gas		2
Mining		13
Manufacturing		24
Beverages	4	
Shoemaking	1	
Sugar	3	
Processed foods	5	
Paper and paperboard	1	
Rubber products	2	
Textiles	4	
Tobacco	3	
Construction materials	1	
Total number of products		40

Production data were arranged in accordance with the International Standard Industrial Classification of All Economic Activity (ISIC), in order to obtain standardization and to allow international comparability. The ISIC industrial classification scheme is a

classification by kind of economic activity (or industry) and not by kind of occupation or commodity. The classification does not draw distinctions according to kind of ownership, type of economic organization or mode of operation. Thus, establishments engaged in the same type of economic activity are classified in the same group of the ISIC, irrespective of whether they are owned by incorporated enterprises, individual proprietors or governments or whether or not the parent enterprise owns other establishments. Similarly, manufacturing establishments are classified according to the

[23] For a brief summary of the conditions leading its creation as well as its record, see, Cuban Economic Research Project, *Cuba: Agriculture and Planning*, pp. 188-190.

[24] Joaquin Martínez Sáenz, *Por la Independencia Económica de Cuba* (La Habana: Editorial Lex, 1959), pp. 120-141.

[25] The text of the Law, as well as an indication of the extent to which new industries were established under the auspices of the legislation are available in Cuba, Consejo Nacional de Economía, *La Estimulación Industrial en Cuba* (La Habana Publicaciones del Consejo Nacional de Economía, 14, 1956.)

[26] Cuban Economic Research Project, *A Study on Cuba*, p. 293.

Table 3-3

PRODUCT COVERAGE OF THE CALCULATED INDEX FOR CUBA

Code[a] and ISIC numbers	ISIC categories	Product
D:0	AGRICULTURE, FORESTRY, HUNTING and FISHING	
M:04	Fishing	
G:041	Ocean and coastal water fishing, excluding factory vessel fishing	1. Fish[b]
D:1	MINING AND QUARRYING	
M:12	Metal Mining	
G:121	Iron ore mining	2. Iron ore
G:122	Metal mining except iron ore mining	3. Chromium ore
		4. Copper ore
		5. Gold ore
		6. Manganese ore
		7. Nickel ore
		8. Silver ore
G:130	Crude petroleum and natural gas	9. Petroleum
		10. Naphtha
G:191	Salt mining and quarrying	11. Salt[c]
G:192	Chemical and fertilizer mineral mining	12. Barite
G:199	Nonmetalic mining and quarrying not elsewhere classified	13. Asphalt
		14. Gypsum
D:2-3	MANUFACTURING	
M:20	Food Manufacturing Industries, except beverage industries	
G:202	Manufacture of dairy products	15. Butter
		16. Cheese
		17. Condensed milk
		18. Evaporated milk
G:205	Manufacture of grain mill products	19. Wheat flour
G:207	Sugar factories and refineries	20. Cane sugar
		21. Molasses
		22. Rich molasses and syrups
M:21	Beverage Industries	
G:211	Distilling and blending of spirits	23. Alcohol
		24. Cane brandy
G:213	Breweries and manufacture of malt	25. Beer
G:214	Soft drinks and carbonated water industries	26. Soft drinks
M:22	Tobacco Manufacturing	
G:220	Tobacco manufactures	27. Tobacco
		28. Cigars
		29. Cigarettes
M:23	Manufacture of Textiles	
G:231	Spinning, weaving and finishing textiles	30. Cotton cloth
		31. Rayon filament yarn
		32. Rayon tire cord
		33. Rayon staple
M:24	Manufacture of Footwear, other wearing apparel and made-up textile goods	
G:241	Manufacture of footwear	34. Shoes[d]
M:27	Manufacture of Paper and Paper Products	
G:271	Manufacture of pulp, paper and paperboard	35. Paper
M:30	Manufacture of Rubber Products	
G:330	Manufacture of rubber products	36. Inner tubes
		37. Tires
M:33	Manufacture of Nonmetallic Mineral Products, except products of petroleum and coal	
G:334	Manufacture of cement (hydraulic)	38. Cement

Table 3-3 (Continued)

PRODUCT COVERAGE OF THE CALCULATED INDEX FOR CUBA

Code[a] and ISIC numbers	ISIC categories	Product
D:5	ELECTRICITY, GAS, WATER, and SANITARY SERVICES	
M:51	Electricity, Gas and Steam	
G:511	Electric light and power	39. Electricity
G:512	Gas manufacture and distribution	40. Gas

a. Code: D, division; M, major group; G, group.
b. Fish catch only. Crustacea, molluscs, sponges, and other water products not included.
c. From mining and evaporation.
d. Includes rubber shoes produced, in some cases.

SOURCE: Adapted from United Nations. Statistical Office. *International Classification of all Industrial Activities*, Statistical Papers, Series M, No. 4, Rev. 1 (New York: 1958) and *Indexes to the International Standard Industrial Classification of All Economic Activities*, Statistical Papers, Ser. M, No. 4, Rev. 1, Add. 1 (New York: 1957).

kind of economic activity in which they engage, whether the work is performed by power-driven machinery or by hand or whether it is done in a factory or a household. Unless these principles are followed, it is not possible to maintain comparability between countries which differ in the way the ownership of productive units is distributed or in stage of economic development.[27]

For the purpose of this work, however, the definition of industrial activity differs significantly from the ISIC definition. In general, the ISIC classification is intended to cover the entire field of economic activities: agriculture, forestry, and fisheries; mining; construction; manufacturing; transportation, communication, electric, gas, and sanitary services; and government.[28] The definition used here, however, is more restrictive and parallels somewhat that recommended by the Statistical Commission of the United Nations to member countries in 1950, in an effort to encourage them to construct index numbers of industrial production:

> In its commonly understood form, the index of production does not comprise all activities in the economy. It is convenient and useful to limit its scope to "industry" in the narrow sense of production of commodities, excluding agriculture and services. The components from which it is constructed are the products of industrial establishments and these comprise a very substantial part of the whole economy. Moreover, the products aggregated in the index are generally the more readily measurable elements of the economy.[29]

Thus, the narrower definition of industry above used here is

closer to what are commonly referred to as "transformation industries," that is, those enterprises which, through some productive process, transform a raw material or intermediate commodity into a finished product. Activities such as commerce, services, transport, communications, and storage, which are under the rubric of industry under the broader ISIC definition, do not pertain to industry under the stricter definition used here.

The United Nations Statistical Commission report further sets forth that

> Water and sanitary services involve a considerable non-industrial element and should be omitted. All the other activities — mining, manufacturing, construction, electricity and gas — appear to belong to the scope of the index. There can be little, if any disagreement about mining and manufacturing. Construction is a rather more difficult case, but the difficulties arise because the problems of measurement are particularly troublesome in this field. Construction is an important industry, however, and it is desirable that efforts should be made to overcome the practical difficulties in the way of its inclusion.[30]

Despite the U.N. recommendation for including the construction industry, the calculated index does not because the fragmentary data available for this industry give rise to insurmountable measurement problems.[31] Rather, the method here excludes construction activities following the approach

[27] United Nations, Statistical Office, *International Standard Industrial Classification of All Economic Activities*, Statistical Papers, Series M, no. 4, Rev. 1 (1958), p. 2.

[28] Cf., United States, Bureau of the Budget, *Standard Industrial Classification Manual* (Washington: U.S. Government Printing Office, 1957), p. 1.

[29] United Nations, Statistical Office, *Index Numbers of Industrial Production*, Studies in Methods, Series F, 1 (1961), p. 6.

[30] *Ibid*, pp. 10, 12.

[31] Fragmentary data concerning budgeted value of building construction and number of structures is available from the Ministerio de Hacienda. There is no indication as to the composition of the structures, i.e., the breakdown between residential and nonresidential construction. Data are available from the Colegio de Arquitectos de La Habana, which attempt to throw light upon the square footage of new construction. The data are not useful because the report of two provinces (Las Villas and Camagüey) is incomplete. See Banco Nacional de Cuba, *Memoria 1957-1958* (La Habana: Banco Nacional de Cuba, 1958), pp. 173-186.

of other international industrial production studies.[32] The fishing industry was included because of the geography of Cuba and the great potential it had in its economic development.[33]

The use here of the ISIC methodology in the collection, presentation, and analysis of production data is consistent with efforts to apply this methodology to Cuban economic statistics which were being carried on by the Tribunal de Cuentas since 1952. The result of these efforts was the publication in 1955 of *Clasificación Industrial de las Actividades Económicas de Cuba*, a useful manual based on the ISIC framework that aimed at enlisting all government agencies to use the classification in their work in order to serve as a point of departure for the preparation of high quality Cuban statistical data.[34] The Cuban version did not differ significantly from the ISIC, except for some specific changes in product coverage to account for the types of products produced in Cuba vis-à-vis those produced in other countries.

Each of the forty output series used in the study can be classified under one of the following industrial divisions or groups: electricity and gas, fishing, mining, and manufacturing (see Tables 3-2 and 3-3). Availability of data was the deciding factor in determining the output series to be included in the study. Omission of numerous industrial series makes the calculated index fall short of a fully comprehensive measure. Industrial products such as clothing, furniture, chemical products, matches, paints, detergents, glass products, bricks and tiles, tin products, machinery, and others are not included because of incomplete statistical coverage. Nevertheless, the basis for this study can be defended by examining in some detail the role that the forty output series considered played in total Cuban industrial production for the period under consideration.

Table 3-4 shows the total monetary value of all Cuban industrial activities (industrial activities as defined in this study) for 1953, and also the monetary value of the economic activities corresponding to the sectors and subsectors from which industrial products considered in this study originate. The industrial sectors covered here were responsible for 77.4 percent of the total value of Cuban industrial production for 1953. These same sectors accounted for 77.6 percent of total value added by industry in 1953.

For the non-sugar manufacturing sector, where the omission of certain products was most severe, Table 3-4 points out that the value of total production included in the study amounts to 62.8 percent of total income and 56.0

Table 3-4

PARTICIPATION OF PRODUCT SAMPLE IN TOTAL CUBAN INDUSTRIAL PRODUCTION, 1953

(in C$)

Category	Total Cuban industrial activities[a] (1)	Product sample (2)	Percent coverage (2)/(1)
Sales and other income	1,540,101,682	1,192,500,631	77.4
Value added	539,009,728	418,615,665	77.6
Sales and other income (manufacturing only)[b]	934,601,452	587,000,401	62.8
Value added (manufacturing only)[b]	273,727,729	153,333,666	56.0

a. Industrial activities as defined in this study.
b. Sugar excluded.

SOURCE: Calculated from Cuba, Tribunal de Cuentas, Dirección de Fiscalización Preventiva y Control de Presupuestos del Estado, "Analisis de los Sectores Económicos en Cuba y su Tributación, Años 1953 y 1954" (La Habana, mimeographed, July 22, 1957), Tables A and B.

percent of total value added. Although the product-omission problem was rather serious in some instances (such as in the processed foods group and, to a lesser extent, in the beverages and construction-materials group), I assumed that the quantum series of the missing products followed the general movements of the products sampled. Thus, the movements of the individual omitted products are imputed to the movements, if the sampled products within an industrial group.[35]

This problem of incomplete coverage of products is one that permeates the calculation of historical industrial production indexes. Chang, in his study of industrial development in pre-Communist China, operated with an industrial product sample that represented somewhere between 40 percent and 70 percent of net value added by industry.[36] Hodgman, analyzing industrial production in the Soviet Union for the period 1928-51, faced data problems that forced his coverage to vary from 137 product series in 1934 to 18 in 1951.[37] Solomon Fabricant, in his classic study of United States manufacturing industries, experienced problems created by limitations of data and studied them in detail. Fabricant's conclusions indicate as a rule of thumb a "40 percent coverage" as sufficient to warrant the computation of an index of industrial production.[38] Even if Table 3-4 were to overestimate somewhat the true coverage of the

[32] The construction industry is omitted from the calculation of industrial output indexes in three major international studies. Cf. United Nations, *Patterns of Industrial Growth, 1939-1958* (New York: 1960); idem, *The Growth of World Industry, 1938-1961* (New York: 1963); and idem, *The Growth of World Industry, 1953-1966* (New York: 1969).

[33] Lee in his study of North Korean industrial production includes fisheries as an industrial product. See Pong S. Lee, "An Index of North Korean Industrial Output, 1946-1963."

[34] Hugo López Sanabria, *Clasificación Industrial de las Actividades Económicas de Cuba* (La Habana: Tribunal de Cuentas) 1955.

[35] This imputation procedure has been suggested in United Nations, Statistical Office, *Index Numbers of Industrial Production*, p. 12. Variations in coverage are treated at length by Solomon Fabricant, *The Output of Manufacturing Industries, 1899-1937* (New York: National Bureau of Economic Research, 1940), pp. 362-369.

[36] Chang, *Industrial Development in Pre-Communist China*. Chap. 3, esp. pp. 35-36.

[37] Hodgman, *Soviet Industrial Production*, pp. 49, 81-82.

[38] Fabricant, *The Output of Manufacturing Industries*, pp. 351-352.

product sample used here, it still exceeds Fabricant's rule of thumb and is in line with the coverage of Chang's and Hodgman's studies.

Production and Price Data for the
Calculated Index

The calculation of an industrial output index requires data on the physical volumes of industrial products, prices of those products and weights indicative of each product's importance in the industrial sector. This section deals first with the quantum data for the industrial products used in the analysis, and then with the prices used to calculate the industrial output indexes. The aggregation weights are discussed in the next section.

Production Data

My calculated industrial output index utilizes production series for forty industrial products (Table 3-3) for the period 1930-58. The raw production data and sources are presented in Appendix A. This section discusses briefly the quality of Cuban industrial production statistics for the period under consideration, and the estimation methods used to fill the statistical gaps and discontinuities that existed in some of the quantum series.

Production data for Cuban industrial activities for the period 1930-58 are available but of varied quality. The collection of official Cuban statistics was carried out by the departments, bureaus, ministries, offices, organizations, under which the activity took place. These different statistical offices often lacked the budget, personnel, and technical knowledge to do a thorough job. Worse, the work of the different statistical offices lacked coordination and central guidance, hence statistics were often duplicated in some areas and nonexistent in others. In 1952, there were 380 different departments with a combined budget of over 1 million pesos involved in the gathering of social, economic, and demographic statistics.[39] The lack of a central statistical office to direct, compile, present, and update this wealth of information led to the waste of valuable statistical data and resources.

In some areas, statistical data available were satisfactory.[40] Vital statistics, in general, were of a high quality and were published with regularity. The first population census after the Spanish domination took place in 1899 during the United States intervention. The censuses of 1899 and 1907, conducted by the U.S. War Department, were thorough in their analysis of population, citizenship, education, and the budget. The censuses of 1919, 1931, 1943, and 1953, conducted by the Dirección Nacional del Censo (called Oficina General de los Censos Demográfico y Electoral after 1931), were also very comprehensive, although coverage varied. The Census of 1943 was by far the most comprehensive, including statistical data on population, production, housing, education, social and sanitary conditions, wages, and salaries.[41]

Before the beginning of operations by the Banco Nacional de Cuba in 1950, there were little systematic data available in the monetary and fiscal areas. The Banco, especially through its Departamento de Investigaciones Económicas, contributed to filling the gap by collecting, preparing, and presenting in its annual report, *Memoria*, a detailed assessment of the state of the economy, including a consumer price index, national income, money in circulation, loans and obligations, national debt, availability of foreign currencies, deposits, and other banking statistics.[42] An independent journal, *Cuba Económica y Financiera*, which was published between 1926 and 1960, supplied much data in the areas of public finance and banking.

The only attempt to gather and publish statistical data from many sources on an annual basis was made by the Dirección General de Estadística del Ministerio de Hacienda which published very irregularly (1914, 1952, 1956, 1957) an *Anuario Estadístico*[43] The yearbook included vital and health statistics, data on banking and public finance, sugar production (including prices, availability, yields), tobacco cattle production, and foreign trade. Although it was a good attempt at a statistical yearbook, the irregularity of publication diminished its usefulness as source of data.

Foreign commerce statistics were comprehensive and of a high quality. The annual *Comercio Exterior*,[44] published throughout the period 1902-58, gives useful foreign commerce data under numerous classifications. A corollary to the influence of the foreign commerce sector is the ready availability of data for sugar production and tobacco manufacturing, two sectors closely connected with exports. The *Anuario Azucarero de Cuba*, published from 1937 to 1960 by Cuba Económica y Financiera, with information from the Instituto Cubano de Establización del Azúcar, presented data concerning the sugar industry: sugar cane cultivated, sugar cane processed, yields, production of sugar and

[39] "Las Estadísticas en Cuba," *Cuba Económica y Financiera*, 27:314 (May, 1952), p. 14, and "La Falta de Estadísticas en Cuba," *Cuba Económica y Financiera*, 25:294 (September, 1950), p. 23.

[40] For a general appraisal of Cuban Statistics, and in particular of vital statistics, see Cuban Economic Research Project, *Cuba: Geopolítica y Pensamiento Económico*, pp. 359-365. For employment and unemployment statistics, see Mesa-Lago, *The Labor Force, Unemployment and Underemployment in Cuba*.

[41] Cuba, Dirección Nacional del Censo, *Censo de la República de Cuba, 1929* (La Habana: Maza, Arroyo y Caso, 1920), 977 pp.; idem, *Censo de 1931* (La Habana: Carasa, 1932), 106 pp.; *Censo de 1943* (La Habana: P. Fernández, 1945), 1,373 pp.; idem, *Censo de Población, Viviendas y Electoral, 1953* (La Habana: P. Fernández, 1955), 325 pp.

[42] Cuba, Banco Nacional de Cuba, *Memoria 1949-1958*. The monthly *Revista* of the Banco Nacional provided up-to-date banking data as well as incisive reports concerning special aspects of the economy. It was published during the period 1955-60.

[43] Cuba, Dirección General de Estadística, *Anuario Estadístico, 1914, 1952, 1956, 1957*. Other important publications that lacked periodicity were, e.g., *Resúmenes Estadísticos Seleccionados* (La Habana: P. Fernández, 1959); idem, *Riqueza Minera, 1903* (La Habana: Imprenta La Propagandista, 1903); idem, *Producción Forestal, Años 1933 y 1935* (La Habana, 1937).

[44] Cuba, Dirección General de Estadística, *Comercio Exterior*, 48 volumes.

by-products, labor force employed in agriculture and industrial sugar-related occupations, world market prices for sugar, and so forth.[45] An earlier period, 1902-36, was also comprehensively covered by *Industria Azucarera y sus Derivador.*[46] Statistics on production, export, and consumption of cigars, cigarettes, and tobacco were compiled and published by the Commisión de Propaganda y Defensa del Tabaco Habano, an association of tobacco manufacturers.[47]

Mineral production statistics are plentiful, although their reliability varies depending on the mineral and the source of data. Metallic minerals (nickel, copper, iron, chrome, and manganese) were mined primarily for export, and are adequately covered by various statistical publications. Even when production data are not available, export data can be used as valid approximations. Nonmetallic minerals (gypsum, naphtha, petroleum, asphalt, salt) and metallic minerals, which were not very significant in terms of production and foreign trade (barite, gold, silver), merited limited coverage. Production statistics from the *Minerals Yearbook*[48] series, whenever available, are preferred over Cuban statistics because of continuity and consistency, standardization of percentages of mineral contents in the ore, and clear specification of the unit of volume used.

Electricity and gas production and distribution in Cuba were controlled by the Compañía Cubana de Electricidad (CCE). It has been estimated that 90 percent of all electric power and virtually all gas sold in Cuba were produced by CCE.[49] Small independent plants, sugar mills, and some industrial plants also produced electricity, but statistical data for these producers are available only for isolated years. Data on electricity consumption, per capita consumption, consumption by households, businesses, industries, and government are available for CCE, but production figures are not. United Nations data, which give estimates of total production of electricity and gas for Cuba,[50] presumably from CCE only, are the data used in this study.

The Instituto Cubano de la Pesca was responsible for regulating and developing the Cuban fishing industry. Statistical data on catches of fish, shrimp, lobster, crab, oysters, sponges, and other marine products were published, as released by the Instituto, in various statistical publications.[51] Data for the output of fishing activities other than fish landings are fragmented. Thus fish landings is the only fisheries category whose output series has been included in this study. Reported production is probably 25 percent lower than the actual fish catch.[52]

The most serious weaknesses in Cuban industrial production statistics occur in the area of non-sugar manufacturing. Exceptions are manufacturing industries prominent within the industrial sector and/or as a source of exports which are covered thoroughly by independent organizations, as discussed above. Comprehensive and systematic data are not readily available for manufacturing products of lesser importance or those destined primarily for domestic consumption.

The production of construction and building materials is not covered properly by the statistical data available. Cement production is reported in various sources, and the data appear to be complete and reliable since during the period under study only three cement plants were in operation.[53] However, there are no data for bricks, tiles, nuts, bolts, rivets, nails, plaster, sand, asbestos, roofing, soil pipe, and other construction materials production.

Data for the production of some processed foods can be obtained from official Cuban sources and from publications of the U.S. Departments of Agriculture and Commerce.[54] Comprehensive data exist for condensed and evaporated milk and for wheat flour.[55] Fairly complete data are available for the production of butter and cheese. There are no data for the production of candy and bakery goods, the slaughtering of cattle, meat preparation, fruits, vegetables, and fish canning and similar activities.

Shoe manufacturing was regulated by the Comisión Reguladora de la Industria del Calzado (CRIC), an organization directed by representatives of shoe manufacturers, tanning industry, and employees of the shoe industry, whose main purpose was to promote and protect the development of their industry. In 1952, about 1,500 shoe factories were

[45] Cuba Económica y Financiera, *Anuario Azucarero de Cuba*, 23 volumes.

[46] Cuba, Dirección General de Estadística, *Industria Azucarera y sus Derivados 1901/1905, 1904/1905-1913/1914, 1923/1924-1929, 1930/1931; idem, Azúcar: Síntesis Estadístico-Analítica* (La Habana, March, 1939, and October, 1939).

[47] Cf. Cuba, Comisón Nacional de Propaganda y Defensa del Tabaco Habano, *Nuestro Comercio de Exportación de Tabaco en Rama y Manufacturado* (La Habana, 1959).

[48] United States, Bureau of Mines, *Minerals Yearbook* (Washington, D.C.: U.S. Government Printing Office).

[49] "After 1948, the Compañía Cubana de Electricidad had been supplying 90 percent of the electric energy requirements of the country" (Cuban Economic Research Project, *A Study on Cuba* p. 580). According to a study for the year 1958, however, CCE was responsible for only 50 percent of all generating power in the country that year. In the same year, CCE produced 69 percent of all electric power generated in the country. Sugar mills produced 15 percent, industries (nonsugar) 12 percent and independent generating plants 4 percent. See Cuba, Junta Central de Planificación Revolucionaria, *Estudio de Producción y Consumo de Energía Eléctrica y de Uso de Combustibles en los Centrales Azucareros* (La Habana, 1960), p. 19.

[50] United Nations, Statistical Office, *Statistical Yearbook*.

[51] Fishing data can be obtained from Cuba, Dirección General de Estadística *Anuario Estadístico*, and *idem, Resúmenes Estadísticos Seleccionados.*

[52] *Ibid., Anuario Estadístico, 1957.*

[53] For very detailed information see, Cuba, Junta Central de Planificación Revolucionaria, *Consumo y Producción de Cemento, 1938-1958* (La Habana, 1959).

[54] Cf. U.S. Bureau of Foreign Commerce, American Republics Division, *Investment in Cuba* (Washington, D.C.: 1956); U.S. Department of Agriculture, *Cuba as a Market for U.S. Agricultural Products*, Foreign Agricultural Report No. 81 (Washington, D.C.: 1954); U.S. Department of Commerce, International Reference Service, *Cuba*, Foreign Service Yearbook Series, 3:30 (1946).

[55] A wheat flour mill, the first of its type in Cuba, was established in Havana in 1953 (United Nations, Economic Commission for Latin America, *Economic Survey of Latin America, 1953* [New York: 1954], p. 217).

operating in Cuba. Of these, 927 were duly registered and followed the regulations set up by CRIC: local license, minimum salary, payment of taxes, social security contributions.[56] In 1951, CRIC made it compulsory for each pair of shoes manufactured in Cuba to carry a seal (face value: 5 centavos) to indicate that it was produced in a registered factory. In 1958, approximately 16 million seals were sold, indicating a volume of production from registered plants of about 16 million pairs of shoes.[57] Despite the regulations, probably about 20 percent of production was carried out in small shops and avoided CRIC stamps and control.[58] The data used in this study come from CRIC sources, and thus underestimate the true production of shoes in Cuba during the period 1930-1958. Gaps in the data have been filled through simple interpolation.

In other manufacturing areas, the compilation and presentation of production statistics is wanting. For some industries, such as paper and paperboard, textiles, and beverage production, estimates of output volumes reported in official and semi-official publications had been arrived at indirectly.

Little if any data on the national production of paper and paperboard are available from Cuban sources. Two United Nations publications describe the conditions facing the pulp and paper industries and provide statistics on production, imports, and apparent consumption of paper, paperboard, and newsprint, for the periods 1925-50 and 1955-60.[59] Production data are estimates of domestic production based on imports of raw materials. The production estimates assumed that the raw materials utilized in the manufacturer of paper and paperboard were imported (with the exception of a certain amount of waste paper from domestic sources) and used imports of raw materials to estimate probable paper and paperboard output volumes. United Nations figures are used in this study, after interpolating production statistics for the period 1951-54.

A similar situation exists for textile manufacturing. Rayon production statistics are plentiful since only one manufacturing plant operated during the period under study. Cotton textiles, however, were produced by more than 75 factories, although one concern, Compañía Textilera Ari-

guanabo, controlled most of the spinning capacity.[60] Although fragmentary production data are available, no comprehensive statistics on cotton textile production can be obtained for the period under study.[61] Instead, imports of cotton fiber have been used to estimate the production of cotton textiles, following a suggestion in the *Economic Survey of Latin America.*[62] Thus, data on raw cotton imports published in foreign trade journals have been used to derive a series of cotton cloth production numbers.[63] Lags have not been introduced in the series to account for the time elapsed between the import of the raw materials and the manufacture of the finished product.

The beverage industry did not publish its production data. Estimates of production were computed by the government from available tax-revenue figures. In 1904, the Republic of Cuba contracted with Speyer, a New York banking firm, for a loan of US$35 million to cover the obligations incurred during the liberation war against Spain. Income for the amortization and service of the debt was to be generated by special permanent taxes levied on the production and import of hard liquor, wines, cider, beer, beverages, matches, tobacco, sugar, and playing cards.[64] A special department of the Ministerio de Hacienda was created to administer and collect revenues generated by these taxes. Data on the contribution of beverages produced domestically to total revenue collected by the special taxes were used to derive production series for alcoholic beverages and soft drinks. These data were prepared by the Ministerio de Hacienda and reported in various statistical sources.[65] This material is used here.

Detailed notes describing the source of each production data number, or the estimation method used in calculating them, are in Appendix A, below.

Product Prices

The aggregate monetary value of an industry's output is likely to change over time because of the variability in two factors: the physical production volume of the products and

[56] "La Producción Nacional de Calzado," *Cuba Económica y Financiera*, 27:313 (April, 1952), p. 15.

[57] In writing this section, I have benefited greatly from conversations with Ulises Prieto, a former CRIC officer.

[58] Although this figure is an estimate, it is not unreasonable, given the large number of small factories not regulated by CRIC. In fact, one of the main functions of CRIC was to track down and regulate these outlaw producers (*fábricas clandestinas*). See Walter E. Reiners, "Estudio de la Industria del Calzado Cubano," Report Commissioned by CRIC (La Habana: Typewritten, September 1, 1958), p. 13.

[59] United Nations, Economic Commission for Latin America, *Possibilities for the Development of the Pulp and Paper Industry in Latin America* (New York: 1953), and United Nations, Economic Commission for Latin America, *Pulp and Paper Products in Latin America* (New York: 1963).

[60] A comprehensive study of the textile industry in Cuba can be found in Economic and Technical Mission to Cuba, *Report on Cuba* (Baltimore: Johns Hopkins Press, 1951), pp. 953-965.

[61] Fragmentary data appear in Great Britain, Overseas Trade Department, *Economic and Commercial Conditions in Cuba, 1954* (London: 1955), p. 111. A presumably detailed analysis of the Cuban textile industry, *Industria Textil: Datos Estadísticos*, published by the Junta Central de Economía in 1949, has not been located in Libraries in the United States. It was cited in *Report on Cuba* p.953. The same applies to a "thorough study of the textile industry ordered by the Revolutionary government in 1959," authored by Carlos A. Quintana and Octavio A. Martínez, titled "El Desarrollo de la Industria Textil Cubana" (La Habana, mimeographed, 1960), cited by James O'Connor, *The Origins of Socialism in Cuba* (Ithaca: Cornell University Press, 1970), pp. 148n, 171-173n.

[62] United Nations, Economic Commission for Latin America, *Economic Survey of Latin America,1957*, p. 189.

[63] Import data from Cuba, Dirección General de Estadística, *Comercio Exterior.*

[64] Luis V. de Abad, *Los Impuestos Especiales del Empréstito de los 35 Millones* (La Habana: Editora Mercantil, 1941), pp. 109-111.

[65] See n. 51, above.

the price at which they are transacted. An index of industrial output should only be concerned with changes in the aggregate monetary value of an industry's products that arise because of changes in physical quantities. In order to isolate changes in the physical quantum series, it is necessary to maintain prices constant over the time period examined. To this effect, the year 1952 was chosen as the reference period for the prices of the forty industrial products used in the analysis.

The different output series within each industrial sector or subsector, as indicated earlier in this section and in Appendix A, were first combined by a Laspeyres quantity index of the form:

$$I_j = \frac{\Sigma\ P_{oi}\ \cdot Q_{ti}}{\Sigma\ P_{oi}\ \cdot Q_{oi}} \qquad (1)$$

where I_j is the output index for the jth sector or subsector, P_{oi} is the base period price of the ith commodity in the sector or subsector, Q_{oi} its output volume in the base year, and Q_{ti} its output volume in the year t.

Comprehensive price statistics for Cuban industrial products are not generally available, but fragmentary data from different sources for the year 1952 allowed the collection and computation of relatively reliable prices. Whenever feasible, domestic wholesale prices for the products under consideration were used. In other cases, unit values or other estimates were used as proxies for the domestic wholesale prices.

For most processed foods and beverages in the sample, the average wholesale price in the city of Havana for the months August through December, 1952, was available.[66] For these products, the price used in this study is merely an arithmetic average of the monthly prices reported.

For some of the products in the sample, export unit values for the year 1952 were used because domestic wholesale prices were not available. Average export values were used to approximate the domestic prices of tobacco products (cigarettes, cigars, and tobacco), products of the rayon industry (rayon filament yarn, rayon tire cord, and rayon staple) and some minerals (iron ore, chromium ore, salt, gypsum).[67] In those cases where Cuba did not export the commodity in question, average import values were computed and used as an approximation.[68] This was the procedure used to estimate prices for rubber products (rubber tires and inner tubes) and cotton cloth. Domestic unit values were also used for a large number of products. In all three situations, the underlying assumption is that export, import or domestic unit values can be used as a valid approximation for the domestic wholesale prices of the same or similar commodities.

[66] The data were gathered by the Departamento de Econometría de la Junta Nacional de Economía, and published in the *Anuario Estadístico*. The data used here are from *Anuario Estadístico, 1956*, pp. 638-639.

[67] Data obtained from Cuba, Dirección General de Estadística, *Comercio Exterior 1952-1953.*

[68] *Ibid.*

For products for which foreign or domestic trade data were not available, the domestic price was estimated by linking the calculated unit values of two closely related products for the United States with the unit value for a product for which the Cuban unit value was known (or had been calculated) and one for which it was unknown. This approximation method assumes that, in general, the ratio of the unit values (prices) of two commodities in a given country at a specific time reflects the relative costs of production of one product to the other. For countries that are similar in resource endowment, economic structure, and stage of economic development, the ratio of the prices of two commodities produced in the two countries should be similar. Thus, for those products in the sample for which a price could not be obtained from published materials, the ratio of the prices of two closely associated commodities in a country whose economic conditions were basically similar to those of Cuba and which produced similar commodities could be determined. Once this ratio is calculated, the price of a commodity for which the Cuban price was known and the one for which it was not could be linked with the known ratio calculated earlier, and the equation solved for the unknown Cuban price. The difficulty in obtaining wholesale industrial product prices for Latin American countries prevented the use of this method.

As a result, instead of using data for a Latin American country, the ratio of unit values of two closely associated commodities in the United States was used, in some instances, to determine the relative unit values of those same two commodities in Cuba. There are wide differences in structure, resources, and level of technology between the United States and Cuban economies, but since the procedure was used exclusively to estimate the prices of mineral products, the technological differences here are less important than they might be in another sector of the economy (e.g., manufacturing), and the ratio of unit values of some minerals in the United States was assumed to be valid to estimate the relative unit values of corresponding Cuban minerals.

Appendix B and its notes contain data indicating the prices or unit values for the commodities used in this study as well as their sources and/or methods of determination.

Value-Added Weights in the Calculated Index

The indexes for the twelve sectors of the economy were combined into indexes for each of the four divisions (not given here), and then further aggregated into a global index of industrial production (Table 3-7). A weighting system that reflects the relative importance of the various industrial goods represented in the index was used in the aggregation.

The formula of aggregation used is

$$I = \sum_{j=1}^{k} I_j \cdot \frac{W_j}{\sum\limits_{j=1}^{k} W_j} \qquad (2)$$

where I is the aggregate index of industrial output, I_j is the index of production for sectors and subsectors as determined by formula (1), W_j is the weight assigned to the jth industrial sector or subsector, and k is the total number of sectors and subsectors.

The criterion used to determine the relative importance of each of the industrial sectors or subsectors was the percentage of total gross value added by industry which was created in each of them. The value added by a firm or industry, that is, the value created by the activities of a firm or industry and its employees alone, is the difference between the market value of the goods produced and the cost of the goods and materials purchased from other producers. Since value added excludes from the total value of an individual firm or industry's production, the contributions made by other producers, it is essentially equal to the market value created by a firm or industry.[69]

The value-added figures described above are actually measures of gross value added. In order to calculate net value added, items such as depreciation, rent, taxes, interest on short-term debt, maintenance and repairs, expenses, and other purchases of supplies and services (e.g., advertising, light, office supplies, professional services) would have to be deducted from gross value added.[70] The lack of data referring to depreciation allowances and overhead items for the Cuban economy at the time of this study, prevented the use of net value added as the weighting standard. Thus, gross value added shares were used as weights indicative of the

relative importance of each of the industrial activities in the economy.

Official Cuban data on value added by industries are not readily available. Thus, they were calculated from raw data originating from the Tribunal de Cuentas, released in a mimeographed report during 1957.[71] The data in question describe the activities of the different sectors of the Cuban economy for 1953 and 1954. For each sector or subsector of the economy, total income from sales and other activities and total amount spent in the purchase of both domestic and foreign raw materials and services, other than labor are available. The difference between total income from sales and total expenditures for materials and services (from the domestic economy and/or foreign countries) for an industry has been used as the gross value-added weight assigned to each industrial sector or subsector. The weights and their source are indicated in Table 3-5.

Gross value added by fishing could not be computed in the same manner as the rest because data from the Tribunal de Cuentas aggregate agriculture, forestry, hunting, and fishing into a single sector. It was assumed that a worker in each of these four activities contributed equally to total income and to expenditures in the purchase of materials and services from domestic sources (there were no expenditures in other countries). Thus, considering that the 1953 census listed 818,706 persons as employed in agriculture, forestry, hunting, and fishing, and 5,814 indicated fishing as their

[69] Richard Ruggles and Nancy R. Ruggles, *National Income Accounts and Income Analysis* (New York: McGraw-Hill, 1965), p. 50.

[70] Fabricant, *The Output of Manufacturing Industries, 1899-1937*, p.347.

[71] Cuba, Tribunal de Cuentas, Dirección de Fiscalización Preventiva y Control de Presupuestos del Estado, "Análisis de los Sectores Económicos en Cuba y su Tributación, Años 1953 y 1954" (La Habana, mimeographed, July 22, 1957), Tables A and B.

Table 3-5

GROSS VALUE-ADDED WEIGHTS FOR SOME SECTORS AND SUBSECTORS OF CUBAN INDUSTRIAL PRODUCTION, 1953

(In current C$)

Sector	Sales and other income	Purchase of Materials and other Services		Value added	Percent of total value added
		Cuba	Other countries		
Beverages	115,357,684	67,501,723	6,611,800	41,244,161	9.85
Tobacco	43,501,150	21,620,574	925,906	20,954,670	5.00
Textiles	44,686,639	20,190,530	7,602,974	16,893,135	4.03
Processed foods	286,697,085	219,801,223	29,199,531	37,696,331	9.01
Sugar	499,013,045	302,896,383	12,995,462	183,121,200	43.74
Shoemaking	20,340,370	9,971,384	6,595,994	3,772,992	0.90
Rubber products	15,161,302	5,541,667	3,775,021	5,884,614	1.40
Paper and paperboard	24,692,173	9,629,235	6,980,402	8,082,536	1.93
Construction materials	36,563,998	15,009,100	2,709,671	18,845,227	4.50
Fishing	3,353,776	696,226	#	2,657,550	0.63
Mining	46,537,814	12,336,504	#	34,201,310	8.17
Electricity and gas	56,595,595	3,568,495	7,725,161	45,301,939	10.84
Total	1,192,500,631	688,763,044	85,121,922	418,615,665	100.00

SOURCE: Adapted from data from Cuba, Tribunal de Cuentas, Dirección de Fiscalización Preventiva y Control de Presupuestos del Estado, "Análisis de los Sectores Económicos en Cuba y su Tributación, Años 1953 y 1954" (La Habana, mimeographed, July 22, 1957), Tables A and B.

occupation, total income and value added by fishing were estimated.[72]

The manufacturing sector, formed by beverages, tobacco, textiles, sugar, processed foods, shoemaking, rubber products, construction materials, and paper and paperboard, contributed 80.36 percent of the total gross value added by the industries examined. The sugar subsector alone represented 43.74 percent of total value added, or 54.43 percent of the total value added by the manufacturing sector. Beverages were responsible for 9.85 percent of total value added, followed by processed foods (9.01), tobacco (5.00), textiles (4.03), and construction materials (4.50). Rubber products, paper and paperboard, and shoemaking contributed 1.40, 1.93 and .90 percent of total gross value added, respectively.

Electricity and gas, mining, and fishing, the nonmanufacturing components of industrial production, combined for 19.64 percent of the total gross value added by industry. The percentage of total gross value added originating from electricity and gas production and distribution amounted to 10.84 percent. Mining contributed 8.17 percent, and fishing .63 percent.

The percentages of gross value added for each individual sectors or subsectors were used as the weights through which the relative importance of each industrial activity was determined. The use of value-added weights, and particularly fixed value-added weight for each industrial activity throughout the period under study, creates some conceptual problems and disadvantages that have been analyzed in detail elsewhere.[73] Two implicit assumptions in the procedure are that, over the time interval under consideration, no changes occur in the quantity, quality, and kinds of inputs going into the creation of the final products, or in the quality of the outputs produced and that no changes occur in the efficiency with which raw materials and fuels are used to generate final output,[74] that is, it is assumed that over the time period examined, no changes occur in the demand schedule for productive services or in the level of technology.

[72] Value added by fishing was determined in the following manner: Data from *ibid.* indicate that agriculture, forestry, hunting, and fishing accounted for C$472,362,780 in sales and other income for the year 1953 while purchasing materials and services amounting to C$98,060,069. Thus, gross value added by the division totaled, C$374,302,711. From Cuba, Oficina General de los Censos Demográfico y Electoral, *Censo de Población, Vivienda y Electoral, 1953,* Table 50, p. 185, it can be learned that total employment in the agriculture, forestry, hunting, and fishing subgroups amounted to 818,706 workers, of which 5,814 were fishermen. Thus, 0.71 percent of workers within the division were fishermen. Applying this percentage to the income and value added of the entire industrial division yields sales and other income generated by the fishing industry alone of C$3,353,776; C$696,226 were spent for the purchase of raw materials and services; and value added for the fishing industry resulted in C$2,657,550. These figures have been entered in Table 3-5.

[73] Cf., Fabricant, *The Output of Manufacturing Industries,* pp. 29-30, and Chang, *Industrial Development in Pre-Communist China,* pp. 33-34.

[74] See, e.g., Richard Brumberg, "*Ceteris Paribus* for Supply Curves," *Economic Journal,* 63 (June, 1953). pp.462-467.

The calculated index assumes that the gross value-added weights computed for 1953 (Table 3-5) hold for the entire interval 1930-58, that is, the gross value-added weights calculated for 1953 are considered as representative of the gross value added by each industrial sector or subsector during 1930-58, despite the year-to-year variations that probably took place. Although the index suffers from the limitations in this restrictive assumption, constancy of the weighting system is necessary in order to construct an industrial output index for which each year's output volume may be compared with the volume during the base year.

The gross value-added weights computed here measure up well when compared with a priori conceptions of the structure of the Cuban economy for the period analyzed. The preponderance of the sugar industry in Cuban industrial production stands out clearly. Industrial production of sugar and by-products constituted by far the most important subsector of industry: 43.74 percent of total gross value added by industry occurred in this subsector. Other industrial sectors and subsectors were secondary to sugar and by-products in their relative importance in the economy.

Some comments are in order concerning the degree to which 1953 value-added weights may be representative of the entire period 1930-58. Sugar production in Cuba during the period 1930-58 was marked by wide variability in both the quantity of sugar produced and the price. The period under study saw the end of the sugar expansion period, the establishment of restrictive measures to control production and exports beginning with the Great Depression years, and finally the slow recovery of the industry stimulated by World War II. The culmination of the recovery period occurred in 1952, when a record 7,011,393 long tons of raw sugar was produced as a result of a crop free of restrictions. Throughout the period, the price of sugar underwent wide fluctuations. Variations in price and quantity of sugar produced were instrumental in causing significant differences in the total income generated by the sugar industry. Data in Table 3-6 suggest the acuteness of the year-to-year fluctuations. Whereas the estimated value of raw sugar produced in 1954 amounted to about C$425.1 million, this figure was approximately C$35 million less than in 1953, but C$35 million more than in 1955. That is, the value of the *zafras* (sugar crops) corresponding to the years 1953 and 1955 differed by approximately C$70 million (or about 20 percent of total value of the sugar crop for 1954) over a two-year period.

Assuming that gross value added by the sugar industry would tend to move proportionately with the value of the crop, it can be argued that acute fluctuations in the value of the sugar crop had serious repercussions in value added by the sugar industry. Taking into consideration the magnitude of value added by sugar production relative to total value added by other industrial activities (particularly fishing, production of paper and paperboard, shoemaking), it is logical to assume that value-added weights for different years for the sugar industry, and other sectors or subsectors of the economy probably fluctuated quite significantly.

Table 3-6

CUBAN PRODUCTION, PRICES, AND ESTIMATED VALUE OF RAW SUGAR, 1930-58

Year	Raw sugar production (1,000 long tons)	Average official price in public warehouses (centavos/lb)	Total estimated value of production (C$ million)
1930	4,620,973	1.23	141.3
1931	3,120,796	1.11	88.8
1932	2,604,292	0.71	50.8
1933	1,994,238	0.97	50.5
1934	2,225,869	1.19	68.2
1935	2,537,951	1.58	98.9
1936	2,556,937	1.73	108.3
1937	2,974,584	1.76	128.6
1938	2,975,949	1.45	108.0
1939	2,723,814	1.51	102.5
1940	2,779,350	1.36	95.2
1941	2,406,954	1.69	100.3
1942	3,345,056	2.53	201.6
1943	2,843,077	2.44	171.3
1944	4,174,041	2.47	251.4
1945	3,454,983	2.94	240.6
1946	3,940,728	3.55	385.7
1947	5,672,238	4.80	632.3
1948	5,876,761	4.18	578.0
1949	5,073,968	4.35	518.2
1950	5,393,541	4.64	586.1
1951	5,589,232	5.08	662.6
1952	7,011,393	4.13	764.3
1953	5,007,060	3.89	461.4
1954	4,752,720	3.76	425.1
1955	4,404,443	3.74	390.4
1956	4,604,942	3.84	418.9
1957	5,505,990	5.05	653.7
1958	5,613,823	4.18	554.2

SOURCE: Adapted from Cuba Económica y Financiera, *Anuario Azucarero de Cuba.*

The use of gross value-added weights for 1953 as representative of the entire period 1930-58, introduces certain biases into the index of industrial production. The year 1953 yielded a relatively small and medium-priced sugar crop. As a result, the value added weight assigned here to the sugar sector is probably too low for the period after 1945, and higher than it should be for the period before that year.

A similar situation, although perhaps not so acute, occurs in several other industrial sectors or subsectors. For example, total income generated by the mining industry was heavily influenced by the production of nickel owing to the relatively high price of that product in relation to other minerals. Nickel production in Cuba fluctuated considerably during the 1930-58 period, and the price of nickel also wavered significantly. During World War II, nickel was of strategic importance. The United States invested heavily in Cuba and built a plant to extract and condense the mineral. The plant, which operated from 1943 to 1947, shut down at the end of the war and did not resume production until 1951. In 1953, the year selected for the determination of gross value-added weights, the plant was again in full opera-

tion. As a consequence, income generated by nickel production was high, and this carried over to the entire minerals sector. It is likely that the value-added weight computed for the minerals sector in this study may be unduly high for the earlier part of the period under examination.

The only record of Cuban value-added data in published materials occurs in an unofficial source. In 1965, Philip Newman, a one-time economic consultant to the Cuban government, calculated and published value-added data for the Cuban economy based on "previously unpublished data from the Tribunal de Cuentas, Government of Cuba, for 1954, the latest year for which these data are available."[75] The value-added figures reported by Newman, for the year 1954, are presumably derived from the same raw data as those used in this study.[76] Except for what appear to be typographical errors in Newman's report, his calculations would be identical with mine,[77] if the year 1954 had been used as the weight-base year.

The Calculated Index of Industrial Output

The calculated index of growth of total Cuban industrial activity for the period 1930-58, the index of nonsugar industrial production, and that of the sugar subsector alone are presented in Table 3-7 and in Figure 3-1. Although the three indexes are found generally to increase throughout the period, some remarks concerning each of the individual series are in order.

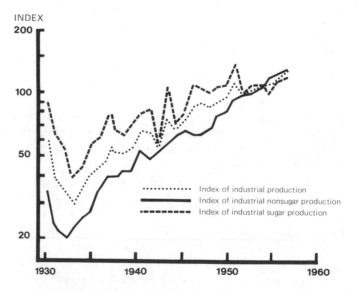

Figure 3-1. Calculated Indexes of Cuban Industrial Production, 1930-58 (1953=100).

The index of industrial activity in the sugar subsector varies greatly during the period 1930-58. Activity is generally strong during the first year of the study (when, despite the poor condition of the national economy, sugar output was

[75] Philip C. Newman, *Cuba before Castro: An Economic Appraisal* (Bombay: Foreign Studies Institute, 1965), Table 12, p. 35.
[76] See n.71, above.
[77] Cf., Newman, *Cuba Before Castro*, p.35; and Table 3-5, above.

Table 3-7

CALCULATED INDEXES OF CUBAN INDUSTRIAL PRODUCTION, 1930-58

(1953 = 100)

Year	Index of total industrial production	Index of industrial production	
		Nonsugar	Sugar
1930	59.18	34.01	91.57
1931	40.25	24.09	61.04
1932	33.77	19.83	51.70
1933	29.61	22.04	39.36
1934	33.69	25.40	44.35
1935	39.81	27.54	55.59
1936	45.95	34.15	61.13
1937	56.31	39.55	77.88
1938	51.80	40.15	66.78
1939	51.34	42.20	63.10
1940	55.05	42.59	71.08
1941	64.40	53.29	78.69
1942	63.16	48.87	81.54
1943	53.74	52.05	55.91
1944	76.86	56.47	103.09
1945	66.21	62.85	70.52
1946	71.57	66.56	78.02
1947	84.76	63.73	111.82
1948	87.31	64.23	106.99
1949	81.93	67.12	100.97
1950	90.59	77.96	106.84
1951	94.67	82.11	110.82
1952	114.24	94.67	139.41
1953	100.00	100.00	100.00
1954	104.04	102.05	106.59
1955	108.12	107.59	108.80
1956	110.53	117.49	101.57
1957	117.82	124.93	108.68
1958	124.40	130.00	117.21

1945-48 and 1954. The index of nonsugar industrial production shows gains during 23 years and losses in only 5 (Table 3-8).

Table 3-8

RATES OF GROWTH OF CALCULATED INDEXES OF CUBAN INDUSTRIAL PRODUCTION, 1930-58

(percentages)

Year	Index of total industrial production	Index of industrial production	
		Nonsugar	Sugar
1931	−18.93	−9.92	−30.53
1932	−6.48	−4.26	−9.34
1933	−4.16	+2.21	−12.34
1934	+4.08	+3.36	+4.99
1935	+6.12	+2.14	+11.24
1936	+6.14	+6.61	+5.54
1937	+10.36	+5.40	+16.75
1938	−4.51	+.60	−11.10
1939	−.46	+2.05	−3.68
1940	+3.71	+.39	+7.98
1941	+9.35	+10.70	+7.61
1942	−1.24	−4.42	+2.85
1943	−9.42	+3.18	−25.63
1944	+23.12	+4.42	+47.18
1945	−10.65	−6.38	−32.57
1946	+5.36	+3.71	+7.50
1947	+13.19	−2.83	+33.80
1948	−2.55	+.50	+5.17
1949	−5.38	+2.89	−16.02
1950	+8.66	+10.84	+5.87
1951	+4.08	+4.15	+3.98
1952	+19.57	+12.56	+28.59
1953	−14.24	+5.33	−39.41
1954	+4.04	+2.05	+6.59
1955	+4.08	+5.54	+2.21
1956	−2.41	+9.90	−6.23
1957	+7.29	+7.44	+7.11
1958	+6.58	+5.07	+8.53

high), contracts significantly during the Great Depression and the overthrow of the Machado government, and shows modest signs of recovery thereafter, particularly during the periods around World War II and the Korean War. Despite the stimulus of the two wars on Cuban sugar production, the volume of sugar produced in 1930 and in the decade of the 1920s was not consistently matched or surpassed by the Cuban economy until after 1947. Production per capita did not reach the marks set in 1930 and in the sugar expansion period that preceded it. Table 3-8 and Figure 3-1 indicate that the index of sugar industrial production exhibited a positive rate of growth on a yearly basis for 18 years, and a negative one for 10 years during the period spanned by this study.

The behavior of the nonsugar industrial component (Table 3-7 and Fig. 3-1) traces a different picture. After the collapse of the sugar industry in the early 1920s and the passage of the Tariff Reform of 1927, industrial diversification was encouraged by government policies. Cuban nonsugar industrial production increased modestly but persistently throughout the 1930-58 period, with the exception of the Great Depression years and short time periods around

The activity of the nonsugar industrial sector can best be examined by considering the behavior of its individual components (Table 3-9, 3-10 and Fig. 3-2). Electricity and gas production, one of the key indicators of industrial activity, and one of the components of nonsugar industrial production, showed impressive growth throughout the period, with no inflection points in its expansionary path other than during the Great Depression. Electricity and gas production increased more than fivefold over the period 1930-58, with output of electricity almost doubling between 1950 and 1958. The mining sector underwent serious fluctuations over the period. This seemingly erratic behavior can be explained in the light of export markets for Cuban minerals and the strategic importance that some of the minerals gained during the Korean War and World War II. Fishing grew modestly during the period analyzed: It underwent a prolonged decline during 1937-45; fluctuated between 1946-54; and grew beginning in 1955 to finish at a very high level of activity.

The nonsugar manufacturing sector showed a remarkable growth record during the period 1930-58, despite slow-

Table 3-9

CALCULATED INDEXES OF SECTORS OF CUBAN NONSUGAR INDUSTRIAL PRODUCTION, 1930-58

(1953 = 100)

Year	Manufacturing	Mining	Electricity and gas	Fishing
1930	34.25	40.43	26.32	68.60
1931	22.16	30.20	23.34	69.60
1932	18.42	20.48	21.13	71.10
1933	20.29	27.80	20.63	73.10
1934	24.65	27.70	23.33	75.10
1935	27.62	26.71	25.04	77.10
1936	34.28	39.37	27.23	78.34
1937	38.29	53.61	30.51	85.55
1938	41.12	43.06	32.30	83.02
1939	44.81	38.16	34.08	82.62
1940	44.51	40.62	35.38	80.93
1941	59.80	54.32	36.77	62.60
1942	51.17	53.48	37.68	47.41
1943	54.26	59.14	39.48	48.01
1944	61.29	53.38	42.76	52.47
1945	67.24	63.15	48.51	51.14
1946	71.70	62.64	52.89	53.70
1947	69.98	42.38	56.76	96.83
1948	69.94	37.94	63.52	85.65
1949	72.39	40.14	68.61	84.71
1950	86.01	44.48	75.37	88.51
1951	88.13	55.19	83.12	64.32
1952	99.25	80.17	91.27	74.36
1953	100.00	100.00	100.00	100.00
1954	103.64	87.69	108.11	91.34
1955	106.50	98.54	119.17	88.62
1956	119.61	88.80	131.44	126.17
1957	128.45	92.25	134.40	181.31
1958	132.85	93.18	145.17	180.50

Table 3-10

RATES OF GROWTH OF CALCULATED INDEXES OF SECTORS OF CUBAN NONSUGAR INDUSTRIAL PRODUCTION, 1930-58

(percentages)

Year	Manufacturing	Mining	Electricity and gas	Fishing
1931	−12.09	−10.23	−2.98	+1.00
1932	−3.74	−9.72	−2.21	+1.50
1933	+1.87	+7.32	−.50	+2.00
1934	+4.36	−.10	+2.70	+2.00
1935	+2.97	−.99	+1.71	+2.00
1936	+6.66	+12.66	+2.19	+1.24
1937	+4.01	+14.24	+3.28	+7.21
1938	+2.83	−10.55	+1.69	−2.53
1939	+3.69	−4.90	+1.88	−.40
1940	−.30	+2.46	+1.30	−1.69
1941	+15.29	+13.70	+1.39	−18.33
1942	−8.63	−.84	+.91	−15.19
1943	+3.09	+5.66	+1.80	−.60
1944	+7.03	−6.76	+3.28	+4.46
1945	+5.95	+9.77	+5.75	−1.33
1946	+4.46	−.51	+4.38	+2.56
1947	−.72	−20.26	+3.87	+43.13
1948	−.04	−4.44	+6.76	−11.18
1949	+2.45	+2.20	+5.09	−.94
1950	+13.62	+4.34	+6.76	+3.80
1951	+2.12	+10.71	+7.75	−24.19
1952	+11.12	+34.98	+8.15	+10.04
1953	+.75	+19.83	+8.73	+25.64
1954	+3.64	−12.31	+8.11	−8.66
1955	+2.86	+10.85	+11.06	−2.72
1956	+13.11	−9.74	+12.27	+37.55
1957	+8.84	+3.45	+2.96	+55.14
1958	+4.40	+.93	+10.77	−.81

downs during the Depression years, during the period 1944-48, and in 1954. The behavior of the manufacturing sector resembles the behavior of total nonsugar industrial production (Figure 3-1) more closely than any of the other sectorial indexes. This result is expected, given the heavy weight assigned to manufacturing relative to mining, fishing, and electricity and gas production in total nonsugar industrial production.

Data in Appendix C indicate the behavior of the output indexes for the eight individual subsectors that compose the index of nonsugar manufacturing. A cursory observation of the data points out the overall tendency of the series to increase over the period analyzed. However, producer goods subsectors (construction materials, textiles, rubber products, and paper and paperboard) tended to show more dramatic expansion than consumer goods subsectors (beverages, shoemaking, processed foods, and tobacco).

In analyzing the growth of nonsugar industrial concerns devoted primarily to the production of producer goods (i.e., involved primarily in activities that produce goods not exclusively for final demand), the importance of the forward-linkage effects of these activities should be noted. In general, expansion in the output of producer goods tends to

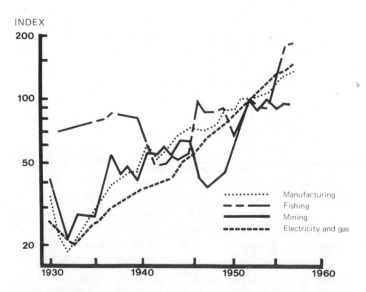

Figure 3-2. Calculated Indexes of Sectors of Cuban Nonsugar Industrial Production, 1930-58 (1953=100).

induce expansion of other industries which would use the outputs of the former as inputs in their activities. Unfortunately, data limitations have prevented the investigation in this area. Construction materials and paper and paperboard began the period with relatively high production levels and expanded over the time span, although exhibiting fluctuations (particularly in the case of paper and paperboard). Textiles and rubber products began from almost negligible levels and expanded rapidly during 1930-58. Tobacco manufacturing underwent serious fluctuations during the period, showing a very modest growth rate.

The calculated index is given in Table 3-7 and Figure 3-1. Table 3-8 gives the yearly percentage rates of growth of the index. They show that the index of industrial production had a tendency to increase over the period examined. Sugar production, in particular, has a large influence on the behavior of the index given the relatively heavy weight of the sugar subgroup in total value added by industry. Thus, during the early years of the study, when sugar production was high relative to the volume of other industrial production, the industrial output index resembles closely the index of sugar production. Beginning with 1945, however, the calculated index shows fewer fluctuations than the sugar-production index owing to the influence of nonsugar industrial production, which followed a steady growth pattern. In all, the calculated index realized positive changes for 16 years in the study, with industrial output more than doubling in the interim.

It is useful to calculate the average annual rate of change for the different sectors that compose the index, as well as for the industrial output index itself. Table 3-11 presents the average annual growth rate of industrial output in Cuba for the entire period 1930-58, as calculated from the industrial product index developed in this study (Table 3-7). Average growth rates for the sectors of the industrial production index (from Table 3-9) are also included, as are average growth rates for the post-World War II period, 1946-58. The data indicate that industrial production in Cuba expanded at an annual average rate of 2.69 percent for the period 1930-58, and at the more rapid pace of 4.71 percent in the post-World War II era. Nonsugar industrial production, meanwhile, advanced at an annual rate of 4.91 percent during the 1930-58 period, and at the rate of 5.74 percent per annum in the post-World War II period. Sugar production grew at a very modest .89 percent per annum during 1930-58 while for the post-World War II period, it advanced at a yearly rate of 3.45 percent. The last result must be qualified, however, since a comparatively small sugar crop was produced in 1946. If, instead, the period 1947-58 is considered, the result is drastically different; the annual rate of growth of sugar production becomes .43 percent (Tables 3-6 and 3-11). Nonsugar manufacturing and electricity and gas production, the two main components of nonsugar industrial production, displayed impressive growth rates (4.96 and 6.29 percent, respectively) during the period 1930-58, and even higher rates of advancement in the post-World War II period (5.27 and 8.78 percent, respectively). The rate of growth of mining increased modestly during the post-World War II period in comparison with the entire period covered by the study

Table 3-11

GROWTH RATE OF THE CALCULATED INDEX OF INDUSTRIAL OUTPUT IN CUBA, 1930-58

Category	Annual percentage growth rate	
	1930-1958	1946-1958
All industrial activity	2.69	4.71
All industrial activity (sugar excluded)	4.91	5.74
Sugar and by-products	.89	3.45[a]
Manufacturing (sugar excluded)	4.96	5.27
Electricity and gas	6.29	8.78
Mining	3.03	3.36
Fishing	3.52	10.63

a. This figure is misleading since sugar production was very low in 1946. If the period is changed to 1947-58, the result is drastically different, .43 percent.

SOURCE: Tables 3-7 and 3-9, above.

(3.03 v. 3.36 percent), whereas fishing, despite serious fluctuations, grew at an annual rate of 3.52 percent over the entire span of the study, and at a brisk 10.63 percent in the post-World War II period.

Table 3-12, compares the rate of growth of industrial output in Cuba with that of selected Latin American countries for the period 1948-58. The determination of the countries in Latin America to be compared with the calculated index of Cuban industrial production developed in this study was centered on the availability of data. Official industrial production index data, as compiled and presented by the Statistical Office of the United Nations, were only available for nine Latin American countries, mainly for the period 1948-58. In the case of two countries (Guatemala and Uruguay), the data covered a shorter time period than would have been preferred, but they were nevertheless considered in order to increase the sample size.

Average rates of growth of the industrial sector for Cuba and the nine Latin American countries were calculated from raw data for the Latin American countries from a United Nations survey and from Cuban data from Tables 3-7 and 3-9. Whenever the absolute value of the indexes decreased in absolute terms between 1948 and 1958, no rate of growth was calculated. Table 3-12 contains two different sets of data for Cuba, one that refers to the activities of the industrial sector, and another that refers only to nonsugar industrial activities.

Table 3-12 indicates that industrial production in Cuba for the period 1948-58 grew at an annual rate of 3.6 percent, as measured by the industrial production index developed in this study. This compares with much faster rates of growth for Venezuela, Peru, and Brazil, and is more in line with the growth rates of Chile, Guatemala, Uruguay,

Table 3-12

RATE OF GROWTH OF THE INDUSTRIAL SECTOR IN SELECTED LATIN AMERICAN COUNTRIES, 1948-58

(percentages per annum)

Country	All Industrial Activities	Mining	Manufacturing	Electricity and gas
ARGENTINA	1.8	4.6	1.5	3.3
BRAZIL	9.1	5.6	9.3	7.0
CHILE	3.3	(–)	4.2	8.3
COLOMBIA	6.3[a]	4.6[a]	7.5[a]	9.3[a]
GUATEMALA	4.4	~	3.9	8.1
MEXICO	5.8	2.0	6.2	8.6
PERU	11.1	17.5	7.2	~
URUGUAY	5.1[b]	(–)[b]	3.8[b]	16.1[b]
VENEZUELA	10.1	8.6	14.9	19.4
CUBA (all industrial production)	3.6	9.4	2.7	8.6
CUBA (nonsugar)	7.3	*	6.6	*

(–) indicates a decrease in absolute numbers

a. 1950-58
b. 1954-58

Calculated from:

> For Latin American Countries: United Nations, Statistical Office, *The Growth of World Industry, 1938-1961* (New York: 1963), various tables.
> For Cuba: Tables 3-7 and 3-9, above.

and Mexico. The mining sector in Cuba expanded by 9.4 percent per annum for 1948-58, a rate only exceeded by Peru, and approached by Venezuela. Cuban manufacturing expanded at a yearly rate of 2.7 percent, which is considerably slower than that of Venezuela, Brazil, Peru, and Mexico. Finally, the rate of growth of electricity and gas production in Cuba was 8.6 percent per annum, which although comparable with that of most of the countries of the sample, was significantly slower than the rates of Venezuela and Uruguay.

Although examination of Table 3-12 and the preceding discussion appears to indicate that Cuban industrial production expanded at a rate at least comparable with the bulk of the Latin American countries analyzed, a simple modification of the data points out significantly different results. If the rates of growth of the industrial sector for the Latin American countries in Table 3-12 are compared with the rate of growth of Cuban nonsugar industrial production, the situation changes dramatically. The average rate of growth of Cuban nonsugar industrial production over the period soars to 7.3 percent per annum and moves Cuba among the leaders, in roughly the same category as Venezuela, Peru, and Brazil. Furthermore, the nonsugar manufacturing sector in Cuba indicates an annual rate of growth of 6.6 percent topped only by Venezuela, Brazil, Peru, and Colombia. The

implications of this approach to the study of the rate of Cuban industrialization are very significant. If the stagnating sugar sector is excluded, the record of the Cuban industrial sector in the period under analysis is quite impressive, and certainly well in line with the development of the industrial leaders in Latin America during the same period.

Comparison of Calculated Index and Banco Nacional de Cuba Index

Although the invention of index numbers to measure the magnitude of a variable relative to a specified value of another variable is more than 200 years old,[78] the first attempts at the preparation of index numbers of economic activity did not take place in Cuba until the mid 1930s. At about that time, the Ministries of Agriculture and Finance undertook the task of developing a cost-of-living index and an index of wholesale prices for food products, in order to aid in the determination of minimum wages. Hugo Vivó, Chief of the Office of Index Numbers, Ministry of Agriculture, can probably be credited with pioneering the preparation of index numbers in Cuba. The publication of his essay, *Los Números Indices en Cuba*,[79] is the first recorded attempt at using index numbers in Cuba.[80]

In the 1950s, the newlyfounded Banco Nacional de Cuba assigned to its Department of Economic Research the task of preparing indexes of economic activity encompassing all sectors of the Cuban economy. The Banco Nacional de Cuba's *Memoria, 1954-1955* first presented preliminary figures of the indexes of economic activity for the agricultural and industrial sectors.[81] Subsequent editions of the annual report updated and revised these indexes. The behavior of the calculated index of industrial production developed in this study will now be compared with the industrial activity index prepared by the Banco Nacional de Cuba.

The economic-activity index presented in *Memoria, 1954-1955*, which uses as its base the year 1953, is broken down into agricultural and industrial components, with the agricultural sector further divided into sugar cane and non-sugar cane agricultural activities. The industrial sector is disaggregated into sugar, mining, construction, electricity

[78] Wesley C. Mitchell, *The Making and Using of Index Numbers* (New York: Augustus Kelley, 1965, reprint of Bulletin of Labor Statistics, 1938), p.7.

[79] Hugo Vivó, *Los Números Indices en Cuba* (La Habana: Secretaría de Agricultura, Oficina de los Números Indices, 1938).

[80] There is little evidence to indicate that the making and using of index numbers of economic activity was very widepread in Cuba. For instance, an international bibliographical study, W. F. Maunder, ed., *Bibliography of Index Numbers*, 2d ed. (London: Athlone Press for the International Statistical Institute, University of London, 1970), lists three entries of over a total of 2,000 which refer to index numbers in Cuba. Besides the mentioned book by Vivó, Maunder also lists the following: Hugo Vivó, *Números Indices. Naturaleza de los Números Indices: Números Indices de Precios al por Mayor: Otras Clases de Números Indices* (La Habana: Talleres Tipográficos de Editorial Lex, 1945), 61 pp., and Hugo Vivó, "El Movimiento de Precios en Cuba," *Estadística y Análisis Económico* (La Habana), 1 (January, 1953), p. 3,

[81] Banco Nacional de Cuba, *Memoria, 1954-1955*, pp. 154-163.

and gas, and manufacturing subsectors. The period covered by the indexes is 1946-54.

The index numbers are presented as preliminary and tentative. A special publication of the Banco Nacional, to be made available to the public later on, would supply further information on the indexes, and would clarify such areas as the method of aggregation, base, and method of computation. The Banco's report reminded the reader of the difficulties in obtaining and compiling Cuban statistics and stressed the efforts being undertaken to prepare comprehensive indexes. Further, in reference to the industrial activity index it indicated that reliable statistical series dealing with the production of beverages, tobacco, textiles, footwear, rubber products, petroleum refining and by-products, and others were available, although there was no mention of whether these series were the ones used to compute the industrial output index. Presumably these were the series used, for the report indicated that statistical data were not available concerning the production of foodstuffs, clothing, paper, printing, metal products, and other areas, and therefore they were not included in the preparation of the index. In all, the index claimed to cover 53 percent of all nonsugar manufacturing activities.[82]

Research has failed to locate the announced special supplemental publication of the Banco Nacional, if indeed it was ever published. If it was released, circulation must have been very limited, hence there is no clear and readily available explanation of how the index was computed or of which products were included.[83] Thus, the usefulness of the Banco Nacional de Cuba's industrial output index as a tool of economic analysis is weakened.

The validity of conclusions based on the Banco Nacional index may be further weakened because it suffers from both limited product coverage and a short time span. There is very little information concerning the industrial activities included in the computation of the index. The only available data point out that the index accounts for 53 percent of all nonsugar manufacturing activities. The percentage of construction, mining, and other activities presumably included is not explicitly mentioned. This raises doubts regarding the completeness of the coverage of these industries. A further complicating factor is the short time period covered. The first figures published correspond to 1946 and the latest ones available to 1957, so that a period of just over one decade is covered. Thus, although the index may be appropriate for short-term studies, it is not useful whenever long-term implications are concerned.[84]

Despite its weaknesses the Banco Nacional de Cuba production index has been widely used as an indicator of Cuban industrial activity ever since it was published. It was included in official government documents and appraisals of the economy, and appeared in international publications as the official (and only) index of economic activity for Cuba. Its usefulness to students of the Cuban economy has been very significant.[85]

The calculated industrial output index strives to avoid some of the problems of the Banco's index, and yet they both share some weaknesses that are inherent in this undertaking. The methodology of the calculated index is clearly spelled out and the data and sources used included in Appendixes A and B below. The time period covered by the calculated index is considerably longer than that of the Banco's index, 28 years versus just over a decade. The product coverage, however, remains incomplete, a similar problem to that faced by the Banco Nacional index.

The industries covered by the calculated index account for 62.8 percent of all sales and other income generated in nonsugar manufacturing for 1953. These industries represent 56 percent of all value added by nonsugar manufacturing for the same year.[86] Sugar, fishing, electricity and gas, and mining sectors are represented by a much higher percentage of all production in their respective sectors than is the case in manufacturing. In all, the calculated index probably covers a slightly greater share of all nonsugar manufacturing activities and a comparable share of mining, electricity and gas, and sugar activities than that covered by the Banco Nacional index.[87]

A comparison of the industrial output index for Cuba prepared by the Banco Nacional de Cuba and the calculated index for the period applicable is given in Table 3-13 and Figure 3-3 below. Table 3-14 and Figures 3-4, 3-5 and 3-6 offer a comparison of Banco Nacional de Cuba and calculated index of industrial output for some sectors of the economy. A close comparison of the official and calculated indexes indicates very similar behavior.

The two production indexes for electricity and gas are remarkably alike, with the exception of an abrupt difference for 1956 (see Fig. 3-5). The close correspondence lends authority to the calculated index, but this correspondence is not very surprising considering that the production series represent two homogeneous goods produced mainly by one large enterprise. The large difference for 1957 could have been caused by a typographical error either in the data used

---

[82] *Ibid*., pp. 161-163.

[83] The presumed publication is not listed as existing in the collection at the Library of Congress or in other libraries in the United States. No summary (or even mention) of it is made in the *Revista* of the Banco Nacional de Cuba. See "Indice Quinquenal: Enero de 1955-Diciembre de 1959," *Revista del Banco Nacional de Cuba,* 5:11-12 (November-December, 1959), pp. 1401-1412.

[84] For the most part, indexes are more reliable for short-period comparisons and, theoretically, more reliable for periods close to the weight base. Longer-period indexes are very useful in tracing changes

in a variable or variables over time and allowing for the examination of long-term processes. Although reliability is lost by moving from the base year, long-term indexes throw light upon relatively long-term tendencies in economic activity.

[85] E.g., Universidad Católica de Santo Tomás de Villanueva, Instituto de Investigaciones Económicas, *Cuba y Canadá: Investigación Económica Comparativa* (La Habana: Editorial Lex, 1957).

[86] Refer to sections on Industrial Product Coverage and Value-Added Weights in this study.

[87] There is no evidence to indicate that the fishing industry was covered by the "official" index while it is covered by the calculated index. See Banco Nacional de Cuba, *Memoria, 1954-1955*.

Table 3-13

BANCO NACIONAL DE CUBA INDEX AND CALCULATED INDUSTRIAL OUTPUT INDEX FOR THE CUBAN ECONOMY, 1946-58

(1953 = 100)

Year	A Banco Nacional de Cuba[a]	B Calculated
1946	81.0	71.6
1947	99.0	84.8
1948	92.1	87.3
1949	88.9	81.9
1950	99.5	90.6
1951	103.9	94.7
1952	114.4	114.2
1953	100.0	100.0
1954	103.3	104.0
1955	104.4	108.1
1956	106.8	110.5
1957	~	117.8
1958	~	124.4

a. The Banco Nacional de Cuba often revised its figures. These are the latest ones available.

SOURCE:

    A. 1946-51, Banco Nacional de Cuba, *Memoria, 1954-55.*
       1952-56, *ibid., 1956-57.*
    B. Table 3-7 in this study.

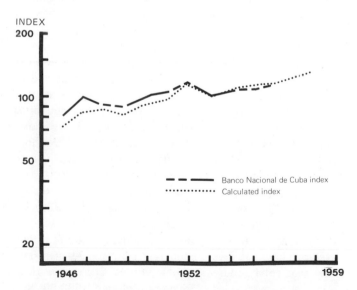

Figure 3-3. Banco Nacional de Cuba Index and Calculated Output Index for the Cuban Economy, 1946-58 (1953=100).

for the calculation of the official index or in the computations of the calculated index. The Banco Nacional de Cuba may have revised this latter figure in a more recent publication, but those data are not available.

The indexes representing the mining industry (Fig. 3-4) are also quite compatible. Although the magnitude of year-to-year change in the two indexes is quite different at times, the direction of change is, generally, the same. These differences in the magnitude of the changes could be influenced

Table 3-14

BANCO NACIONAL DE CUBA INDEX (1) AND CALCULATED INDUSTRIAL OUTPUT, INDEX (2) FOR SOME SECTORS OF THE CUBAN ECONOMY, 1946-58

(1953 = 100)

Year	Mining (1)	Mining (2)	Electricity and gas (1)	Electricity and gas (2)	Manufacturing[a] (1)	Manufacturing[a] (2)
1946	58.4	62.7	53.7	52.9	83.9	71.7
1947	38.6	42.4	57.1	56.8	96.4	70.0
1948	25.0	37.9	63.9	63.5	76.7	69.9
1949	22.5	40.1	69.0	68.6	82.3	72.4
1950	36.4	44.5	76.0	75.4	94.0	86.0
1951	36.6	55.2	83.2	83.1	99.4	88.1
1952	59.2	30.2	91.2	91.3	104.4	99.3
1953	100.0	100.0	100.0	100.0	100.0	100.0
1954	86.7	87.7	108.7	108.1	102.1	103.6
1955	80.5	98.5	118.6	119.2	104.5	106.5
1956	78.6	88.8	132.2	131.4	110.7	119.6
1957	85.0	93.0	146.0	134.4	115.3	128.5
1958	~	93.2	~	145.2	~	132.9

a. Sugar excluded.

SOURCE:

   Mining
     (1) 1946: Banco Nacional de Cuba, *Memoria, 1954-1955.*
         1947-57: *Ibid., 1956-1957.*
     (2) 1946-58: Calculated. See Table 3-9, above.

   Electricity and gas
     (1) 1946-54: Banco Nacional de Cuba, *Memoria, 1954-1955.*
         1955-57: *Ibid., 1955-1957.*
     (2) 1946-58: Calculated. See Table 3-9, above.

   Manufacturing
     (1) 1946-57: Banco Nacional de Cuba, *Memoria, 1956-1957.*
     (2) 1946-58: Calculated. See Table 3-9, above.

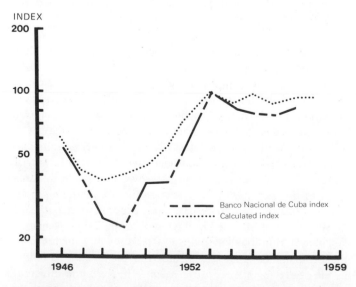

Figure 3-4. Comparison of Banco Nacional de Cuba Index and Calculated Mining Production Index for the Cuban Economy, 1946-58 (1953=100).

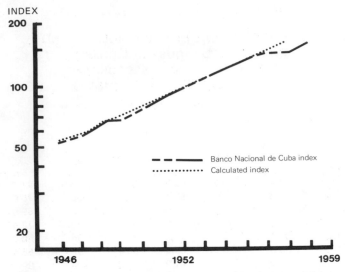

Figure 3-5. Comparison of Banco Nacional de Cuba Index and Calculated Electricity and Gas Production Index for the Cuban Economy, 1946-58 (1953=100).

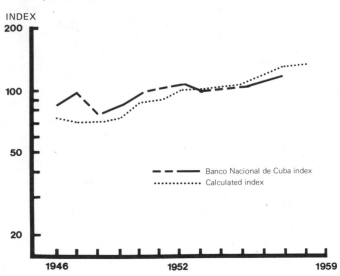

Figure 3-6. Comparison of Banco Nacional de Cuba Index and Calculated Nonsugar Manufacturing Production Index for the Cuban Economy, 1946-58 (1953=100).

by differences in product coverage and different relative price composition. If the latter consideration were true, a situation very much like the one that takes place here could be expected. In all, the two indexes appear to move together and the relative changes to be of an order of a magnitude that would validate the behavior of the calculated index.

As expected, the greatest divergences between the two indexes are found in the nonsugar manufacturing industrial sector. The product coverage of the two indexes in this area is quite different, with the calculated index including foodstuffs, construction materials, and paper and paperboard presumably not included in the index of the Banco Nacional. Petroleum refining and by-products, probably included in the official index, are not included in the calculated index. In all, the two indexes move roughly in the same direction although the magnitudes of period-to-period changes are quite different.

A comparison of the two indexes of total industrial production bears out a close correspondence (Table 3-13 and Figure 3-3). Differences can probably be explained in terms of the role played by the sugar sector in influencing the behavior of the total industrial output index. Thus, the calculated index shows a slightly faster and steadier pattern of growth of the industrial production than the Banco's index, which is probably more heavily influenced by the volatile sugar sector. Despite these differences, the two indexes have a degree of correspondence which tends to justify the calculated index.

Conclusion

The index of Cuban industrial output calculated here indicates a modest but significant growth rate of Cuban industrial production in the period under study. Particularly in the post-World War II period, Cuban industrial production underwent significant growth to levels never before accomplished.

Several interpretations can be set forth concerning the industrialization process in Cuba and specifically the impressive growth of nonsugar industrial production during the period spanned by this work. The resurgence of native entrepreneurship after the banking collapse of the late 1920s and the relative political stability after the overthrow of Machado in 1933 offered a climate for investment activity which was conducive to laying the foundations for later development. Government economic policies geared to the diversification of production led to a more developed internal economy which was not so dependent on a single export product. The active involvement of government in protecting nascent industries, large public investments in public works and in the infrastructure, social and economic reform legislation, together with favorable prices for sugar during and after world War II, brought prosperity and the flourishing of numerous industrial enterprises throughout the island. Development institutions created during this period were instrumental in directing and financing the growth of Cuban industry.

Table 3-11 presents the annual average growth rate of industrial output in Cuba for the period 1930-58 and 1946-58, as calculated from the industrial output index developed here and presented in Tables 3-7 and 3-9. The data show that total industrial production in Cuba grew at an annual average rate of 2.69 percent during 1930-58, and 4.71 percent in the post-World War II era. Nonsugar industrial production meanwhile advanced at a rate of 4.91 percent per year during 1930-58, and 5.74 percent yearly in the post-World War II period. Sugar production grew at a modest .89 percent per annum during 1930-58 and at 3.45 percent yearly during 1946-58. The last figure must be qualified, however, since a comparatively small sugar crop was obtained in 1946. If instead the period 1947-58 is considered, the annual rate of growth of sugar production becomes .43 percent (Tables 3-6 and 3-11). Nonsugar manufacturing and electricity and gas production, the two main components of nonsugar industrial production, displayed impressive rates of growth (4.96 and 6.29 percent, respectively) during 1930-1958, and the post-World War II period (5.27 and 8.78 percent, respectively). Mining and fishing production underwent a more turbulent, but still positive, growth pattern during the period. The rate of growth of mining increased modestly in the post-World War II period in comparison with the entire period covered by the study (3.36 v. 3.03 percent) whereas fishing, despite serious fluctuations, expanded at an annual rate of 3.52 percent over the entire span of the study and at a brisk 10.63 percent in the post-World War II period.

A brief comparison between the calculated index and the official industrial output indexes for selected Latin American countries for the period 1948-58 (Table 3-12) suggests that the rate of expansion of Cuban industrial production for the period analyzed was in line with the rates observed by Latin American countries of moderate growth. If the calculated index for nonsugar manufacturing production and nonsugar industrial production are compared with the record of all Latin American countries (for which data are available), the rates of expansion of these two indexes assume magnitudes comparable even with the fast-growing countries, while exhibiting a more balanced pattern of growth.

A comparison between the indexes calculated here and those of the Banco Nacional de Cuba indicates a close relationship between the movements of the two sets of indexes. The calculated index for all industrial production exhibited slightly faster and steadier rates of growth than its counterpart prepared by the Banco. The divergences that do exist may be explained in terms of differences in product coverage and weighting systems employed in the preparation of the two indexes.

The calculated industrial output index probably underestimates the industrial accomplishments of the Cuban economy, particularly in the latter years of the period examined. Absent from the product sample are such dynamic industrial product areas as chemicals, petroleum refining and by-products, iron and steel, glass, and pharmaceutical products, for which data are not available. These products were gaining in importance among industrial production in Cuba particularly in the years closer to the end of the period. Taking into account the importance of the sugar sector in the product sample and the erratic and stagnant behavior of sugar production during the 1930-58 period (Table 3-6), the gap left open by the series not included and the limited coverage in others probably tends to introduce a downward bias in the calculated index.

It may be asserted that the index of industrial activity is not an appropriate measure of industrial development in Cuba. I suggest that a more meaningful measure of the extent and rate of industrialization in Cuba is the index of nonsugar industrial production. The heavy weight of sugar production significantly influences the index of industrial activity. The volume of sugar produced is a function of the processing

capacity in the industry, level of technology, quality and quantity of inputs, etc., as is generally the case in most production processes. But, in addition, it is largely influenced by an exogenous variable: the annual sugar quota assigned to Cuba by the United States (which is then reflected in individual quotas for each of the sugar mills). An indication of the production potential of the sugar industry once quota restrictions were removed can be observed in 1952, when a free zafra was declared, and Cuban sugar production soared to over seven million metric tons, a record high for the prerevolutionary period.[88] Fluctuations in the volume of sugar produced caused by changing United States sugar requirements tend to distort the industrial output index to such an extent that the contributions of nonsugar industrial activities to the economy become obscured. Thus, a superior measure of the rate and extent of industrialization in Cuba is the index of nonsugar industrial activity: this index, as indicated in Table 3-11, advanced at an annual average rate of 4.91 percent over the entire period and 5.74 percent over the post-World War II period, a very impressive performance.[89]

However moderate it might be, the rate of growth of Cuban industrial production calculated in this study dispels the contentions that the Cuban economy, and particularly its industrial sector, were stagnant during the prerevolutionary period.[90] The calculations carried out here show quite

[88] An idea of the extent to which industrial capacity in the sugar industry was underutilized can be obtained from the following. Out of 152 sugar mills active during the 1971 sugar crop in Cuba, the 12 most recently constructed were built between 1920 and 1927; 45 were built during the first two decades of the 20th century; and the rest, 95, before 1900. Cf. Juan Ferrán, "Las Microinversiones y la Productividad en la Industria Azucarera," *Economía y Desarrollo* (La Habana), 14 (November-December, 1972), p. 115. Cuban sugar production since the establishment of the last sugar mill (in 1927) to the overthrow of Batista (December 31, 1958), varied greatly, from a low of 1,994,238 long tons in 1933 to a record high of 7,011,393 long tons in 1952. Although production in 1952 was more than three times that of 1933, there was no increase in productive capacity over the period. Industrial sugar production capacity in Cuba has been calculated at between 7.5 and 8.0 million metric tons per year. Orlando Borrego Díaz, "Problemas que Plantea a la Industria una Zafra de 10 Millones de Toneladas," *Cuba Socialista* (La Habana), 5:44 (April, 1963), p. 18, and Juan F. Noyola, "La Revolución Cubana y sus Efectos en el Desarrollo Económico," *El Trimestre Económico* (México), 28:111 (July-September, 1961), p. 425.

[89] An attempt at measuring the extent and rate of industrial development by an industrial production index of commodities for domestic consumption was carried on in the early 1950s by the Junta Nacional de Economía. Presumably, the index covers 18 products, important for the domestic market, and explicitly excludes products primarily produced for export. The index has serious shortcomings: the time period covered is short (1945-49), the product coverage is not indicated, and the aggregation formulas, and weights are not presented. See Gustavo Gutiérrez, *El Desarrollo Económico de Cuba* (La Habana: Publicaciones de la Junta Nacional de Economía, 12, 1952), pp. 218-220.

[90] For different (and not always consistent) expositions of the Cuban economic stagnation hypothesis see, e.g., Seers, ed., *Cuba: The Economic and Social Revolution,* particularly part III, "Industry," by Max Nolff and pointedly pp. 286-295; Benjamin Higgins, *Economic Development: Problems, Principles and Cases* (New York:

conclusively that the industrial sector of the Cuban economy expanded at a considerable rate during the period considered, and especially in the 1946-58 period. The rate of population expansion for Cuba in the period 1930-58 can be estimated at 1.91 percent per annum, and at 2.29 percent per annum after World War II.[91] Thus, the rates of expansion of the industrial sector calculated in this study are still quite significant even after adjusting for population growth.

That is not to suggest that the standard of living of each member of the population rose at an annual rate of 4.91 or 5.74 percent for each of the periods studied in detail. Inequities in the distribution of national income, corruption in the national government, the extraction of profits from the country by foreign corporations and by Cuban nationals, among other factors, prevented the Cuban people from sharing equitably in the benefits of industrial development, and did much to attenuate the impact of the growth of the industrial sector upon the welfare of the average citizen. While there is no single economic indicator that can be used to measure the development of a country or the welfare of its citizens.,[92] the growth of the industrial sector has tradi-

tionally been accepted as one aspect and an integral part of the development process of a country, and it is in this light that the present study has been carried out.[93] Although industrial growth per se does not mean that development has taken place, its absence generally prevents development from occurring.

The industrial output index developed here, despite weaknesses and limitations,[94] offers for the first time a long-run index of Cuban industrial activity and fills a serious gap in Cuban economic statistics for the pre-revolutionary period. Perhaps data from sources unavailable to me now will allow additions and revisions to the present work in order to update it and increase its reliability. This work is the first attempt at an independently calculated index of Cuban industrial output and serves as a point of departure for serious studies of the Cuban economy in the prerevolutionay period and comparisons with the record in the revolutionary stage.

W. W. Norton, 1968), Chapter 34; O'Connor, *The Origins of Socialism in Cuba,* and the review of the O'Connor volume by Carmelo Mesa-Lago in *Journal of Economic Literature,* 9:2 (June, 1971), pp. 478-481. This list is not exhaustive.

[91] Calculated from raw data presented by Cuban Economic Research Project, *Stages and Problems of Industrial Development in Cuba,* p. 97. The data originate from census sources and logistic interpolations.

[92] The problems in finding an economic indicator of the degree and rate of change of economic development is a topic well treated in any elementary economics or economic development textbook. Higgins, *Economic Development: Problems, Principles and Cases,* for

instance, has a good discussion on this point. The disenchantment of economists with traditional measures (such GNP) to indicate economic welfare has led to the development of new concepts, among them the Measure of Economic Welfare (MEW). See William Nordhaus and James Tobin, "Is Growth Obsolete?" in *Fiftieth Anniversary Colloquim V* (New York: Columbia University Press for the National Bureau of Economic Research, 1972). Of related interest, Edward F. Denison, "Welfare Measurement and the GNP," *Survey of Current Business,* 51:1 (January, 1971).

[93] For an interesting view of industrial expansion as one aspect of economic development see Fabricant, *The Output of Manufacturing Industries, 1899-1937,* pp. 19-22.

[94] See Simon Kuznets, "Quantitative Economic Research: Trends and Problems," in *Fiftieth Anniversary Colloquim VII* (New York: Columbia University Press for the National Bureau of Economic Research, 1972), pp. 7-10, 22-23.

Appendix A

RAW DATA OF INDUSTRIAL-OUTPUT SERIES, 1930-58

Year	Fish (1,000 lbs.)	Iron ore (metric tons)	Chromium ore (metric tons)	Copper concentrate of ore (metric tons)	Gold ore (fine ounces)	Manganese ore (metric tons)	Nickel ore (short tons)	Silver (fine ounces)	Petroleum (1,000 gallons)	Naptha (1,000 gallons)
1930	13,700	190,270	41,640	15,693	3,000	762	- - -	100,000	400.0	85
1931	13,900	92,407	15,197	13,507	2,800	96	- - -	95,000	366.6	85
1932	14,200	82,610	- - -	5,927	2,600	9,800	- - -	90,000	330.0	90
1933	14,600	169,490	24,154	8,957	2,500	28,000	- - -	88,000	300.0	90
1934	15,000	181,121	50,162	6,192	2,400	68,064	- - -	90,000	280.0	109
1935	15,400	228,408	48,509	6,960	2,300	35,269	- - -	92,000	254.8	300
1936	15,650	456,827	71,086	11,163	2,140	48,471	- - -	94,000	200.0	861
1937	17,100	496,258	94,592	13,191	3,707	131,299	- - -	96,000	180.0	1,783
1938	16,600	234,061	40,163	14,431	3,889	123,844	- - -	99,000	170.0	2,524
1939	16,500	166,739	67,061	9,964	3,851	102,415	- - -	102,915	160.0	5,400
1940	16,165	160,339	52,789	9,559	1,251	119,852	- - -	45,836	150.0	7,238
1941	12,500	192,851	163,175	9,838	607	251,385	- - -	27,150	130.0	6,719
1942	9,470	132,847	286,470	8,916	195	249,255	- - -	36,238	120.0	5,937
1943	9,600	47,113	354,152	6,405	51	311,214	2,430	142,420	106.7	4,291
1944	10,480	28,370	192,191	6,584	39	257,864	4,679	42,985	622.9	3,955
1945	10,215	- - -	172,626	9,067	423	198,247	10,900	107,195	3,334.2	2,267
1946	10,725	- - -	174,350	11,323	1,105	130,764	11,241	127,222	3,698.0	2,516
1947	19,340	63,276	159,209	13,729	364	50,397	2,014	146,932	5,375.1	1,533
1948	17,105	36,595	116,624	16,300	334	29,073	- - -	185,216	4,285.8	1,103
1949	16,920	11,961	97,368	17,400	5,692	62,503	- - -	157,411	2,904.1	786
1950	17,675	12,000	65,696	20,447	6,915	79,193	- - -	221,779	797.3	818
1951	12,845	17,000	79,049	19,681	835	154,059	- - -	172,318	542.4	600
1952	14,850	101,000	61,812	17,868	881	251,625	8,924	163,211	435.1	407
1953	19,970	229,000	70,025	16,145	1,181	353,146	13,844	167,895	279.5	326
1954	18,245	25,400	63,490	15,873	677	269,198	14,545	179,479	723.2	276
1955	17,700	45,122	74,158	17,700	2,024	314,439	15,138	366,673	6,591.7	179
1956	25,200	137,000	31,428	15,800	1,008	234,002	16,062	284,202	12,253.0	96
1957	36,215	107,000	51,938	8,600	705	248,744	22,267	252,728	7,161.6	92
1958	36,050	15,000	115,303	25,700	310	67,505	16,782	325,278	7,000.0	88

Appendix A (Continued)

RAW DATA OF INDUSTRIAL-OUTPUT SERIES, 1930-58

Year	Salt (metric tons)	Gypsum (metric tons)	Barite (metric tons)	Asphalt (1,000 metric tons)	Butter (million lbs.)	Cheese (million lbs.)	Condensed milk (cases)[a]	Evaporated milk (cases)[b]	Wheat flour (metric tons)	Cane sugar (long tons)
1930	24,947	27,200	---	5.0	3.80	2.4	56,708	---	---	4,670,973
1931	22,680	25,000	---	9.7	3.40	2.1	129,878	---	---	3,120,796
1932	31,751	22,000	---	8.0	3.00	2.0	200,755	---	---	2,604,292
1933	35,000	18,000	---	7.0	3.60	2.4	312,111	---	---	1,994,238
1934	20,964	15,000	---	6.0	4.00	2.5	475,492	1,900	---	2,255,869
1935	36,921	12,000	---	5.0	4.20	2.9	547,208	22,756	---	2,537,951
1936	34,339	10,000	166	4.0	4.40	3.1	579,316	25,273	---	2,556,937
1937	36,806	15,028	3,849	2.5	4.60	3.3	660,263	27,704	---	2,974,584
1938	57,970	7,257	---	3.8	4.70	3.5	835,177	28,288	---	2,975,949
1939	113,398	6,270	12,000	3.5	4.63	4.0	733,694	56,182	---	2,723,814
1940	113,398	12,000	16,105	2.2	5.02	4.5	843,185	63,751	---	2,799,350
1941	41,909	12,000	13,223	4.6	5.51	5.0	1,191,996	90,624	---	2,406,954
1942	43,545	4,303	3,787	2.6	6.02	5.0	868,152	100,672	---	3,345,056
1943	18,416	2,921	3,158	11.1	4.20	5.0	795,390	66,158	---	2,843,077
1944	15,422	9,008	4,787	2.7	2.60	5.0	695,327	58,616	---	4,174,041
1945	52,335	10,400	2,094	9.1	2.00	5.5	562,458	12,766	---	3,454,983
1946	56,782	14,300	2,200	---	2.50	6.0	771,083	10,377	---	3,940,728
1947	51,225	14,900	2,400	---	2.50	7.0	714,650	827	---	5,672,238
1948	55,339	16,500	2,600	---	2.60	6.9	691,423	18,942	---	5,876,761
1949	59,874	13,880	2,800	---	3.30	5.2	879,666	29,617	---	5,073,968
1950	59,300	15,550	3,000	---	2.80	5.4	1,059,335	---	---	5,393,541
1951	50,983	30,000	3,400	---	3.20	5.1	963,239	---	---	5,589,232
1952	56,960	30,000	3,900	---	3.20	5.1	1,313,606	---	30,327	7,011,393
1953	51,734	30,000	4,448	---	5.00	5.8	1,348,780	54,052	67,257	5,007,060
1954	54,708	30,000	7,000	---	5.10	11.2	1,135,981	80,545	48,203	4,752,720
1955	64,092	31,751	10,000	---	4.90	11.4	1,405,738	18,839	49,145	4,404,443
1956	69,000	21,768	15,000	---	4.10	11.8	1,570,100	145,560	66,309	4,604,942
1957	68,000	40,815	20,676	---	4.10	12.4	1,671,248	319,200	64,887	5,505,990
1958	68,000	40,815	10,821	---	4.50	12.9	1,501,799	335,500	66,000	5,613,823

a. 1 case contains 48 cans at 14 ounces each.
b. 1 case contains 48 cans at 14.5 ounces each.

Appendix A (Continued)

RAW DATA OF INDUSTRIAL-OUTPUT SERIES, 1930-58

Year	Molasses (gallons)	Rich molasses and syrups (gallons)	Alcohol (liters)	Cane brandy (liters)	Beer (liters)	Soft drinks (million cases)c	Tobacco (1,000 lbs.)	Cigars (million units)	Cigarettes (million units)	Cotton cloth (1,000 kgs.)
1930	210,448,586	?	20,040,540	10,862,050	36,199,007	5.00	529	230.3	5,615	275
1931	129,332,412	?	21,137,100	31,890,240	22,098,907	4.00	447	148.4	5,011	249
1932	170,946,398	?	26,569,330	35,228,350	16,083,926	3.00	367	90.2	2,899	227
1933	112,448,133	?	29,037,370	35,516,610	18,609,172	2.00	332	88.6	2,825	270
1934	112,267,767	?	29,522,910	33,244,500	22,943,500	6.00	389	110.2	3,454	524
1935	122,849,628	61,468,875	23,286,370	31,157,350	30,313,168	6.50	337	116.6	4,113	1,210
1936	127,081,101	116,438,093	35,573,250	34,900,280	35,674,239	7.00	284	140.3	4,380	2,944
1937	149,883,854	207,726,114	25,653,340	29,876,080	43,712,130	7.50	157	160.9	4,964	3,012
1938	145,121,641	89,044,140	30,676,720	34,011,360	40,594,049	8.00	139	157.6	5,043	3,143
1939	150,270,640	100,482,106	33,121,110	33,644,320	38,461,023	9.00	120	154.8	4,959	3,536
1940	124,902,620	178,025,796	37,269,680	34,822,030	40,269,113	10.00	120	229.8	5,030	3,969
1941	101,241,049	338,711,699	34,601,132	28,272,581	45,385,173	9.00	139	265.9	5,187	10,544
1942	163,628,245	169,562,702	25,072,882	19,164,562	43,258,088	5.19	157	309.1	6,076	6,288
1943	139,504,013	465,633	109,139,695	18,611,339	43,568,223	6.79	225	321.2	6,290	8,240
1944	233,881,260	222,141,171	211,154,606	14,794,075	57,863,066	10.04	220	421.5	6,773	9,559
1945	206,252,783	23,447,452	202,650,082	3,591,846	77,983,951	14.40	304	370.5	6,724	8,261
1946	240,807,705	124,270	191,557,401	5,118,357	81,365,182	17.02	240	362.4	7,164	7,988
1947	307,779,182	17,385	153,031,437	3,036,115	84,383,615	18.59	126	390.3	7,327	7,595
1948	394,981,397	2,413,415	90,063,620	1,614,178	99,747,629	19.91	163	399.8	7,684	6,091
1949	291,547,299	8,039,178	122,489,579	1,260,088	96,545,922	20.23	200	366.9	7,963	5,906
1950	271,774,732	8,178,469	134,644,878	1,911,931	104,293,328	23.50	159	350.1	8,156	12,150
1951	299,642,231	7,315,344	133,457,762	2,446,831	125,538,031	22.23	156	364.0	8,334	7,005
1952	406,929,172	9,385,567	144,760,488	2,196,630	143,668,840	23.44	187	390.8	8,975	8,796
1953	291,736,056	11,285,265	184,603,517	2,207,906	118,768,320	19.43	68	375.1	8,740	7,209
1954	247,185,140	139,659,409	174,150,922	2,560,510	120,212,398	20.13	75	316.0	9,357	9,912
1955	211,265,368	239,146,797	190,806,074	2,726,373	117,919,422	20.39	117	339.7	9,341	9,056
1956	220,801,995	119,445,495	205,468,706	3,069,399	120,458,000	22.24	114	377.2	9,539	10,210
1957	253,264,511	7,300,000	173,146,589	3,818,225	129,200,000	24.44	121	409.0	10,370	11,754
1958	230,684,742	79,600,000	119,013,534	3,045,348	132,200,000	23.75	123	378.0	10,016	12,178

c. Cases of 24 bottles

Appendix A (Continued)
RAW DATA OF INDUSTRIAL-OUTPUT SERIES, 1930-58

Year	Rayon filament yarn (metric tons)	Rayon tire cord (metric tons)	Rayon staple (metric tons)	Shoes (1,000 pairs)	Paper and paperboard (metric tons)	Rubber inner tubes (units)	Rubber tires (units)	Cement (1,000 metric tons)	Electricity (million kwh)	Gas (million cu.m.)
1930	- - -	- - -	- - -	2,754	28,586	- - -	- - -	276.6	265	13.0
1931	- - -	- - -	- - -	2,500	18,175	- - -	- - -	48.9	235	11.8
1932	- - -	- - -	- - -	2,000	19,182	- - -	- - -	32.9	213	8.0
1933	- - -	- - -	- - -	1,800	18,807	- - -	- - -	31.0	208	7.0
1934	- - -	- - -	- - -	3,000	14,412	- - -	- - -	51.1	235	11.0
1935	- - -	- - -	- - -	3,600	5,937	- - -	- - -	70.4	252	14.3
1936	- - -	- - -	- - -	4,200	14,494	- - -	- - -	106.9	274	15.7
1937	- - -	- - -	- - -	4,800	19,575	- - -	- - -	121.7	307	17.2
1938	- - -	- - -	- - -	5,300	30,299	- - -	- - -	111.3	324	19.0
1939	- - -	- - -	- - -	4,600	57,535	- - -	- - -	128.8	343	19.2
1940	- - -	- - -	- - -	4,800	17,069	- - -	- - -	152.6	356	19.8
1941	- - -	- - -	- - -	5,000	29,710	- - -	- - -	155.5	370	20.5
1942	- - -	- - -	- - -	6,000	22,000	- - -	- - -	166.1	379	23.2
1943	- - -	- - -	- - -	7,200	17,249	8,000	20,000	169.6	397	25.3
1944	- - -	- - -	- - -	8,700	10,434	13,000	30,600	173.8	430	26.8
1945	- - -	- - -	- - -	9,000	56,992	25,000	40,000	180.2	488	29.9
1946	- - -	- - -	- - -	9,500	48,517	42,527	54,981	240.4	532	32.5
1947	- - -	- - -	- - -	13,740	19,979	40,464	60,038	276.4	571	34.1
1948	51.7	209.1	31.6	10,560	25,990	33,275	58,595	285.0	639	38.5
1949	879.5	1,664.3	801.8	8,906	22,150	33,702	32,810	312.3	690	43.1
1950	1,527.7	2,871.9	3,096.7	9,761	34,349	45,881	85,662	316.3	758	48.0
1951	1,573.3	4,116.3	3,423.4	9,881	36,000	51,162	109,916	383.0	836	52.3
1952	1,265.9	3,536.7	3,403.8	9,825	38,000	46,238	94,421	420.0	918	57.1
1953	731.4	4,686.6	3,458.4	11,000	40,000	39,640	84,822	406.6	1,006	60.0
1954	519.4	4,963.3	4,256.1	11,800	41,500	45,972	101,801	420.1	1,088	59.8
1955	728.3	4,379.4	4,269.6	12,600	43,645	46,994	101,069	455.3	1,200	58.3
1956	819.1	4,968.9	4,378.1	13,900	49,003	57,991	129,137	591.1	1,324	59.9
1957	574.4	4,454.1	4,757.6	15,300	50,750	59,543	156,313	644.0	1,354	59.1
1958	620.0	4,700.0	4,100.0	16,000	51,400	79,664	264,914	715.1	1,463	58.8

Sources and Notes

1930-34. Extrapolated.

1935-51. Cuba, Dirección General de Estadística, *Anuario Estadístico, 1952.*

1952-55. *Ibid., 1957.*

1956. Estimate for 12 months based on production of 23,132,494 pounds for 11 months. It includes crustacea, molluscs, sponges, and other water products. *Ibid.*

1957. Includes crustacea, molluscs, sponges, and other water products. *Ibid.*

1958. Extrapolated from previous data assuming the same rate of growth obtained from United Nations, Economic Commission for Latin America, *Statistical Bulletin of Latin America,* i.e., 22,000 metric tons produced in 1957 and 21,900 metric tons in 1958. It includes crustacea, molluscs, sponges, and other water products.

Fish

Iron Ore

1930-56. U.S. Bureau of Mines, *Minerals Yearbook.*

1947-55. U.S. Department of Commerce, *Investment in Cuba,* p. 62.

1956-58. Pan American Union, *América en Cifras.*

Chromium Ore

1930-54. U.S. Bureau of Mines, *Minerals Yearbook.*

1955. U.S. Department of Commerce, *Investment in Cuba.*

1956. Cuba, Dirección General de Estadística, *Anuario Estadístico, 1957.*

1957-58. U.S. Bureau of Mines, *Minerals Yearbook.*

Sources and Notes (Continued)

Copper Concentrate of Ore
1930-54. *Ibid.*
1955-58. United Nations, *Statistical Yearbook*.

Gold Ore
1930-35. Extrapolated.
1936-58. U.S. Bureau of Mines, *Minerals Yearbook*.

Manganese Ore
1930-56. *Ibid.*
1957. Pan American Union, *América en Cifras, 1958*, mineral content: 45 percent.
1958. U.S. Bureau of Mines, *Minerals Yearbook, 1960*, average manganese content: 36-50 percent.

Nickel Ore
1930-58. *Ibid.*

Silver
1930-38. Extrapolated.
1939-58. U.S. Bureau of Mines, *Minerals Yearbook*.

Petroleum
1930. Extrapolated.
1931. Cuba, Oficina General de los Censos Demográfico y Electoral, *Censo del Año 1943*.
1932-34. Interpolated.
1935. Cuba, Oficina General de los Censos Demográfico y Electoral, *Censo del Año 1943*.
1936-42. Interpolated.
1943-57. U.S. Bureau of Mines, *Minerals Yearbook*.
1958. Extrapolated.

Naphtha
1930-33. Extrapolated.
1934. Cuba, Oficina General de los Censos Demográfico y Electoral, *Censo del Año 1943*.
1934. Interpolated.
1936-49. *Cuba Económica y Financiera*, 25:286 January, 1950, p. 8.
1950. *Ibid.*, 25:303 (1950). p. 6.
1951-52. Great Britain, Overseas Trade Department, *Economic and Commercial Conditions in Cuba, 1954*, p. 116. Naphtha from Motembo.
1953-57. Cuba, Dirección General de Estadística, *Anuario Estadístico, 1956*.
1958. Extrapolated.

Salt
1930-49. U.S. Bureau of Mines, *Minerals Yearbook*.
1950. United Nations, *Statistical Yearbook, 1954*.
1951-55. U.S. Department of Commerce, *Investment in Cuba*, p. 66.
1956. United Nations, *Statistical Yearbook, 1958*.
1957-58. Pan American Union, *América en Cifras, 1961*.

Gypsum
1930. U.S. Bureau of Mines, *Minerals Yearbook*.
1931-36. Interpolation.
1937-51. *Ibid.*, various years.
1952-55. U.S. Department of Commerce, *Investment in Cuba*.
1956-58. U.S. Bureau of Mines, *Minerals Yearbook*.

Barite
1930-58. *Ibid.*

Asphalt
1930. Extrapolation.
1931. Cuba, Oficina General de los Censos Demográfico y Electoral, *Censo del Año 1943*.
1932-36. Interpolated.
1937-45. Banco Nacional de Cuba, *Memoria, 1950-1951*, p. 196.

Butter
1930-34. Extrapolated.
1935-39. Calculated given that average production for the period was 4.5 million pounds per annum. U.S. Department of Commerce. *Investment in Cuba*, p. 76.
1940-44. *Ibid. Cuba* (Foreign Service Yearbook Series), p. 4.
1945-55. U.S. Department of Commerce, *Investment in Cuba*.
1956-58. Cuban Economic Research Project, *A Study on Cuba*, p. 558.

Cheese
1930-34. Extrapolated.
1935-39. Calculated given that average production for the period was 3.3 million pounds per annum. U.S. Department of Commerce, *Investment in Cuba*.
1940-44. U.S. Department of Commerce. *Cuba* (Foreign Service Yearbook Series).
1945-55. U.S. Department of Commerce, *Investment in Cuba*.
1956-1958. Extrapolated.

Condensed Milk
1930-51. *Cuba Económica y Financiera*, 32:373 (April, 1957), p. 28.
1952-58. *Ibid.*, 35:406 (January, 1960), p. 22.

Evaporated Milk
1930-51. *Ibid.*, 32:373 (April, 1957), p. 28.
1952-58. *Ibid.*, 35:406 (January, 1960), p. 22.

Wheat Flour
1930-58. United Nations, Economic Commission for Latin America, *Economic Survey of Latin America, 1957*, p. 196.

Cane Sugar
1930-58. Cuba Económica y Financiera, *Anuario Azucarero de Cuba*.

Molasses
1930-56. Cuba, Dirección General de Estadística, *Resúmenes Estadísticos Seleccionados*, p. 54.
1957-58. Cuba Económica y Financiera, *Anuario Azucarero de Cuba*.

Rich Molasses and Syrups
1930-56. Cuba, Dirección General de Estadística, *Resúmenes Estadísticos Seleccionados*.
1957-58. Cuba Económica y Financiera, *Anuario Azucarero de Cuba*, various years.

Alcohol
1950-58. *Ibid.*

Cane Brandy
1930-58. *Ibid.*

Sources and Notes (Continued)

Beer

1930-55. "Producción y Consumo de Cerveza Nacional," *Cuba Económica y Financiera,* 31:359 (February, 1956), p. 31.

1956. Cuba, Dirección General de Estadística, *Resúmenes Estadísticos Seleccionados,* p. 72.

1957-58. Cuban Economic Research Project, *A Study on Cuba,* p. 558.

Soft Drinks

1930-39. Extrapolated.

1940. U.S. Department of Commerce, *Economic Conditions in Cuba, 1945,* p. 4

1941. Interpolated

1942-55. Cuba, Dirección General de Estadística, *Anuario Estadístico, 1956.*

1956-58. *Cuba Económica y Financiera,* 35:416-417. (November-December, 1960), p. 4.

Tobacco

1930-57. Cuba, Dirección General de Estadística, *Anuario Estadístico, 1957.*

1958. Extrapolated.

Cigars

1930-56. *Ibid.*

1957-58. United Nations, *Statistical Yearbook.*

Cigarettes

1930-58. *Ibid.*

Cotton Cloth

1930-58. Estimates based on consumption of raw cotton. Import of raw cotton figures from Cuba, Dirección General de Estadística, *Comercio Exterior.* Production figure for 1944 from Economic and Technical Mission to Cuba, *Report on Cuba,* p. 960.

Rayon Filament Yarn

1930-53. United Nations, Economic Commission for Latin America, *Economic Survey of Latin America, 1953,* p. 217.

1954-57. *Ibid, 1957,* p. 195.

1958. Extrapolation.

Rayon Tire Cord

1930-53. United Nations, Economic Commission for Latin America, *Economic Survey of Latin America, 1953,* p. 217.

1954-57. *Ibid, 1957,* p. 195.

1958. Extrapolation.

Rayon Staple

1930-53. United Nations, Economic Commission for Latin America, *Economic Survey of Latin America, 1953,* p. 217.

1954-57. *Ibid, 1957,* p. 195.

1958. United Nations, *Statistical Yearbook, 1960.*

Shoes

1930. "La Producción Nacional de Calzado." *Cuba Económica y Financiera,* 27:313 (April, 1952), p. 15.

1931-34. Interpolated.

1935-39. Estimated from previous data and given that production for the period 1935-39 averaged 4,500,000 pair per annum according to "La Producción Nacional de Calzado," *Cuba Económica y Financiera.* Production for 1949 given as 4,600,000 pair in Cuban Economic Research Project, *Stages and Problems of Industrial Development in Cuba,* p. 53.

1940-44. Estimated from previous data and given that production for the period 1940-1944 averaged 6,340,000 pair per annum according to "La Producción Nacional de Calzado," *Cuba Económica y Financiera.* Production for 1944 given as 8,700,000 pair in Cuban Economic Research Project, *Stages and Problems of Industrial Development in Cuba.*

1945. Interpolated.

1946-48. Cuban Economic Research Project, *Stages and Problems of Industrial Development in Cuba,* p. 53, and Economic and Technical Mission to Cuba, *Report on Cuba,* p. 130. *Stages and Problems of Industrial Development in Cuba* reports leather shoe production as 9,500,000 pair in 1946, 10,000,000 in 1947 and 8,000,000 in 1948. In addition, *Report on Cuba* cites rubber shoe production of 3,740,000 pair in 1947 and 2,560,000 pair in 1948. The sum of the two figures is given as total production.

1949. Economic and Technical Mission to Cuba, *Report on Cuba,* 5,850,000 pair leather shoes and 3,056,000 pair rubber shoes.

1950-52. Great Britain, Overseas Trade Department, *Economic and Commercial Conditions in Cuba, 1954,* p. 111. For 1950, production consisted of 6,351,000 pair leather shoes and 3,409,146 pair of rubber shoes. For 1951, 6,300,000 pair leather shoes and 3,581,000 pair rubber shoes. For 1952 the breakdown was 6,600,000 pair leather shoes and 3,250,000 pair rubber shoes.

1953. United Nations, Economic Commission for Latin America, *Economic Survey of Latin America, 1953,* p. 217. Industry operating at 45 percent of full capacity.

1954-55. Interpolated.

1956-57. Cuban Economic Research Project, *Stages and Problems of Industrial Development in Cuba,* p. 53.

1958. Estimate of Mr. Ulises Prieto, former officer of the Comisión Reguladora de la Industria de Calzado (CRIC), based on sale of CRIC compulsory seals.

NOTE: After the completion of all calculations, the excellent study of the Cuban shoe industry "Estudio de la Industria del Calzado Cubano," by Walter E. Reiners, under contract authorized by CRIC (September 1, 1958), became available. Reiners' data on cuban shoe production reflect sale of CRIC seals, and thus, only include official production, with no estimates of production outside of CRIC. His figure of 16,000,000 pair in 1958 coincides exactly with the Prieto estimate used in this study. Other production data, shown below, also follow quite closely the estimates obtained through interpolations and data from other sources used here. Although the Reiners data are probably superior to others, they are not incorporated in the calculations in order to expedite the completion of this study and under the assumption that these changes will not significantly affect the results of this work.

Year	Production (Pairs)
1952-53	12,602,000
1953-54	13,373,000
1954-55	14,059,000
1955-56	14,075,000
1956-57	16,000,600
1957-58	15,684,000

Walter E. Reiners, "Estudio de la Industria del Calzado Cubano," p. 30.

Sources and Notes (Continued)

Paper and Paper board

1930-50. United Nations, Economic Commission for Latin America, *Possibilities for the Development of the Pulp and Paper Industry in Latin America*, p. 108.

1951-54. Interpolated.

1955-58. United Nations, Economic Commission for Latin America, *Pulp and Paper Prospects in Latin America*, pp. 16-21. Data include paper and paperboard produced, and printing and writing paper.

Rubber Inner Tubes

1943. Extrapolated.

1944. Cuba, Dirección General de Estadística, *Anuario Estadístico, 1957.*

1945. Interpolated.

1956-57. Cuba, Dirección General de Estadística, *Anuario Estadístico, 1957.*

1958. *Cuba Económica y Financiera*, 35:407 (February, 1960), p. 18.

Rubber Tires

1943. Extrapolated.

1944-57. Cuba, Dirección General de Estadística, *Anuario Estadístico, 1957.*

1958. *Cuba Económica y Financiera*, 35:407 (February, 1960), p. 18.

Cement

1930-50. Banco Nacional de Cuba, *1950-1951*, pp. 202-203.

1951-58. Cuba, Junta Central de Planificación Revolutionaria, *Consumo y Producción de Cemento 1938-1958*, p. 2. All figures rounded.

Electricity

1930-54. Cuba, Dirección General de Estadística, *Anuario Estadístico, 1956.*

1955-58. United Nations, *Statistical Yearbook.*

Gas

1930-34. Extrapolated

1935-49. *Cuba Económica y Financiera*, 26:301 (April, 1951), p. 88.

1950-58. *Ibid.*, 34:395 (February, 1959), p. 33.

Appendix B
PRODUCT UNIT PRICES FOR 1952[a]

Product	Unit	Price (current C$)
Iron ore	Metric ton	10.05
Chromium ore	Metric ton	14.77
Copper concentrate of ore	Metric ton	423.48
Gold ore	Troy ounce	30.62
Silver ore	Troy ounce	0.79
Manganese ore	Metric ton	31.97
Nickel ore	Short ton	660.43
Petroleum	1,000 gallons	52.63
Naphtha	1,000 gallons	63.88
Salt	Metric ton	17.71
Barite[1]	Metric ton	5.90
Asphalt	Metric ton	2.37
Gypsum[2]	Metric ton	132.00
Butter	100 pounds	102.46
Cheese	100 pounds	61.20
Condensed milk	Case of 48 cans	9.20
Evaporated milk	Case of 48 cans	9.49
Wheat flour	Metric tons	83.38
Cane sugar	Spanish long ton	92.51
Molasses	1,000 gallons	58.20
Rich molasses and syrups	1,000 gallons	435.60
Alcohol	Liter	0.19
Cane brandy	Liter	0.20
Beer	100 liters	38.30
Soft drinks	Case of 24 bottles	0.81
Tobacco	1,000 pounds	1,014.00
Cigars	1,000 units	158.39
Cigarettes	1,000 units	4.65
Cotton cloth[1]	1,000 kilograms	2,801.50
Rayon filament yarn	Metric ton	1,418.32
Rayon tire cord	Metric ton	1,688.03
Rayon staple	Metric ton	822.90
Rubber inner tubes[1]	Units	7.96
Rubber tires[1]	Units	15.62
Electricity[3]	Million kwh	53,514.11
Gas	Million cubic meters	48,800.00

1. 1953
2. Average 1954-55
3. 1954
a. No prices are given for fish, shoes, paper, and cement since they are the only products in their sectors and do not have to be aggregated by using the Laspeyres quantity index of formula(1).

Source and Notes

Iron ore	Export unit value for 1952 calculated from *Comercio Exterior, 1952-1953*, p. 464.
Chromium ore	Export unit value for 1952 calculated from *ibid.*, p. 464
Copper Concentrate of ore	Estimate based on unit value of copper ore (32 percent mineral content) in *Resúmenes Estadísticos Seleccionados*, p. 111.
Gold ore	Estimate obtained linking U.S. unit values for domestic production of copper concentrate and gold for 1952 from *Statistical Abstract of the United States: 1954*, pp. 736-738 with estimated unit value for copper concentrate.
Silver ore	Estimate obtained using the same procedure as above.
Manganese ore	Export unit value for 1952 calculated from *Comercio Exterior, 1952-1953* p. 465.
Nickel ore	Export unit value for 1952 calculated from *ibid.*
Petroleum	Estimate obtained linking U.S. unit values for domestic production of petroleum and copper concentrate for 1952 from *Statistical Abstract of the United States: 1954*, pp. 727, 736-738 with estimated unit value for copper concentrate.
Naphtha	Estimate obtained using the same procedure as above.
Salt	Export unit value for 1952 calculated from *Comercio Exterior, 1952-1953*, p. 506.
Barite	Export unit value for 1953 calculated from *ibid.*, p. 464.
Asphalt	Estimate obtained using linking procedure similar to that used to estimate petroleum unit value.
Gypsum	Export unit value for 1954-1955 calculated from *Comercio Exterior, 1954-1955*.
Butter	Average wholesale price in the city of La Habana for the year 1952. Calculated from *Anuario Estadístico de Cuba, 1956*, p. 638.
Cheese	Same as above.
Condensed milk	Same as above.
Evaporated milk	Same as above.
Wheat flour	Same as above.
Sugar	Average official price of sugar in public warehouses for 1952 from Cuban Economic Research Project, *A Study on Cuba*, p. 481.
Molasses	Domestic unit value calculated from *Resúmenes Estadísticos Seleccionados*, p. 54.
Rich molasses and syrups	Domestic unit value, calculated from *ibid*.
Alcohol	Domestic unit value, calculated from *ibid.*, p. 55.
Cane brandy	Domestic unit value, calculated from *ibid.*, p. 56.
Beer	Average wholesale price in the city of La Habana for 1952. Calculated from *Anuario Estadístico, 1956* p. 638.
Soft drinks	Same as above.
Tobacco	Export unit value for 1952 calculated from *Comercio Exterior, 1952-1953*, p. 501.
Cigars	Export unit value for 1952 calculated from *ibid*.
Cigarettes	Export unit value for 1952 calculated from *ibid*.
Cotton cloth	Import unit value of white cotton cloth for 1953 calculated from *ibid.*, pp. 202-203.
Rayon filament yarn	Export unit value for 1952 calculated from *ibid.*, p. 514.
Rayon tire cord	Export unit value for 1952 calculated from *ibid.*, p. 480.
Rayon staple	Export unit value for 1952 calculated from *ibid.*, p. 478.
Rubber inner tubes	Import unit value for 1953 calculated from *ibid.*, p. 444.
Rubber tires	Same as above.
Electricity	Domestic unit value for 1954 calculated using value of production from Cuban Economic Research Project, *Stages and Problems of Industrial Development in Cuba*, pp. 84-90 and production volume from Appendix A.
Gas	Domestic price for 1952 from *Cuba Económica y Financiera* 34:395 (February 1959), p. 33.

APPENDIX C

CALCULATED INDEXES OF SUBGROUPS OF CUBAN
NONSUGAR MANUFACTURING PRODUCTION, 1930-58
(1953 = 100)

Year	Beverages	Shoes	Processed foods	Paper and paperboard	Rubber products	Textiles	Tobacco	Construction materials
1930	27.19	25.04	21.63	71.47	?	2.41	63.05	68.04
1931	21.02	22.73	21.92	45.44	?	2.18	47.20	12.03
1932	18.00	18.18	22.59	47.96	?	1.98	28.10	8.09
1933	19.32	16.36	29.52	47.02	?	2.36	27.47	7.63
1934	23.56	27.27	36.84	36.03	?	4.59	33.87	12.57
1935	27.19	32.73	41.65	14.84	?	10.60	37.89	17.32
1936	32.29	38.18	44.02	36.24	?	25.78	42.82	26.30
1937	33.66	43.64	48.05	48.94	?	26.38	48.66	29.94
1938	35.12	48.18	54.81	75.75	?	27.52	48.49	27.38
1939	34.57	41.82	53.21	143.84	?	30.97	47.64	31.68
1940	36.71	43.64	59.76	42.67	?	34.76	59.84	37.54
1941	38.17	45.46	75.49	74.28	?	92.43	66.30	38.25
1942	32.97	54.55	66.79	55.00	?	55.07	77.28	40.86
1943	43.25	65.46	56.28	43.12	22.93	72.16	80.25	41.72
1944	64.11	79.09	46.60	26.09	35.69	83.71	98.36	42.75
1945	75.80	81.82	39.38	142.48	50.22	72.34	90.15	44.33
1946	77.97	86.36	49.36	121.29	70.69	69.95	90.85	59.13
1947	75.95	124.91	49.36	49.95	76.80	66.51	95.90	67.99
1948	78.41	96.00	54.91	64.98	71.94	54.75	99.10	70.10
1949	80.26	80.96	58.52	55.38	66.64	66.46	95.83	76.82
1950	87.81	88.73	56.11	85.87	103.79	136.29	93.43	77.80
1951	99.63	89.83	77.25	90.00	129.49	98.85	96.45	94.21
1952	112.10	89.32	100.00	87.24	112.34	110.43	103.70	103.31
1953	100.00	100.00	100.41	100.00	100.00	100.00	100.00	100.00
1954	100.06	107.27	107.39	103.75	119.24	126.24	93.52	103.34
1955	100.71	114.55	120.50	109.11	119.04	116.63	97.24	112.00
1956	104.77	126.36	130.89	122.51	151.10	130.52	104.09	145.40
1957	107.48	139.10	128.70	126.88	177.73	141.22	112.99	158.41
1958	102.75	145.46		128.50	290.91	144.74	106.44	175.90

References

(All official Cuban works published in Havana; Great Britain works, London;
United Nations works, New York; United States works, Washington, D.C.)

Abad, Luis V. de. *Los Impuestos Especiales del Empréstito de los 35 Millones.* La Habana: Editora Mercantil, 1941.

Alienes Urosa, Julián. *Características Fundamentales de la Economía Cubana.* La Habana: Banco Nacional de Cuba, 1950.

_____ . *Los Problemas de la Economía de la Paz y las Soluciones que se Apuntan.* La Habana: Molina, por la Cámara de Comercio de la República de Cuba, 1945.

_____ . *Tésis Sobre el Desarrollo Económico de Cuba.* La Habana: Publicaciones de la Asociación Nacional de Industriales de Cuba, 2, 1952.

American Petroleum Institute. *Petroleum Facts and Figures.* 1967 edition. New York: American Petroleum Institute, 1968.

Anuario Estadístico Interamericano. Bajo los auspicios de la Comisión Argentina de Altos Estudios Internacionales. Paul C. Migone, Director. Buenos Aires: El Ateneo, 1940.

Aranda, Sergio. *La Revolución Agraria en Cuba.* México: Siglo XXI Editores, 1968.

Arrendondo, Alberto, *Reforma Agraria: La Experiencia Cubana.* San Juan, Puerto Rico: Editorial San Juan, 1969.

Asociación Nacional de Industriales de Cuba. "Estudio Sobre la Industria Textil." Report prepared by Insúa, Fernández y Alvarez Díaz, Public Accountants. La Habana, September 9, 1960. Typewritten.

_____ . *Informe y Plan de Desarrollo Industrial.* La Habana: Publicaciones de la Asociación Nacional de Industriales de Cuba, 1959.

Banco de Fomento Agrícola e Industrial de Cuba. División Industrial. *Informe Anual Sobre Operaciones de la División Industrial (1956-1957).*

_____ . *Labor, 1959, por la Industrialización de Cuba.*

Banco Nacional de Cuba. *La Economía Cubana 1955/56, 1956/57.*

_____ . *Economic Development Program: Progress Reports.* Various years.

_____ . *Memoria 1949-1958.* 11 vols.

_____ . *Revista.* 1955-1960.

Bernardo, Roberto M. *The Theory of Moral Incentives in Cuba.* University: University of Alabama Press, 1971.

Boorstein, Edward. *The Economic Transformation of Cuba.* New York: Monthly Review Press, 1968.

Borrego Díaz, Orlando. "Problemas que Plantea a la Industria una Zafra de 10 millones." *Cuba Socialista* (La Habana), 5:44 (April, 1965).

Brumberg, Richard. "*Ceteris Paribus* for Supply Curves." *Economic Journal,* 63 (June, 1953).

Carter, C. F., W. B. Reddaway, and Richard Stone. *The Measurement of Production Movements.* Cambridge: Cambridge University Press, 1965.

Center for Intercultural Information. *Latin America in Charts, Maps, Tables.* Mexico, 1964.

Chang, John K. *Industrial Development in Pre-Communist China.* Chicago: Aldine, 1969.

Comercio Exterior. See Cuba. Dirección General de Estadística.

Commission on Cuban Affairs. *Problems of the New Cuba.* New York: Foreign Policy Association, 1935.

Cuba, Cámara de Comercio, La Habana. *Directorio Comercial e Industrial Cubano (1951, 1952, 1955, 1958).*

_____ . Comisión del Censo Agrícola Nacional. *Memoria del Censo Agrícola Nacional, 1946.*

_____ . Comisión Nacional de Estadística y Reformas Económicas. *Cuadros Estadísticos.* 1926.

_____ . _____ . *Cuadros Estadísticos de los Empleados del Estado y los Sueldos que les Corresponden tomados de los Presupuestos Generales en Vigor en el Ejercicio de 1924-1925.*

_____ . _____ . *Cuadros Estadísticos en Relación con los Ingenios y su Zafra en 1925 a 1926.*

_____ . Comisión Nacional de Propaganda y Defensa del Tabaco Habano. *Nuestro Comercio de Exportación de Tabaco en Rama y Manufacturado.* 1959.

_____ . Consejo Nacional de Economía. *El Aprovechamiento de los Derivados de la Caña y el Azúcar.* 1955.

_____ . _____ . *La Estimulación Industrial en Cuba.* Publicaciones del Consejo Nacional de Economía, 14. (1956).

_____ . Dirección de Montes y Minas. *Boletín de Minas.* 1-12 (1916-1928).

_____ . Direccion General de Estadística. *Anuario Estadístico (1914, 1952, 1956, 1957).*

_____ . _____ . *Azúcar: Síntesis Estadístico-Analítica.* 1939.

_____ . _____ . *Comercio Exterior, 1902-1961.* 48 vol.

_____ . _____ . *Estadística de Plantas Eléctricas. Servicio Público, Año 1935.*

_____ . _____ . *Industria Azucarera v sus Derivados (1901/1905, 1904/1905-1913/1914, 1923/1924-1929, 1930/1931).*

_____ . _____ . *Organizaciones Patronales y Obreras, 1937.*

_____ . _____ . *Producción Forestal, Años 1933 y 1935.*

_____ . _____ . *Resúmenes Estadísticos Seleccionados.*

_____ . _____ . *Riqueza Minera, 1903.*

_____ . Dirección Nacional del Censo. *Censo de la República de Cuba, 1919.*

_____ . _____ . *Censo de 1931.*

_____ . Instituto Cubano de Investigaciones Tecnológicas. *Serie de Estudios Sobre Trabajos de Investigación.* 1959.

_____ . Junta Central de Planificación. Dirección Central de Estadística. *Boletín Estadistico 1968.*

_____ . _____ . _____ . *Compendio Estadístico de Cuba (1965, 1966, 1967).*

_____ . Junta Central de Planificación Revolucionaria. *Consumo y Producción de Cemento, 1938-1958.*

_____ . _____ . *Estudio de Producción y Consumo de Energia Eléctrica y de Uso de Combustibles en los Centrales Azucareros.* 1960.

_____ . Junta Nacional de Economía. *Boletín Informativo,* 1, 1952-

_____ . Oficina General de los Censos Demográfico y Electoral. *Censo de 1943.*

_____ . Oficina General de los Censos Demográfico y Electoral. *Censo de Población, Viviendas y Electoral, Enero 28 de 1953: Informe General.*

_____ . Secretaría de Agricultura, Comercio y Trabajo. *Cuba: A Pamphlet Descriptive of the Island of Cuba Containing Unembellished Data for General Information.* (Prepared by Leon J. Canova). 1910.

_____ . _____ . *Sinópsis Económica de Cuba: Lo que Cuba Produce. El Comercio Internacional de Cuba. La Hacienda Pública en Cuba.*

_____ . Secretaría de Hacienda. *Aportaciones para una Política Económica Cubana.*

————. Secretaría de Obras Publicas. *Boletín,* 1 (1926-   ).

————. Tribunal de Cuentas. Dirección de Fiscalización Preventiva y Control de Presupuestos del Estado. "Análisis de los Sectores Económicos en Cuba y su Tributación, Años 1953 y 1954." Mimeographed. 1957.

Cuba Económica y Financiera. 1926-1960.

Cuba Económica y Financiera. *Anuario Azucarero de Cuba.* 23 vols. 1938-1960.

Cuban Economic Research Project. *Cuba: Agriculture and Planning.* Miami: Editorial AIP, 1965.

————. *Cuba: Geopolítica y Pensamiento Económico.* Miami: Duplex, 1964.

————. "Stages and Problems of Industrial Development in Cuba." Miami: 1965(?), Mimeographed.

————. *A Study on Cuba.* Miami: University of Miami Press, 1965.

Denison, Edward F. "Welfare Measurement and the GNP." *Survey of Current Business,* 51:1 (Jan., 1971).

"El Desarrollo Industrial de Cuba." *Cuba Socialista,* Part I (April, 1962) and Part II (May, 1966).

Directorio Mercantil de la Isla de Cuba (Para el Año 1901). La Habana: Imprenta Avisador Comercial, 1901.

Dumont, René. *Cuba ¿Es Socialista?* Caracas: Editorial Tiempo Nuevo, 1970.

————. *Cuba: Socialism and Development.* New York: Grove Press, 1970.

Echeverría Salvat, Oscar. *La Agricultura Cubana: 1934-1966.* Miami: Ediciones Universal, 1971.

Economic and Technical Mission to Cuba. *Report on Cuba.* Baltimore: Johns Hopkins Press, 1951.

"Las Estadísticas en Cuba." *Cuba Económica y Financiera,* 27:314 (May, 1952).

Fabricant, Solomon. *The Output of Manufacturing Industries, 1899-1937.* New York: National Bureau of Economic Research, 1940.

"La Falta de Estadísticas en Cuba." *Cuba Económica y Financiera,* 25:194 (Sept., 1950).

Ferrán, Juan F. "Las Microinversiones y la Productividad en la Industria Azucarera." *Economía y Desarrollo* (La Habana), 14 (Nov.-Dec., 1972).

Financiera Nacional de Cuba. *Memoria 1956-1957.*

Fors, Ing. Alberto J. *Las Maderas Cubanas.* La Habana: Ministerio de Agricultura, Dirección de Minas, Montes y Aguas, 1946(?).

Great Britain. Board of Trade. *Statistical Abstract for the Principal and other Foreign Countries, 1887 to 1896-97.*

————. Commercial Relations and Exports Department. *Cuba: Economic and Commercial Conditions in Cuba (1922, 1949, 1954).*

Guerra y Sánchez, Ramiro. *Filosofía de la Producción Cubana.* La Habana: Cultural, 1944.

Gutelman, Michel. *La Agricultura Socializada en Cuba.* Mexico: Ediciones Era, 1970.

Gutiérrez y Sánchez, Gustavo. *El Desarrollo Económico de Cuba.* La Habana: Publicaciones del Consejo Nacional de Economía, 12 (1952).

————. *La Orientación de la Economía Nacional.* La Habana: Publicaciones de la Economía, 1 (1947).

————. *El Problema Económico de Cuba: Sus Causas y sus Posibles Soluciones.* La Habana: Molina, 1931.

————. *El Programa Económico de Cuba.* La Habana: Publicaciones del Consejo Nacional de Economía, 1955.

Higgins, Benjamin. *Economic Development: Problems, Principles, Cases.* New York: W. W. Norton, 1968.

Hodgman, Donald R. *Soviet Industrial Production, 1928-1951.* Cambridge: Harvard University Press, 1954.

Huberman, Leo, and Paul Sweezy. *Cuba: Anatomy of a Revolution.* New York: Monthly Review Press, 1960.

Kaplan, Norman N., and Richard H. Moorsteen. "An Index of Soviet Industrial Output." *American Economic Review,* 50:3 (June, 1960).

Kuznets, Simon. "Quantitative Economic Research: Trends and Problems." *Fiftieth Anniversary Colloquim VII.* New York: Columbia University Press for the National Bureau of Economic Research, 1972.

Latin American Economic Institute. New York. *The Cotton Textile Industry in Latin América.* New York, 1943.

Lee, Pong S. "An Index of North Korean Industrial Output, 1946-1963." Unpublished, 1971.

León Jiménez, Antonio. *Cuba y su Economía.* La Habana, 1943.

Le Riverend, Julio. *Historia Económica de Cuba.* 2d ed. La Habana: Editorial Nacional de Cuba, 1965.

————. *Los Orígenes de la Economía Cubana (1510-1600).* México: Jornada 46, Centro de Estudios Sociales, El Colegio de México, 1945.

López Sanabria, Hugo. *Clasificación Industrial de las Actividades Económicas de Cuba.* La Habana: Tribunal de Cuentas, 1955.

Martínez Sáenz, Joaquín. *Por la Independencia Económica de Cuba.* La Habana: Editorial Lex, 1959.

Maunder, W. F., ed. *Bibliography of Index Numbers,* 2d ed. London: Athlone Press for the International Statistical Institute, University of London, 1970.

Mesa-Lago, Carmelo. "Availability and Reliability of Statistics in Socialist Cuba." *Latin American Research Review,* 4, 1 (Spring, 1969) and 4, 2 (Summer, 1969).

————. "Cuba: Teoría y Práctica de los Incentivos." *Aportes,* 20 (April, 1971).

————. "Ideological Radicalization and Economic Policy in Cuba." *Studies in Comparative International Development,* 5:10 (1969-1970).

————. *The Labor Force, Employment, Unemployment and Underemployment in Cuba, 1899-1970.* Beverly Hills: Sage Publications, 1972.

————. *The Labor Sector and Socialist Distribution in Cuba.* New York: Praeger, 1968.

————. "La Posición de Cuba en la Polémica de los Incentivos Morales y Materiales." *Revista Cubana,* 1:2 (July-Dec., 1968).

————. "The Revolutionary Offensive." *Trans-Action,* 6:6 (April, 1969).

Mitchell, Wesley C. *The Making and Using of Index Numbers.* Reprints of Economic Classics. New York: Augustus M. Kelley, 1965.

Montias, John Michael. *Economic Development in Communist Rumania.* Cambridge: MIT Press, 1967.

National Foreign Trade Council. *U.S. Business In Cuba: A Background Report.* New York: National Foreign Trade Council, 1960.

Newman, Philip C. *Cuba before Castro: An Economic Appraisal.* Bombay: Foreign Studies Institute, 1965.

Nolff, Max. "El Desarrollo Industrial de Cuba." *Panorama Económico* (Santiago de Chile), 16 (Nov. 1963) and 17 (May, 1964).

Noyola, Juan F. "La Revolución Cubana y sus Efectos en el Desarrollo Económico." *El Trimestre Económico* (México), 28:111 (July-September, 1961).

O'Connor, James. *The Origins of Socialism in Cuba.* Ithaca: Cornell University Press, 1970.

Pan American Union. *América en Cifras.* Washington.

Pariseau, Earl J., ed. *Cuban Acquisitions and Bibliography,* Proceedings and Working Papers of an International Conference held at the Library of Congress, April 13-15, 1970. Washington: Library of Congress, 1970.

Pazos y Roque, Felipe. *Influencia de la Escuela de Ciencias Económicas en el Desarrollo Económico del País.* Santiago de Cuba: Universidad de Oriente, 1955.

Pérez, Luis Marino. *Fuentes de Información sobre los Mercados*

Azucareros. La Habana: Boletín de la Asociación de Colonos de Cuba, 1960.

Pino Santos, Oscar. *El Imperialismo Norteamericano en la Economía de Cuba.* La Habana: Editorial Lex, 1960.

Porter, Robert P. *Industrial Cuba.* New York: Putnam's, 1899.

Primer Anuario Comercial e Industrial de Cuba, 4, (1956-1957).

"La Producción Nacional de Calzado." *Cuba Económica y Financiera,* 27:313 (April, 1952).

Raggi Ageo, Carlos M. *Condiciones Económicas y Sociales de la República de Cuba.* La Habana: Editorial Lex, 1944.

Reiners, Walter E. "Estudio de la Industria del Calzado Cubano." Report Commissioned by CRIC. La Habana, Sept. 1, 1958.

Riera Hernández, Mario. *Historial Obrero Cubano 1574-1965.* Miami: Rema Press, 1965.

Ritter, Arch R. M. "Human Resource Mobilization Strategies in Revolutionary Cuba," *Carleton Economic Papers,* 72-13 (May, 1973).

Roberts, Paul C., and Mukhtar Hamour, eds. *Cuba 1968,* Statistical Abstract of Latin America, Supplement 1. Los Angeles: UCLA Latin American Center Publications, University of California, 1970.

Ruggles, Richard, and Nancy D. Ruggles. *National Income Accounts and Income Analysis.* New York: McGraw Hill, 1965.

Sagra, Ramón de la. *Cuba 1860: Selección de Articulos sobre Agricultura Cubana.* La Habana: Comisión Cubana de la Unesco, 1963.

Sánchez Roig, Mario, and Federico Gómez de la Maza. *La Pesca en Cuba.* La Habana: Seoane, Fernández, 1952.

Schnitter, J. G. *Leather: World Production and International Trade.* Washington: U.S. Department of Commerce, Bureau of Foreign and Domestic Commerce, Trade Promotion Series, 157 (1935).

Seers, Dudley, ed. *Cuba: The Economic and Social Revolution.* Chapel Hill: University of North Carolina Press, 1964.

Silverman, Bertram. *Man and Socialism in Cuba: The Great Economic Debate.* New York: Atheneum, 1971.

Smith, Robert F. *The United States and Cuba: Business and Diplomacy, 1917-1960.* New Haven: College and University Press, 1960.

Statistical Abstract of the United States. See United States. Bureau of the Census.

Stone, Richard. *Quantity and Price Indexes in National Accounts.* Paris: Organization for European Economic Co-Operation, 1956.

Truth about Cuba Committee. *Facts, Data, and Statistics on Pre-Communist Cuba.* Miami: 1964(?).

United Nations. *The Growth of World Industry, 1938-1961.*

_____. *The Growth of World Industry, 1953-1966.*

_____. *Patterns of Industrial Growth, 1938-1958.*

_____. Department of Economic and Social Affairs. *Processes and Problems of Industrialization in Under-Developed Countries.* 1955.

_____ . _____ , *A Study of Industrial Growth.* 1963.

_____. Economic Comission for Europe. *The World Market for Iron Ore.* 1968.

_____ . Economic Commission for Latin America. *Economic Bulletin for Latin America.* 1952-

_____ . _____ . *The Economic Development of Latin America in the Post-War Period.* 1964.

_____ ._____ . *Economic Survey of Latin America,* 1948-

_____ ._____ . *Latin America Timber Trends and Prospects.* 1963.

_____ . _____ . *Possibilities for the Development of the Pulp and Paper Industry in Latin America.* 1954.

_____ . _____ . *Pulp and Paper Prospects in Latin America.* 1955 and 1963.

_____ . _____ .*Statistical Bulletin for Latin America, 1964-*

_____ . Food and Agriculture Organization. *Yearbook of Fisheries Statistics,* 1947-

_____ . _____ . *Yearbook of Food and Agricultural Statistics-Production,* 1947-

_____ . _____ . *Yearbook of Forest Products,* 1947-

_____ . Statistical Office. *Index Numbers of Industrial Production,* Studies in Methods, Series F, 1 (1961).

_____ . _____ . *International Standard Industrial Classification of All Economic Activity,* Statistical Papers, Series M, 4:1. (1958).

_____ . _____ . *Statistical Yearbook.*

United States. Bureau of the Budget. *Standard Industrial Classification Manual.* 1957.

_____ . Bureau of the Census. *Statistical Abstract of the United States.*

_____ . Bureau of Mines. *Minerals Yearbook.*

_____ . Department of Agriculture. *Cuba as a Market for U.S. Agricultural Products.* Foreign Agricultural Rerport 81. 1954.

_____ . Department of Commerce. Bureau of Foreign Commerce. American Republics Division. *Investment in Cuba: Basic Information for United States Businessmen.* 1956.

_____ . _____ . International Reference Service. *Cuba,* Foreign Service Yearbook Series, 3:30 (1946).

_____ . _____ . _____ . *Economic Conditions in Cuba, 1945,* 3:34 (1946).

_____ . Embassy. Cuba. *Economic Development in Cuba* (*1957, 1958*). Published by U.S. Department of Commerce, Bureau of Foreign Commerce.

_____ . Tariff Commission. *Mining and Manufacturing Industries in Cuba.* 1947.

Universidad Católica de Santo Tomás de Villanueva. Instituto de Investigaciones Económicas. *Cuba y Canadá: Investigación Económica Comparativa.* La Habana: Editorial Lex, 1957.

Vivó, Hugo. *Los Números Indices en Cuba.* La Habana: Secretaría de Agricultura, Oficina de los Números Indices, 1938.

Wallich, Henry C. *Monetary Problems of an Export Economy: The Cuban Experience 1914-1947.* Cambridge: Harvard University Press, 1960.

Waterman, Fausto E. *La Minería en Cuba.* Trabajo presentado al I Symposium de Recursos Naturales de Cuba, Sección de Recursos Minerales. La Habana, 1957.

Part Three

LATIN AMERICA

Chapter 4

Projecting the HEC (Health, Education, and Communication) Index for Latin America Back to 1940

James W. Wilkie and Maj-Britt Nilsson

University of California, Los Angeles

Introduction

In *Statistics and National Policy,*[1] Wilkie outlined a health, education and communication (HEC) Index to test the so-called widening gap between the developing and developed countries. Utilizing summary data for 12 items spanning the years 1950 to 1970 the social gap between Latin America (representing the developing world) and the United States (representing the developed world) was measured. For the present study, we set out to project the Index back to 1940 and even 1930.

After an exhaustive search of national and international data sources by Nilsson, we determined that although isolated statistics are available for some countries and/or some items for 1930, it is not possible to locate enough descriptive data to reconstruct a complete profile of the social condition of Latin America before 1940 that would be fully comparable with post-1950 data in the HEC index. In researching data for 1940, we often had to employ inductive analysis to fill in missing descriptive statistics to predict a complete picture for the social situation for that year sufficiently reliable for inclusion in the HEC index, an index that becomes more reliable after 1950. This study discusses the nature of the data for 1940 and how the lacunae were filled.[2]

[Editors' Note: Wilkie's study "The Narrowing Gap," originally planned for publication here, is being expanded into a book and will appear as Supplement 8 entitled *The Narrowing Social Gap: Latin America and the United States, 1940-1970,* forthcoming.]

[1] Statistical Abstract of Latin America Supplement 3 (Los Angeles: UCLA Latin American Center Publications, University of California, 1974), pp. 479-481.

[2] For methodological consultation we are indebted to Professor William J. Rosen, Department of Mathematics, Los Angeles Pierce College.

The HEC Index Introduced

Latin America's level of living or social condition is presented as a differential computed by calculating the gap between Latin America and the United States for individual items in the Index (Table 4-1, Part 1). The items in the Index are not explicitly weighted (but they are implicitly weighted by the fact that there are 5 health items, 4 education items, and 3 communication items (Table 4-1, Part IV). Since it is socially advantageous for 7 items to have a high number (e.g., life expectancy) and for 5 to have a low number (e.g., infant mortality), to get a consistent measure of the closing gap the difference between Latin America and the United States was computed as the percentage of change between low and high numbers, regardless of their Latin American or U.S. origin. Thus, in 1940, Latin America was 1,349 percent worse off than the United States in relation to the HEC items, this figure narrowing to 652 percent by 1970.[3]

The total rate of change in the level of living between 1940 and 1950, between 1950 and 1960, and between 1960 and 1970 was nearly 20 percent or more each decade, the level closing to meet the U.S. standard (Table 4-1, Part II).

Many American nations aspire to improve their relative position within the Latin American region, just as their citizens aspire to improve their living conditions in relation to the HEC components. Table 4-1, Part III, shows the HEC rankings of the 20 Latin American countries.

The 12 items included in the HEC Index (Table 4-1, Part IV) do not, of course, include all the possibilities that might be included in an ideal index; they catalog the data for which we have meaningful time series available for all countries since 1940. Latin America is measured against the

[3] In the subindex for health, e.g., Latin America was 394.1 percent worse off than the United States in 1940.

Table 4-1
HEALTH, EDUCATION, AND COMMUNICATION (HEC) INDEX FOR
LATIN AMERICA, 1940-70

PART I
HEC LEVEL
(DIFFERENTIAL BETWEEN LATIN AMERICA AND THE UNITED STATES)[1]

Year	Health Average 5 items	Education Average 4 items	Communication Average 3 items	Total Average 12 items
1940	394.1	496.1	3,912.3	1,349.3
1950	341.2	403.8	3,282.8	1,097.5
1960	315.0	263.1	2,582.2	864.5
1970	255.3	228.2	1,879.7	652.4

PART II
PERCENTAGE CHANGE

Health	Education	Communication	Total
~	~	~	~
−13.4	−18.6	−19.5	−18.7
−7.7	−34.8	−21.3	−21.2
−19.0	−13.3	−27.2	−24.5

PART III
HEC TOTAL RANKINGS OF THE 20 LATIN AMERICAN COUNTRIES

Country	1940	1950	1960	1970
ARGENTINA	1	2	2	1
BOLIVIA	17	17	17	17
BRAZIL	9	9	10	10
CHILE	5	4	6	6
COLOMBIA	10**	8	9	11
COSTA RICA	6	6**	7	5
CUBA	3	5	3	7
DOMINICAN REP.	16	15**	14	13
ECUADOR	14**	13	13	14
EL SALVADOR	14**	15**	15	16
GUATEMALA	18	18	18	19
HAITI	20	20	20	20
HONDURAS	19	19	19	18
MEXICO	8	12	11	9
NICARAGUA	13	14	16	12
PANAMA	4	3	4	3
PARAGUAY	10**	11	12	15
PERU	12	10	8	8
URUGUAY	2	1	1	2
VENEZUELA	7	6**	5	4

PART IV
HEC COMPONENTS

Health (H)

1. Life expectancy
2. Infant mortality rate
3. Persons per hospital bed
4. Persons per physician
5. Persons per dentist

Education (E)

6. Literacy rate for population age 15 and over
7. Share of school-age population 13-18 enrolled in secondary school
8. Share of school-age population 13-18 enrolled in secondary school
9. Share of students enrolled in higher schools as a share of students enrolled in primary schools

Communication (C)

10. Newspaper circulation, copies per 1,000 persons
11. Number of telephones per 100 persons
12. Number of persons per motor vehicle in use

1. The average HEC differential between Latin America and the United States closed from 1,349.3 in 1950 to 864.5 in 1960, and to 652.4 in 1970. (A zero differential means that Latin America would have the same HEC standard as the United States, which represents a convenient yardstick to which many Latin Americans compare their national level of living.)

SOURCE: James W. Wilkie, *The Narrowing Social Gap: Latin America and the United States, 1940-1970,* Statistical Abstract of Latin America Supplement 8 (Los Angeles: UCLA Latin American Center Publications, University of California, forthcoming).

United States for the following reasons: (1) Items chosen are neutral in that they deal with better living conditions regardless of ideology. All countries strive to improve these levels, eventually if not immediately, except notably for Castro's Cuba which turned away from the communication component in its attempt to create a "New Man." (2) Because of possible debate over the communication component as involving a material, economic, or nonsocial basis, data are presented in Table 4-1 for the subindexes health, education, and communication in order that we may see how the components affect the total as well as to permit other investigators to develop their own indexes. (3) Regardless of the wishes of leaders or intellectuals who would like to see Latin America become "independent" of the United States, U.S. influence in Latin America has been paramount not only directly in international affairs but also indirectly in establishing a standard of living accepted by a large share of the population. (4) It is conceptually more intelligible to speak here of a concrete U.S. HEC standard than of an average standard for many countries of the developed world which would include both better levels (e.g., infant mortality rates) and worse levels (e.g., share of students enrolled in higher schools as a share of students enrolled in primary schools).

The HEC Index differs in an important respect from the Wilkie Poverty Index for Mexico.[4] The latter is based upon census data of 7 items for each person surveyed individually by census takers; the former is based upon a per capita approach. If the Poverty Index for Mexico declines for each of the 7 items, we can know how the population censused is faring; the same is not true for the HEC Index, because if, for example, the number of persons per motor vehicle declines, we cannot say definitely that more people own vehicles: per capita data covers the situation where fewer persons are acquiring a larger number of autos, not necessarily that more persons are acquiring them. All we can say is that the chances for ownership of or access to vehicles in general, including buses and trucks, increase. With these considerations in mind, it is appropriate to assess the data for 1940.

HEC-Index Data for 1940

Writing in 1942 Charles Morrow Wilson painted a bleak picture of health conditions in Latin America:

> There are roughly a hundred and twenty million people in Latin America. . . . At this very moment it is a good bet that at least fifty million of them are sick. Sick of everything from sprue to leprosy. Sick of almost all the diseases that we in the United States encounter in our lives, and of other savage and highly fatal diseases about which we know almost nothing.[5]

About the specific conditions in Haiti, in 1941 James G. Leyburn called attention to problems faced:

> Historians who seek to explain the rise and fall of nations in terms of a single cause might do worse than hit upon health and disease as the all-important explanation. Unless spectacular epidemics have appeared in a country's history, the average person is rarely aware of how diet may affect a people, or of how backwardness in achievement is often directly related to disease. It may well be that the development of *medical* history will yet cause a radical revision of certain philosophies of history. . . .
>
> The "triple threat" to Haitian health is the morbid group: malaria, hookworm, and yaws. The first two are familiar enough in part of the United States, and

require only short comment. For centuries malaria has sapped the vitality of people in southern lands, giving them a reputation for indolence which is not wholly deserved. Haitian peasants were during the entire nineteenth century accused of laziness; when a strapping man lay all day in the shade of a tree, it was logical enough for a white visitor to suppose that he was willfully loafing. The critics might have been more temperate if they had known what it was to be perpetually full of malaria, with a body apparently hale and hearty, but lassitude sapping all energy. A group of doctors from the Rockefeller Foundation discovered that among 4,439 persons examined in various surveys two decades ago sixty-seven per cent showed malarial parasites in the blood. Since the American Occupation steps have been taken to control the disease and much progress has resulted: some of the towns are now practically free of it. But the battle against malaria will never be won so long as the anopheles mosquito breeds in the island; it means an endless war of constant vigilance as well as education — one which must be carried on simultaneously in the neighboring Dominican Republic.

Hookworm, like malaria, is also ordinarily quite undramatic in its symptoms. There is no specific pain, but rather a progressive inertia. Since practically every country person goes barefoot it would be miraculous if hookworm were not widespread, for sanitation is entirely lacking in peasant communities. Dr. Lhérisson reported in 1935 that twenty-six per cent of the mass of Haitian people examined up to that time had been found infested by hookworms. The final figure will probably be revised upward, for the persons most easily examined are townspeople who have better sanitation and more shoes. . . .

Yaws is, of the morbid triad, the most virulent and the commonest. It was brought over from Africa apparently as early as 1509. Oviedo describes it in 1526 as "a terrible pustular disease." It so closely resembles syphilis that it has often been mistaken for that malady. Untreated or wrongly treated it ravages the bodies of its victims, making them loathesome to behold. . . .

Hard work and a simple mode of outdoor life prove, in Haiti at least, not to be the keys to good health which a romantic might fancy them. Haiti has been one of the unhealthiest places in the world. One feels that it has been lucky to escape such scourges as typhus, cholera, and bubonic plague; that smallpox has not been violent in its epidemics, and that the people developed an immunity to yellow fever. It has, indeed, been luck rather than cleanliness and proper medical care which has protected the people in these instances. . . .

Dysentery, when caused by bacilli, is epidemic in nature. In Haiti this form, known as "colerin,"

---

[4] Items included in the Poverty Index involve population regularly wearing sandals, eating tortillas, living in isolated areas under 2,500 persons, being illiterate, living without sewage disposal, going barefoot, and speaking only an Indian language. See James W. Wilkie, *The Mexican Revolution: Federal Expenditure and Social Change Since 1910* (2d ed.; Berkeley: University of California Press, 1970), pp. 204-245; and followup methodological analysis in Wilkie "On Quantitative History: The Poverty Index for Mexico," *Latin American Research Review* 10:1 (1975), pp. 63-75.

[5] Charles Morrow Wilson, "How Latin Americans Die," *Harper's Magazine*, July 1942, p. 140.

annually affects about a quarter of the rural population. Another type, caused by a variety of amoeba, affects another ten or twenty per cent, according to the region. Enteritis is less serious than dysentery but just as prevalent, being caused by protozoa and intestinal worms. Poor diet, the abuse of alcohol, premature weaning, and unwise nursing are also responsible.[6]

Although Leyburn was writing about the region's poorest country, public health campaigns in much of Latin America had yet to get underway in 1940, and Leyburn's comments apply to problems faced in tropical zones throughout Latin America. Too, parasitic diseases and turberculosis have made life difficult for the highland masses who have also suffered from extreme temperature and atmospheric conditions. Only in such capital cities as Buenos Aires, Santiago, Lima, Bogotá, Mexico City, and Havana were modern health facilities firmly established, and even there the masses have not been well cared.

In any event the basis for Latin America's post-1940 health revolution apparently was laid in the 1930s. In one of the few 1930 health indicators that we have to compare with 1940, data on life expectancy at birth in Table 4-2 show that by 1940 the population could expect to live, on the average, 5 years longer, to the age of 40. Although some of the data are projected back to 1930 on a linear regression model (see Method I in the Methodological Appendix, below), actual data for other countries such as Costa Rica, Panama, and Venezuela (where the gain was 6 years) confirm that the computed average figure is relatively reliable. (Actual data for El Salvador and the Dominican Republic show a gain of as much as 8 years in life expectancy at birth, offsetting the low actual data that we would expect to find for Bolivia and Brazil, which experienced only 3-year gains.) Data for a country like Bolivia would appear largely to omit the Indian population, where it has been argued that to survive in the high altitudes Indians must be strong just to be born, even if they then age rapidly, age 40 being considered very old in 1940.

Infant mortality data, the second item in the HEC Index, can be problematic. How do we treat data when the rate for 1940 is lower than for 1950 (as in Bolivia and Paraguay, where the rates were 101 and 145, and 79 and 90, respectively)? Although the rate for Bolivia has been tested with modern statistical analysis by O. Andrew Collver,[7] the official results that he accepts still appear to us to be suspiciously low. Figures of 1940 given in Table 4-3 for Haiti (estimated at 190, the same as the 1970 figure)[8] are lower

[6] James G. Leyburn, *The Haitian People* (New Haven: Yale University Press, 1941), pp. 272-277.

[7] O. Andrew Collver, *Birth Rates in Latin America: New Estimates of Historical Trends and Fluctuations* (Berkeley: Institute of International Studies 1965), p. 72. Collver decided not to modify the rate of 101, noting that it may have involved an underregistration of only 5 to 7 percent.

[8] James W. Wilkie, *The Narrowing Social Gap: Latin America and the United States, 1940-1970,* Statistical Abstract of Latin America Supplement 8 (Los Angeles: UCLA Latin American Center Publications, University of California, forthcoming), Appendix 1.

Table 4-2

HEC ITEM 1: LIFE EXPECTANCY AT BIRTH IN LATIN AMERICA AND THE UNITED STATES, 1930 AND 1940

Country	1930		1940	
	Age	Rank	Age	Rank
Total average	35	*	40	*
ARGENTINA	54.5[a]	2	58.0[a]	2
BOLIVIA	34.7	7	38.8	7**
BRAZIL	34	10**	36.7	14
CHILE	35.2	6	38.1	10
COLOMBIA	34.2	9	38.0	11
COSTA RICA	41.9	4	48.7	3
CUBA	42.3[a]	3	48.3[a]	4
DOMINICAN REP.	26.1	19	34.0	18
ECUADOR	27.5[a]	17	35.0[a]	16
EL SALVADOR	28.7	15	37.5	12**
GUATEMALA	26.6	18	30.4	19
HAITI	18.0[a]	20	26.0[a]	20
HONDURAS	34.0	10**	37.5	12**
MEXICO	33.9	12	38.8	7**
NICARAGUA	28.6	16	34.5	17
PANAMA	35.9	5	42.5	5
PARAGUAY	34.5	8	39.2	6
PERU	29.0[a]	14	36.5	15
URUGUAY	66.7[a]	1	67.7	1
VENEZUELA	32.5	13	38.7	9
UNITED STATES	60.0	*	63.0	*

a. For method used in calculating Argentina, Cuba, Ecuador, Haiti, and Uruguay in 1930 and 1940, and Peru in 1930, see Method I in the Methodolgical Appendix, below.

SOURCE: NLTLA, pp. 2-3. U.S. data are from SHUS, p. 25.

than for Chile's 1940 figure (at 217), suggesting that before World War II Haiti was in better control of infant mortality than was Chile. Is this credible? Or was Haiti still benefiting from the aftermath of the U.S. Marine Corps occupation that introduced radical health measures to the island between 1915 and 1934? At the same time one could only surmise that Chile had a series of infant disease epidemics that Haiti did not have.

On the one hand, it seems to be true that Haitian public health has declined since the marines departed (infant mortality has consistently gotten worse, being lower in 1960 (at 171) than in 1970 (at 190);[9] on the other hand, the marine medical corps may never even have begun to reach the rural Haitian people about whom Leyburn writes. More probably the Chilean data are the most reliable of all countries, a fact meaning that Chile's rank is biased negatively for 1940. Chile's honesty does not go totally unrewarded, however, because the high figure for 1940 infant mortality will show a higher relative decrease by 1950 compared with countries where infant mortality is understated for 1940. In short, given these complex factors, it has seemed best not to

[9] *Ibid.*

Table 4-3

HEC ITEMS 2, 3, AND 4: INFANT MORTALITY RATE, PERSONS PER HOSPITAL BED, AND PERSONS PER PHYSICIAN IN LATIN AMERICA AND THE UNITED STATES, 1940

Country	2: Infant Mortality Rate[†]		3: Persons per Hospital Bed[e]		4: Persons per Physician[f]	
	Rate	Rank	Number	Rank	Number	Rank
Total average	127	*	735	*	4148	*
ARGENTINA	90	5	225	3	1,191	1
BOLIVIA	101[a]	6	2,690	20	5,978	18
BRAZIL	189[b]	18	529	10	2,022[g]	5
CHILE	217	20	251	5	2,439	6
COLOMBIA	141	14	606	11	3,871	10
COSTA RICA	132	13	232	4	3,641	9
CUBA	61[a]	1	277	6	1,384	3
DOMINICAN REP.	149[a]	15	1,759	18	5,024	13
ECUADOR	159	17	429	8	4,110	12
EL SALVADOR	121	9	695	13	6,280	19
GUATEMALA	127[a]	12	766	16	5,555	15**
HAITI	190[d]	19	2,019	19	11,308	20
HONDURAS	106	7	923	17	5,832	17
MEXICO	126	11	683	12	1,965[g]	4
NICARAGUA	109[c]	8	756	15	4,095	11
PANAMA	81[a]	3	173	2	3,560[h]	8
PARAGUAY	79[c]	2	741	14	5,555	15**
PERU	150[a]	16	443	9	5,173	14
URUGUAY	87[c]	4	132	1	1,233	2
VENEZUELA	122	10	371	7	2,748	7
UNITED STATES	47	*	107	*	751	*

[†]Deaths under 1 year of age per 1,000 live births.

a. Data, for 1940-1944, are from BRLA.
b. Data cover 826 places including 21 state capitals.
c. Incomplete.
d. Estimated, see text.
e. Includes some approximate figures, according to source.
f. Data subject to variation of 10 percent or more, according to source.
g. Includes a number of irregular practitioners.
h. Including Canal Zone.

SOURCE: For Item 2: UNSY (1951), pp. 50-53; except Brazil from SBS, p. 60, and see note a above.
For Item 3: LAFW, p. 350; except Mexico from AAA, p. 159, and United States from SHUS, p. 35.
For Item 4: AES, pp. 417-419; except United States from SHUS, p. 34.

tamper with reported data and to estimate each country's data in relation to its own history rather than in relation to other countries in Latin America.[10]

Number of persons per physician (Table 4-3) appears to be one of the less troublesome items in the Index. All medical graduates do not practice medicine though, having been the custom in the past in some Latin American families to have one son study medicine who would practice irregularly or not at all. Also, some physicians who have migrated out of Latin America in search of better working conditions and higher pay may continue to be counted in the statistics for some years, depending upon whether or not the data reflect licensing records or physicians in actual practice. (From a different point of view, data for 1940 may include many cases of unqualified personnel who could practice medicine because of lax enforcement of the laws.) The midwife often substitutes for the doctor, and in Mexico, for example, the national university has offered a degree in midwifery. Although rural areas might be lacking physicians, there has often been a district nurse who is able to treat a number of illnesses, and who sends a patient to the city when in need of more sophisticated care. Finally, the pharmacist, who continues to play a different role in Latin America than in the United States, is often consulted to diagnose minor illnesses of persons, dispensing drugs over the counter — prescriptions are seldom needed in Latin America. According to one source, pharmacists were so common in the 1940s that in some countries there were as many of them as there were doctors.[11]

[10]Thus Haitian data for 1950 are estimated (at 179) to show higher percentage change during the 1940s (5.8 percent) under the Haitian "intellectual revolution" than during the 1950s (4.5 percent) under the dark days of "Papa Doc" Duvalier. See *ibid.*

[11]George Soule, David Effron, and Norman T. Ness, *Latin America in the Future World* (New York: Farrar and Rinehart for the National Planning Association, 1945), p. 351.

The data for persons per hospital bed in 1940 are relatively troublefree except that we are unsure whether or not coverage includes rest homes, nursing homes, and/or private sanitoriums and various kinds of "temporary beds" (Table 4-3). The ratios for persons per dentist are so puzzling that two different estimates have been reported for 1940 (Table 4-4). Both could be considered reliable taken by themselves; both used essentially the same sources and both can be thought of as prepared by reliable reporters. The estimates for 1940-A were calculated by the U.S.-based National Planning Association staff. And using the data reported by Dr. Aristades Moll, the then Secretary for the Pan American Sanitary Bureau, and UNESCO population estimates, we calculated ratios of people per dentist in 1940-B, which for some countries vary greatly compared with ratios in 1940-A. Thirteen countries had fewer persons per dentist in 1940-B than in 1940-A, variation between the ratios ranging from 3 to 283 percent. To know which to consider accurate for a study like this we need to know how the data were gathered and who reported it. Did U.S. officials gather them personally or did officials of the country do so, perhaps inflating their reports in the attempt to disguise the true nature of the situation? What method was used by the National Planning Association? Did it have reliable estimates with which to work? The questions are numerous and cannot be answered here. To resolve it we averaged the two (Table 4-4, last col.). The result appears to give a fair estimate of the situation in 1940 compared with 1950.[12]

For the 1940 figures on literacy (Table 4-5), we found it necessary to adjust the data for all but 5 countries in order to achieve consistency in reporting for persons age 15 and over; figures for Brazil, Chile, Mexico, Peru, and Venezuela were consistently reported for the age group used here. The problem with reporting data for persons ages 6-14 is that it adds to the rate of illiteracy because much of that school-age population is not enrolled in primary school or has not been in school long enough to become literate. The method for adjusting the data meant increasing the literate percentage according to rank of each country in school-age population 7-14 enrolled in primary school (see Table 4-6) by adding percentages as follows: 1 percent for ranks 1-3; 2 percent for ranks 4-7; 3 percent for ranks 8-14; 4 percent for ranks

[12] Wilkie, The Narrowing Social Gap, Appendix I.

Table 4-4

HEC ITEM 5: PERSONS PER DENTIST IN LATIN AMERICA AND THE UNITED STATES, 1940

Country	1940-A		1940-B		Average	
	Number	Rank	Number	Rank	Number	Rank
Total average	17,794[a]	*	12,472	*	15,133	*
ARGENTINA	2,579	1	3,148	2	2,863	1
BOLIVIA	33,265	17	21,520	18	27,392	18
BRAZIL	4,412	4	4,123	4	4,267	4
CHILE	6,250	5	4,186	5	5,218	5
COLOMBIA	13,387	9	13,995	15	13,691	10
COSTA RICA	11,621	8	11,254	9	11,437	7
CUBA	3,877	2	4,087	3	3,982	3
DOMINICAN REP.	10,660	6	17,590	17	14,125	11
ECUADOR	14,537	11	8,220	7	11,378	6
EL SALVADOR	13,608[b]	10	13,608	13	13,608	9
GUATEMALA	38,403	19	23,389	19	30,896	19
HAITI	50,000	20	37,693	20	43,846	20
HONDURAS	34,602	18	11,542	10	23,072	17
MEXICO	21,633	14	12,283	11	16,958	15
NICARAGUA	25,190	15	10,922	8	18,056	16
PANAMA	11,466	7	12,460	12	11,963	8
PARAGUAY	14,848	12	17,092	16	15,970	13
PERU	15,384	13	13,795	14	14,589	12
URUGUAY	4,120	3	1,795	1	2,957	2
VENEZUELA	25,859	16	6,745	6	16,302	14
UNITED STATES	*	*	*	*	1,883	*

a. Subject to a variation of 10 percent or more in many countries, according to source.
b. Data from 1940-B used as no other information available.

SOURCE: For 1940-A: LAFW, Table 14. Ratios prepared by the National Planning Association, Washington, D.C.
For 1940-B: Dentists from AES, p. 309; population data from SNP, table VIII-1.
For United States: SHUS, p. 34.

Table 4-5

HEC ITEM 6: LITERATE POPULATION AGE 15 AND OVER IN LATIN AMERICA AND THE UNITED STATES, 1940

(ADJUSTED)[a]

Country	1940 Percent	1940 Rank
Total average	46	*
ARGENTINA	89	1
BOLIVIA	24	19
BRAZIL	40	13
CHILE	71	3
COLOMBIA	53	5
COSTA RICA	70	4
CUBA	42	10**
DOMINICAN REP.	43	9
ECUADOR	30	15
EL SALVADOR	49	6**
GUATEMALA	29	16**
HAITI	29	16**
HONDURAS	22	20
MEXICO	49	6**
NICARAGUA	34	14
PANAMA	42	10**
PARAGUAY	26	18
PERU	42	10**
URUGUAY	82	2
VENEZUELA	44	8
UNITED STATES	97	*

a. Except for Brazil, Chile, Mexico, Peru, and Venezuela data are adjusted here for consistency for series through 1970. For rationale and methodology, see text.

SOURCE: Data for unadjusted countries are from UNDY (1948); all other data adjusted here were originally estimated by the League of Nations and reported in ACA, p. 60.

15-20. This method was developed from an analysis of Cuban and Mexican data which suggested the above approximate adjustments. Of four countries, Argentina, Colombia, El Salvador, and Haiti, that show a decrease in literacy during the 1940s (Table 4-5) at least two no doubt involve incorrect reports — El Salvador and Haiti. The data are not changed on the assumption that since there are random errors throughout the reporting they may cancel each other out; in any case, the number of other items and the historical trajectory after 1950 assure that the relative overall ranks of Haiti and El Salvador are not affected by the discrepancy.[13]

The U.N. definition for literacy seems to render useless the Latin American simple concept of literacy which is only to be able to read and write on a basic level. According to the United Economic and Social Council, "A person is literate when he has acquired the essential knowledge and skill which enable him to engage in all those activities in which literacy is required for effective functioning in his group and community, and whose attainment in reading,

writing and arithmetic make it possible for him to use these skills toward his own and the community's development, and for the active participation in the life of his country."[14] Clearly this definition would label many "literate" persons in Latin America as "functional illiterates," the situation varying from country to country.

Estimating the percentage of school-age population 7-14 enrolled in primary school (Table 4-6) involved inductive operations. Age-group data for 10 Latin American countries and the United States were projected backward to 1940 using Method II in the Methodological Appendix, below. This age-group data were then used in calculations based upon enrollment data in Table 4-7. To compute the percentage of school-age population 13-18 enrolled in secondary school (Table 4-6), enrollment figures in Table 4-7 were utilized along with Methods II and III in the Methodological Appendix, Method III involving nonlinear analysis. Figures on the higher school enrollment as a percentage of primary school enrollment (Table 4-6), calculated from Table 4-7, were built into the Index to prevent giving undue credit to a country like Paraguay which emphasizes primary education at the expense of education above grade 13.

For newspaper circulation we have data for 1930 and 1940 (Table 4-8). The problem here is one of propaganda, newspapers in the past tending to inflate their circulation figures in order to promote the importance needed to capture advertising and new readers while maintaining political influence. Seven countries showed a decline in circulation from 1930 to 1940, the same pattern as in the United States. Similarly, 10 Latin American countries saw a decline in circulation between 1940 and 1950,[15] as in the United States. With the growing popularity of radio and the expansion of telephone and other communication systems (and television later), this decline makes sense, but some countries, Chile and Peru, show enormous increases during the 1930s, gains that did not hold up during the 1940s.[16]

Although it would be reasonable to expect a correlation between newspaper circulation and the literacy of a country in terms of ranking, only in Argentina, Chile, Honduras, Brazil, Uruguay, and Venezuela are the rankings approximately the same for 1940 (cf. Tables 4-5 and 4-8). Bolivia, Ecuador, and Panama newspapers, to the contrary, seemed to be rather plentiful even though illiteracy was high. It is difficult to assess the apparent contradictions, especially as we do not know if or to what extent the newspapers were subsidized by private political interests or by governments, and the data are therefore used as reported. Owing to the worldwide pressure exerted by the U.S. Audit Bureau of Circulation, leading Latin American newspapers have sought to make their circulation data more reliable and have adopted standard criteria in return for certification by the Bureau.

[13] Ibid.

[14] World Campaign for Universal Literacy (Paris: United Economic and Social Council, 1963), p. 39.

[15] Wilkie, The Narrowing Social Gap, Appendix I.

[16] Ibid.

Table 4-6

**HEC ITEMS 7, 8, AND 9: SCHOOL-AGE POPULATION (7-14 AND 13-18) ENROLLED
IN SCHOOL, AND HIGHER SCHOOL ENROLLMENT AS A SHARE OF PRIMARY
ENROLLMENT IN LATIN AMERICA AND THE UNITED STATES, 1940[†]**

Country	7: Ages 7-14 Enrolled		8: Ages 13-18 Enrolled		9: Higher school enroll-ment as a percentage of primary school enrollment	
	Percent	Rank	Percent	Rank	Percent	Rank
Total average	42	*	4.5	*	1.2	*
ARGENTINA	71[a]	1	13.5[d]	2	2.1	3
BOLIVIA	23[a]	18**	2.2[d]	10**	1.1	6
BRAZIL	37[b]	11**	4.5[b, 1]	8	.6	15**
CHILE	70[b]	2	12.5[b]	3	1.0	7
COLOMBIA	35[b]	13	5.5[b]	6	.6[e]	15**
COSTA RICA	54[b]	6**	2.2[b]	10**	1.2[e]	4**
CUBA	61[a, 1]	4	1.1[d]	18	2.8[e]	2
DOMINICAN REP.	42[a]	9	1.7[d]	14**	.7	12**
ECUADOR	30[a]	14	1.3[d]	17	.9	8**
EL SALVADOR	28[a]	16	1.0[d]	20**	.4	20**
GUATEMALA	23[b]	18**	1.5[b, 2]	16	.7	12**
HAITI	16[a, 2]	20	1.0	20**	.4	20**
HONDURAS	25[b]	17	1.7[b]	14**	.5	18
MEXICO	50[b]	8	2.2[b]	10**	.9	8**
NICARAGUA	29[a, 1]	15	3.0[d]	9	.9	8**
PANAMA	56[b]	5	5.7[b, 1]	5	1.2	4**
PARAGUAY	62[a]	3	8.0[d]	4	.6	15**
PERU	37[b]	11**	5.3[b, 2]	7	.7	12**
URUGUAY	54[a, 3]	6**	16.1[d]	1	5.5	1
VENEZUELA	38[b]	10	2.0[b]	13	.8	11
UNITED STATES	81[c]	*	49.0[d]	*	10.7	*

[†]Calculations based upon data in Table 4-7; and upon Methodological
Appendix, where noted.

1. 1938.
2. 1942.
3. 1939.

a. Population ages 7-14 from ACA.

b. Age distribution from UNDY (1948) predicted for 1940 using
Method II.

c. Age distribution from USA (1952) predicted for 1940 using
Method II.

d. Population ages predicted for 1940 using Method III.

e. 1941.

SOURCE: As cited in notes above.

Of all the items in the HEC Index, telephones and motor vehicles are often considered to be luxury items in Latin America in contrast with the United States where they are considered to be important to the basic standard of living. The telephone is hard to obtain in Latin America, even when one has money; because few lines and telephones are available there are generally waiting periods of one year or more. Used telephones are sold at auction and command hundreds of dollars or more. Often the subscriber must buy stock in the telephone company. Thus the telephone is considered a status symbol in many countries. But it is more than a symbol of luxury. It is a means by which the masses can make contact with the world outside their own immediate locale. It offers a quick way to get medical aid and to report emergencies, as well as a means of communication to obviate expensive or time-consuming travel. Most of all, it is vital to illiterates who cannot otherwise communicate conveniently and inexpensively. Seen in this light, the number of telephones per 100 persons becomes an important item in the HEC Index (Table 4-9).

The number of persons per motor vehicle in use can also be considered a crucial social factor (Table 4-10). Latin American governments tend to treat private motor vehicles as a luxury despite complaints from the middle and lower classes who aspire to the freedom of mobility. Taxes have made automobile imports prohibitive in many countries, where the cost of an auto is doubled or tripled by tariffs; other countries have decreed an outright ban on importation of large-sized autos. Even in Brazil, where autos are manufactured, the internal taxes on ownership may more than double the cost of a vehicle.

A government may limit the use of the auto to protect foreign exchange lost in import of automobile component parts and/or fuel, but in the twentieth century the public does not view the motor vehicle as a luxury except in price. The poor use buses which offer an inexpensive mode of

Table 4-7

EDUCATIONAL ENROLLMENTS IN LATIN AMERICA AND THE UNITED STATES, 1940

Country	Primary Grades 1-6 (thousands)	Secondary Grades 7-12	Higher Grades 13 and Above
ARGENTINA	1,930[a]	140,000[a]	42,000[a]
BOLIVIA	136[g]	10,137[b,1]	1,482[b]
BRAZIL	3,121[a]	347,352[b,1]	20,000[a]
CHILE	633[a]	80,000[a]	6,448[b]
COLOMBIA	614[a]	63,000[a]	3,713[c,3]
COSTA RICA	65[h]	2,000[a]	820[c,3]
CUBA	453[h]	27,423[c,4]	13,949[c,3]
DOMINICAN REP.	132[a]	7,000[a]	868[c]
ECUADOR	181[h]	6,000[a]	1,755[b]
EL SALVADOR	96[a]	3,309[c]	395[b]
GUATEMALA	137[a]	6,552[c,2]	1,000[a]
HAITI	87[d,2]	5,768[c,3]	373[b]
HONDURAS	55[a]	2,544[c,2]	298[b]
MEXICO	1,800[h]	54,000[a]	19,000[a]
NICARAGUA	53[b,1]	1,253[d,2]	450[b]
PANAMA	61[a]	4,060[d,1]	725[b]
PARAGUAY	115[h]	6,000[c,3]	1,238[b]
PERU	566[a]	40,393[e,2]	4,000[a]
URUGUAY	214[b,4]	27,000[c,3]	12,000[i]
VENEZUELA	266[a]	10,000[a]	2,125[b]
UNITED STATES	13,935[f]	7,113,282[f]	1,494,203[f]

1. 1938
2. 1942
3. 1941
4. 1939

SOURCE:
a. SNP   e. FCY
b. ISY   f. SAUS
c. BDOA   g. IVP
d. PAY   h. ACA
          i. UAE

Table 4-8

HEC ITEM 10: NEWSPAPER CIRCULATION IN LATIN AMERICA AND THE UNITED STATES, 1930 AND 1940

(Copies per 1,000 persons)

	1930		1940	
	Ratio	Rank	Ratio	Rank
Total average	48	*	54	*
ARGENTINA	145[a]	2	233	1
BOLIVIA	12	19	29	14
BRAZIL	50	6	38	10**
CHILE	82	4	122	4
COLOMBIA	14[b]	17**	32	12**
COSTA RICA	48	7	43[c]	9
CUBA	99	3	132	2
DOMINICAN REP.	14	17**	22	17
ECUADOR	33	9	38	10**
EL SALVADOR	29	11**	26	16
GUATEMALA	15	16	19	18**
HAITI	5	20	5	20
HONDURAS	21	15	19	18**
MEXICO	32	10	46	8
NICARAGUA	29	11**	27	15
PANAMA	52	5	71	5
PARAGUAY	28	13	32	12**
PERU	24	14	62	6
URUGUAY	201	1	125[d]	3
VENEZUELA	34	8	57[e]	7
UNITED STATES	345[f]	*	328[g]	*

a. Circulation not given for all newspapers.
b. Circulation not given for city of Bogotá.
c. Circulation given for 3 of 5 newspapers.
d. Circulation given for 12 of 60 newspapers.
e. Circulation given for 15 of 30 newspapers.
f. 1929.
g. 1939.

SOURCE: EPIY (1931), 63:37, pp. 260-266; (1941), 74:4, pp. 212-227; (1950), 83:5, pp. 21-46, Part 2. U.S. data from USA (1952), p. 470.

travel, reaching most villages that are accessible by road. Buses are always crowded even when they run frequently. They are used as transportation to markets where the rural people bring their products. This, in turn, leads to contact with people and communities, contact with new ideas and approaches, as well as a way of earning extra income. Trucks are used mainly for transportation of goods, but it is common sight to see them load people to earn money instead of returning empty.

There were fewer persons per vehicle in 1930 than in 1940 for nine countries (Argentina, Brazil, Costa Rica, Cuba, Dominican Republic, Guatemala, Honduras, Nicaragua, and Venezuela), probably because before 1930 cars were freely imported. Cuba ranked fourth in Latin American number of persons per motor vehicle in 1940 but fell to sixteenth in 1970 owing both to external embargo by the United States and to Castro's internal embargo. Bolivia's seventeenth and thirteenth ranks in 1940 and 1950, respectively might appear to be incorrect but any visitor to Bolivia in the late 1960s or early 1970s can verify that there seemed to be more automo-

biles vintage 1945-1950 than all others combined,[17] most of these being in the taxi service.

Conclusion

Despite a number of difficulties we have been able to project the 12-item HEC Index backward to 1940. Although some of the data suffer from problems of reliability, the fact that there are as many as 12 items increases the reliability of the Index as a whole by decreasing the significance of any particularly unreliable statistic. Parsimony of factor analysis that reduces the number of items to a fewer, representative number would override individual variations in the Index from country to country with the result of increasing the significance of unreliability.[18]

[17] ibid.

[18] For factor analysis of the data, see ibid., Appendix IV.

Table 4-9

HEC ITEM 11: NUMBER OF TELEPHONES PER 100 PERSONS IN LATIN AMERICA AND THE UNITED STATES, 1940

Country	1940[a] Number	Rank
Total average	.80	*
ARGENTINA	3.20	1
BOLIVIA	.17	17
BRAZIL	.70	8
CHILE	1.80	3
COLOMBIA	.45	10
COSTA RICA	.40[b]	11
CUBA	1.60[c]	4
DOMINICAN REP.	.20[b]	15
ECUADOR	.28	14
EL SALVADOR	.30[b]	13
GUATEMALA	.10[b]	18
HAITI	.07[d]	19
HONDURAS	.06	20
MEXICO	.90[d]	6
NICARAGUA	.18[b]	16
PANAMA	1.00	5
PARAGUAY	.33	12
PERU	.50	9
URUGUAY	2.30	2
VENEZUELA	.80	7
UNITED STATES	15.90[b]	*

a. Data are for 1941 unless otherwise specified.
b. 1940.
c. 1942.
d. 1939.

SOURCE: BDOA, except U.S. data from ISY (1942), p. 303.

The summary data for four times of measurement — 1940, 1950, 1960, 1970 — indicate that Latin America has been undergoing a structural revolution unparalleled in proportion in the history of the region. The total social gap narrowed by 19 percent between 1940 and 1950, 21 percent between 1950 and 1960, and almost 25 percent between 1960 and 1970. Contrary to any assumption that health gains in Latin America made their greatest advance during the 1940s and 1950s, the highest gain for the region as a whole came during the 1960s, especially in comparison with the 1950s (see Table 4-1). For education factors the rate of change in the region was highest in the 1950s, followed by the 1940s, trailed by the 1960s in spite of the push promised by the Alliance for Progress. The highest change in the communication component of the Index came in the 1960s.

Table 4-10

HEC ITEM 12: NUMBER OF PERSONS PER MOTOR VEHICLE IN USE[a] IN LATIN AMERICA AND THE UNITED STATES, 1930 AND 1940

Country	1930[b] Number	Rank	1940[c] Number	Rank
Total average	472	*	406	*
ARGENTINA	38	1	50	3
BOLIVIA	1,015	19	728	17
BRAZIL	199	8	232	9
CHILE	155	7	111	6
COLOMBIA	485	13	329	10
COSTA RICA	64	3	180	7
CUBA	86	6	96	4
DOMINICAN REP	279	11	609	15
ECUADOR	1,010	18	621	16
EL SALVADOR	645[d]	14	487	12
GUATEMALA	252	9	538	14
HAITI	865[d]	16	1,129	20
HONDURAS	1,942[d]	20	855	18
MEXICO	277	10	192	8
NICARAGUA	908[d]	17	932	19
PANAMA	71[d]	4	45	2
PARAGUAY	676[d]	15	505	13
PERU	362[d]	12	345	11
URUGUAY	42	2	30	1
VENEZUELA	76	5	107	5
UNITED STATES	4.8	*	4.3	*

a. Includes autos, buses, trucks; excludes motorcycles and farm trucks.
b. For 1929 unless otherwise indicated.
c. 1938.
d. 1928.

SOURCE: ISY (1942), pp. 284-285.

With the social gap between the United States and Latin America closing rapidly, it is obvious that not only the aspirations but also the ability of the masses will increase. New demands are certain to be placed upon political leadership, demands that heretofore were limited by a low level of population stamina (owing to ill health), a low level of societal participation (owing to illiteracy and lack of school experience), and a low level of personal communication (owing to the inhibited spread of ideas either through newspapers, telephones, or vehicular mobility). The time is drawing near, then, when dictators will no longer be able to be "president for life" by simply restricting all forms of communication.

Methodological Appendix

Method I

Life expectancies were not available for Argentina, Cuba, Ecuador, Haiti and Uruguay for 1930 and 1940, nor for Peru for 1930. The data reported were predicted for those years based on data for 1950, 1960, and 1970.[19] A linear regression model was used. This is the best model assuming that the relationship is linear.

[19] Ibid., Appendix I.

The formula for finding the prediction of life expectancy given a particular year is:

$$y' = bx - b\overline{x} + \overline{y}$$

where

y' = predicted life expectancy
x = given year
$\overline{x}$ = average of the years known
$\overline{y}$ = average of life expectancies known

and

$$b = \frac{\Sigma (x_i - \overline{x})\, y_i}{\Sigma\, (x_i - \overline{x})^2}$$

Readers who doubt that the linear assumption is reliable are encouraged to use an exponential function or parabolic function to predict these life expectancies.

Method II

Populations of age groups 7-14 and 13-18 were not available for any country. For half the countries population data was given for age groups 5-9, 10-14, and 15-19. We needed the populations for age groups 7-14 and 13-18 in order to calculate the percentages for these age groups which are enrolled in primary and secondary education, respectively. To obtain the necessary information the following method was employed:

1. The mean of each age group was calculated.

Age group	Mean age
5-9	7
10-14	12
15-19	17

2. The total population for each age group was divided by 5 years giving an estimate for the population for ages 7, 12, and 17. For example,

Age	Population	Mean age	Population	
5-9	200	7	40	(200 ÷ 5)
10-14	150	12	30	(150 ÷ 5)
15-19	100	17	20	(100 ÷ 5)

3. The population distribution was assumed to be a linear function of age. Therefore using the data (in the box) a regression line was obtained, $\widetilde{y} = bx + a$, where x = age and $\widetilde{y}$ = predicted population. Thus, given any age we estimated its population size.

4. To get the population for age-group 7-14, we found the estimated populations for ages, 7, 8, and 9, and added these to the existing populations for ages 10-14, giving a total population figure for ages 7-14. For the group 13-18 we took the population for 15-19, added the estimate for ages 13 and 14, and subtracted the estimate for age 19, giving the total population for ages 13-18.

Method III

For countries where these age groups were not available, the data from 1950, 1960, and 1970 were used to estimate the percentage of 13-18 year olds enrolled in 1940. Because of high percentage increases between 1950 and 1960 and between 1960 and 1970 the relationship was assumed *not to be* linear. (The data did not fit a $y = bx + a$ equation — if this equation were used, negative percentages would appear for 1940, which is not possible). Therefore, the relationship was assumed to be exponential, fitting the form $y = ae^{bt}$. Using a logarithmic transformation, we get

$$\log y = (\log a) + b\,(.4343t)$$

This is a linear equation of the form

$$Y' = A + bX \qquad \text{where} \quad \begin{aligned} Y' &= \log y \\ X &= .4343t \\ A &= \log a \\ t &= \text{year} \end{aligned}$$

Using this equation one can apply linear regression techniques in order to estimate the desired percentage for a given year.

Source Abbreviation

AAA   Bustamente, Miguel. "Public Health and Medical Care," *Annals of The American Academy of Political and Social Science,* 208 (1940), pp. 153-161.

ACA   Moreno y García, Roberto. *Analfabetismo y Cultura Popular en América.* México, D.F.: Editorial Atlantes, 1941.

AES   Moll, Aristades A. *Aesculapius in Latin America.* Philadelphia: Saunders, 1944.

BDOA   *Basic Data on the Other American Countries.* Washington, D.C.: Coordinator of Inter-American Affairs, 1945.

BRLA   Collver, O. Andrew. *Birth Rates in Latin America: New Estimates of Historical Trends and Fluctuations.* Berkeley: Institute of International Study, University of California, 1965.

EPIY   *Editor and Publisher International Yearbook.* New York, 1931, 1941, and 1950.

FCY   United States, Department of Commerce. *Foreign Commerce Yearbook.* Washington, D.C., 1948.

ISY   *Inter-American Statistical Yearbook.* New York: MacMillan, 1940, 1942.

IVP   *Bolivia, Informe del Vice-Presidente* [*del Consejo Nacional de Educación*] La Paz: Editorial del Estado, 1942.

LAFW   Soule, George, David Efron, and Norman T. Ness. *Latin American in the Future World*. New York: Farrar and Rinehart for the National Planning Association, 1945.

NLTLA   Arriaga, Eduardo E. *New Life Tables for Latin American Populations in the Nineteenth and Twentieth Centuries*. Berkeley: Institute of International Studies, University of California, 1968.

PAY   *Pan American Yearbook*. New York, 1945.

SBS   United States, Bureau of the Census: *Summary of Bio-Statistics — Brazil*. Washington, D.C., 1944.

SHUS   *Historical Statistics of the United States: Colonial Times to the Present* [1962]. Stanford: Fairfield Publishers, [1965]. (Originally published as U.S. Bureau of the Census, *Historical Statistics of the United States*.)

SNP   Wilkie, James W. *Statistics and National Policy.*

Statistical Abstract of Latin America Supplement 3. Los Angeles, UCLA Latin American Center Publications, University of California, 1974.

SY   *Stateman's Yearbook*. London, 1942.

UAE   Uruguay, Dirección General de Estadística. *Anuario Estadística de la República Oriental del Uruguay*. Montevideo, 1940.

UNDY   United Nations. *Demographic Yearbook*. New York, 1948.

UNSY   United Nations. *Statistical Yearbook*. New York, 1951.

USA   United States Bureau of the Census. *Statistical Abstract of the United States*. Washington, D.C.

WPP   Woytinsky, W. S., and E. S. Woytinsky. *World Population and Production: Trends and Outlook*. New York: Twentieth Century Fund, 1953.

YOE   Usill, Harley V., ed., *Yearbook of Education* London, 1937.

Chapter 5

Research Perspectives on the Revised Fitzgibbon-Johnson Index of the Image of Political Democracy in Latin America, 1945-75

Kenneth F. Johnson

Instituto de las Américas, Buenos Aires
and
University of Missouri, St. Louis

Scholarly opinions may have an impact beyond the circles of academic institutions and governmental policy-making centers when these opinions are widely disseminated via the public media. How this dissemination occurs takes on special importance, critically so, when expert opinions have been aggregated statistically. In the recent past, scholarly opinions about the status of democratic practices in Latin America, formulated by North Americans, have drawn public attention in the southern part of the hemisphere. A case in point involves the Fitzgibbon-Johnson Index which surveys scholarly images of political democracy in Latin America at 5-year intervals.[1]

Commenting on the most recent survey, that of 1975 (see data in Table 5-1), a writer for the then independent and highly influential Mexican newspaper *Excélsior* wrote that "the three most democratic nations in Iberoamerica are Costa Rica, Venezuela, and Mexico, in this order, according to 84 political scholars in the United States."[2] The writer, Armando Vargas, quoted my report on the 1975 survey in such a way as to create a favorable image for his native

country (Costa Rica) and for his host country (Mexico).[3] Thus he ignored my caveat which pointed out that the survey does not involve interval data but only ordinal data (as in this year's "beauty contest" wherein candidates are compared with each other and not with last year's beauties) and therefore we cannot say ex cathedra that Mexico has improved its position from 5 years earlier when it was in fifth place. Nor did the journalist quote my conclusion, based upon my research and interviews with Mexican poltical figures since 1970, that the status of democratic practices in that country had probably declined.[4] (With such traditionally democratic nations as Chile and Uruguay having fallen victim to military coups during the quinqennium 1970-75, Mexico only appeared to have improved its position.) And finally, the journalist for *Excélsior* did not report that my study also contains a revised scale that did not place Mexico among the top three countries in terms of "political democracy" (see Table 5-2), the revision having been developed with the advice of Wilkie to reduce serious methodological problems for the entire series of surveys.[5]

The *Excélsior* article takes on special significance

[Editors' Note: For Professor Johnson's study entitled "Measuring the Scholarly Image of Latin American Democracy, 1945-1970," originally planned for publication here, see Wilkie and Turovsky, eds., *Statistical Abstract of Latin America,* 17 (1976), pp. 347-365. Professor Johnson wishes to thank Merle Kling and James Wilkie for their encouragement and support of this ongoing project.]

[1] A résumé of the time-series results from 1945 through 1970 appeared in the international magazine *Visión,* March 13, 1971. See also Russell H. Fitzgibbon, "Measuring Political Change in Latin America," *Journal of Politics,* 29 (1967), p. 139.

[2] Armando Vargas, *Excélsior,* April 7, 1976.

[3] See my report entitled "Scholarly Images of Latin American Political Democracy in 1975," *Latin American Research Review,* 11:2(1976), pp. 129-140.

[4] *Ibid.,* p. 135.

[5] Full raw data (original and revised) are published for the first time in my "Measuring the Scholarly Image of Latin American Democracy 1945-70," in James W. Wilkie and Paul Turovsky, eds., *Statistical Abstract of Latin America,* Vol. 17 (Los Angeles, UCLA Latin American Center Publications, University of California, 1976), pp. 347-365.

Table 5-1

ORIGINAL FITZGIBBON-JOHNSON INDEX: U.S. VIEW OF DEMOCRACY IN LATIN AMERICA,[a] 1945-75

(15 criteria)[b]

Country	Rank 1945	Rank 1950	Rank 1955	Rank 1960	Rank 1965	Rank 1970	Rank 1975
ARGENTINA	5	8	8	4	6	7	5
BOLIVIA	18	17	15	16	17	18	17
BRAZIL	11	5	5	7	8	10	9
CHILE	3	2	3	3	3	2	11
COLOMBIA	4	6	6	6	7	6	4
COSTA RICA	2	3	2	2	1**	1	1
CUBA	6	4	7	15	18	13	7
DOMINICAN REP.	19	19	19	18	14	14	13
ECUADOR	14	9	10	10	12	9	14
EL SALVADOR	13	14	11	12	11	8	10
GUATEMALA	12	10	14	13	13	13	15
HAITI	16	18	17	19	20	20	20
HONDURAS	17	15	12	14	15	16	16
MEXICO	7	7	4	5	4	5	3
NICARAGUA	15	16	18	17	16	17	18
PANAMA	8	11	9	11	10	11**	12
PARAGUAY	20	20	20	20	19	19	19
PERU	10	13	16	9	9	11**	8
URUGUAY	1	1	1	1	1**	3	6
VENEZUELA	9	12	13	8	5	4	2

a. Excludes Latin American respondents added to the survey beginning in 1970.

b. The fifteen criteria are:
1. Educational level
2. Standard of living
3. Internal unity
4. Political maturity
5. Lack of foreign domination
6. Freedom of press, speech, assembly, radio, etc.
7. Free and honest elections
8. Freedom of party organization
9. Independent judiciary
10. Government accountability
11. Social legislation
12. Civilian supremacy
13. Ecclesiastical separation and freedom
14. Professional governmental administration
15. Local government

SOURCE: Kenneth F. Johnson, "Measuring the Scholarly Image of Latin American Democracy, 1945-1970," in James W. Wilkie and Paul Turovsky, eds., *Statistical Abstract of Latin America* 17 (1976), Table 3200; and Johnson, "Scholarly Images of Latin American Political Democracy in 1975," *Latin American Research Review* 11:2 (1976) p. 137.

because of several factual considerations relevant to North Americans who study Latin American political democracy. During the presidential regime of Luis Echeverría Alverez (1970-76), freedom of speech, which is a key item in the Fitzgibbon-Johnson index, was seriously abridged and academics and journalists were expelled from Mexico or "urged" to leave. Ironically, *Excélsior* itself was taken over under presidential initiative, an act the *New York Times* called totalitarian and likened to the regimes of Lenin and Hitler.[6] Also, efforts by former *Excélsior* staffers to create a new open forum were initially frustrated.[7] In the end, the re-

porter who had disseminated my "good news" about Mexico's democratic status found himself telling the *Washington Post* how he was forced to resign as chief of *Excélsior's* Washington office.[8]

This example taken from Mexico has generic relevance because a basic assumption of the Fitzgibbon-Johnson Index is that some measure of political democracy exists throughout Latin America and that we can compare the relative presence or absence of democracy among the Latin American states without specific reference to, say, the Anglo-American model. Yet, we as North Americans specializing in various aspects of the political life of Latin America may not be able

[6] Quoted by Armando Vargas, "The Coup at *Excélsior*," *Columbia Journalism Review*, September/October, 1976, p. 45.

[7] According to a story in the Argentine newspaper *La Opinión* (November 26, 1976), the former editor of *Excélsior*, Julio Scherer García, who was ousted by president Echeverría's takeover, sought to reestablish a free press on a weekly basis with a journal called *Proceso*. The government's newsprint monopoly denied newsprint to Scherer but when he supplied himself on the open market the first

edition of *Proceso* was completely sold out. It was believed, according to the story, that the Mexican government was one of the principal "buyers" of the new journal to keep it off the street and thereby prevent continued public criticism likely to damage to Echeverría's desired image as a leader of the Third World.

[8] Vargas, "The Coup at *Excélsior*."

Table 5-2

REVISED FITZGIBBON-JOHNSON INDEX: U.S. VIEW OF
DEMOCRACY IN LATIN AMERICA,[a] 1945-75:
FIVE KEY CRITERIA[b]

Country	Rank 1945	Rank 1950	Rank 1955	Rank 1960	Rank 1965	Rank[c] 1970	Rank 1975
ARGENTINA	9	15**	15	4	7	14	5
BOLIVIA	16	13	12	15	16	15	15
BRAZIL	12**	5	4	6	10	17	16
CHILE	3**	2	3	3	2**	2	18
COLOMBIA	3**	6	9	5	5	5	3
COSTA RICA	2	4	2	2	1	1	1
CUBA	5	3	10	16	19	19	14
DOMINICAN REP.	20	20	20	20	14**	10	6
ECUADOR	12**	7	6	9	12	7	10
EL SALVADOR	14	14	8	13	11	8	8
GUATEMALA	11	11	13	12	13	9	9
HAITI	19	17	14	18	20	20	20
HONDURAS	17	8	11	14	14**	12	12
MEXICO	7	9	5	7	6	6	4
NICARAGUA	15	18	19	17	17	16	17
PANAMA	6	10	7	11	9	11	11
PARAGUAY	18	19	18	19	18	18	19
PERU	8	15**	17	10	8	13	13
URUGUAY	1	1	1	1	2**	3	7
VENEZUELA	10	12	10	8	4	4	2

a. Excludes Latin American respondents added to the survey beginning in 1970.
b. The five criteria are:
   1. Free speech
   2. Free elections
   3. Free party organization
   4. Independent judiciary
   5. Civilian supremacy
c. Calculated by Wilkie from data in Johnson's Table 3204, cited in source below.

SOURCE: Johnson, "Measuring the Scholarly Image of Latin American Democracy, 1945-1970," Tables 3201 and 3204; and Johnson "Scholarly Images of Latin American Political Democracy in 1975, p. 137. Cf. discussion of the Index by James W. Wilkie, *Statistics and National Policy,* Statistical Abstract of Latin America Supplement 3 (Los Angeles: UCLA Latin American Center Publications, University of California, 1974), pp. 480-481.

to divorce our judgments from ethnocentric influences, hard as we may try. Also, one must admit the possibility that the concept of democracy is not applicable to the political life of Latin America. Nevertheless, all of the Latin American countries have governments that subscribe to "democracy" as a desirable principle, even though it may be necessary for regimes to suspend the principle's application in operational terms for indefinite periods. Thus, the taking over of *Excélsior* may seem undemocratic to some and not so to others.

In short, Latin America boasts a range of democratic forms: people's democratic dictatorship (Cuba), military-populistic democracy (Panama, Peru), official single- party systems (Mexico), and official two-party systems (Brazil). Even the old-style dictators like Paraguay's Stroessner and Nicaragua's Somoza regularly legitimize themselves via "elections" in which the people have little choice. The Fitzgibbon-Johnson Index, then, may be measuring the degree of "undemocracy" in Latin America. Certainly the onslaught of the Echeverría regime against various organs of the Mexican news media and control of newsprint via a

government monopoly (a common Latin American practice) suggests that "undemocracy" may be a more meaningful concept in terms of freedom of speech and press; so that to say such-and-such countries are the most democratic in Iberoamerica becomes a somewhat empty affirmation.

Ironically one of the goals of the now defunct Alliance for Progress (which cost the United States over US $20 billion) was to promote nonviolent democratic political change throughout Latin America. When the Alliance ended around 1972, most of the area was under some form of dictatorship whereas the reverse was true when the Alliance was initiated in 1961. Since creation of political democracy in Latin America was a foreign policy goal of the United States it could be argued that it is appropriate for U.S. scholars to inquire into the status of Latin American democratic practices, albeit in terms of the paradoxical "undemocracy." Perhaps, it is more appropriate to relate the matter of United States interventionism in Latin America through foreign assistance to the "ups" and "downs" of what we perceive Latin American political democracy to be. This task I have undertaken in a recent study with my colleague Miles

Williams. We find both quantitative and qualitative evidence to support the contention that U.S. aid to Latin America has had a deleterious effect on democratic political development during recent decades.[9] It is, thus, fruitful to compare the scholarly image of political democracy, using statistical tests of significance, with a measurable output of United States foreign "aid" policy.

Also, we are developing a method of reinterpreting the Fitzgibbon-Johnson surveys, for example, to show by how many points a country decreased in its democratic image even as its relative standing in Latin America gained during a given quinquennial period. This method involves the construction of a Democratic Rating Coefficient (DRC) and a Power Rating Coefficient (PRC), the latter based on an experimental supplementary instrument that was appended to the standard Fitzgibbon-Johnson questionnaire for the first time in 1975. I hope that by the time of the 1980 survey we will have perfected a methodology with which to estimate political "distances" between country ranks. Also, I hope to continue measuring the interface between political power, democracy, and interventionism in Latin America, it being important to test political democracy by relating it to both internal and external influences.

With regard to interpretation, users of the Index should consider the composition of the panels of experts who generate the judgments that are aggregated statistically. Prior to 1970 only resident scholars in the United States were surveyed. The overwhelming preponderance of these experts were ethnically "non-Latin." Beginning in 1970, however, I formed a panel of resident Latin American scholars who were ethnically "non-North American." The 1970 survey had nearly equal numbers of resident U.S. and resident Latin American scholars. The latter were drawn from Mexico, Venezuela, and Argentina not only because of financial limitations but also because of my own rapport with persons who could be counted upon to answer the questionnaire competently and promptly.[10]

In the 1970 survey a major effort was successfully made to encourage all the respondents throughout the hemisphere to answer on the same day to avoid the situation of some experts voting before and others after a coup, thus making it difficult to aggregate the data in any meaningful way. By 1975, however, financial constraints were quite severe and no effort was made to secure a Latin American panel of experts from many countries. Because I was in Argentina, I was able to administer a Spanish-language version of the questionnaire during July 1975. The test respondents were journalists and academics from the provinces of Buenos Aires and Tucumán), with most choices dictated by personal rapport. To complicate matters in 1975, however,

Argentina was undergoing a virtual civil war and the Power Rating Coefficient had to be omitted for reasons of political sensitivity. Moreover, I had to promise then, and again in 1976, not to divulge the names of most of the Argentine respondents for at least a year.[11]

Viewing the revised Index results (not given here) for the Argentine scholars in 1975, I find that although the Argentines viewed the status of political democracy in the neighboring republics of Chile and Uruguay more pejoratively than did the North Americans, both the Argentines and the North Americans tended to downgrade the positions of Brazil and Cuba and to upgrade the positions of the other 18 countries. Otherwise, there were few major differences between the Argentines and the North Americans. (Because the Argentine sample was taken in July, and the North American in November, data sets have not been aggregated.)

Although I tried to secure a balanced sample of Latin Americans in both 1970 and 1975, the question of political sensitivity, the legacy of Project Camelot, and the more recent disclosures of United States espionage activity, all have made it extremely difficult to secure meaningful responses in Latin America. As I write these lines from Buenos Aires in November, 1976, I would not think of asking my panel of experts from last year to repeat their survey participation — four of them have been threatened by right-wing death squads, and two are in hiding after having received threats from the left. And in Latin America as a whole, I doubt that at the present time a truly random sample on any political topic could be administered anywhere without hazard except in Costa Rica and Venezuela.

Presuming, however, that in future years it will be possible to conduct political surveys in Latin America, it will be crucial to find panelists who really know about the political systems of other Latin American countries. Since relatively few social scientists in Latin America consider themselves to be specialists on Latin America as a whole, it may be necessary to rely heavily on Latin American journalists. But even Argentine journalists who have cooperated with my survey profess relative ignorance of large areas such as Central America (except for Panama).

For these reasons, and to follow Wilkie's suggestion that it is necessary to maintain the U.S. view of Latin American democracy which the Index originally measured, it is necessary to present findings of the Index without intermingling the Latin American view. Tables 5-1 and 5-2 here offer a consistent summary of the original and revised U.S. views.

In further refining the conceptual basis of the Fitzgibbon-Johnson Index, it is also necessary to make explicit the contention that we need to make a distinction between social and political democracy, the former encom-

[9] Kenneth F. Johnson and Miles W. Williams, "Power, Democracy, and Interventionism in Latin America: Reflections and Measurements," paper presented to the Midwest Association for Latin American Studies, October 7-9, 1976, University of Nebraska, Lincoln.

[10] For 1970 Latin American ranking of countries from most to least democracy, see my "Measuring the Scholarly Image of Latin American Democracy," Tables 3200 and 3204.

[11] I had been invited to present my findings on the Argentine survey to the Sociedad Argentina de Sociología in November 1976, but could not do so because of terrorist threats, some of which declared the entire field of sociology to be "subversive" and condemned the collaboration of Argentine scholars with North Americans.

passing social welfare made possible by leaders for the masses without regard to the latter's requirement that leaders and policies be chosen by secret ballot elections. In this view, social democracy was heavily weighted in the original Index, which had the purpose, as originally conceptualized, of measuring political democracy. If we accept this distinction, then the issue of whether or not "democracy" can exist under military regimes can be answered quite simply. In the words of Juan Pereira Fiorilo, a Bolivian scholar with whom I visited recently in La Paz,[12] social democracy is still possible under generals who came to power via politically undemocratic methods.

[12] Interview in La Paz, Bolivia, September 1976. See also development of his argument in Juan Pereira Fiorilo, *Sociopolítica de los Paises Subdesarrollados* (Cochabamba, Editorial Canelas, 1971).

In conclusion, if we see the Fitzgibbon-Johnson Index not so much as a measure of which country is "democratic" but how Latin American countries appear, in relation to each other, to U.S. observers as reflecting more or less democratic tendencies, then the Index will have sophisticated meaning, especially if the revised (political) Index is compared with the original (social) Index for the 5-year intervals since 1945 — an Index with a time depth now of 30 years. In further developing this Index, my motivating concerns are humanitarian and academic, hoping thereby to provide policymakers and scholars with concepts, methods, standards, and data with which to guide and assess their practical programs and academic teachings.

About the Contributors

Roderic A. Camp, associate professor of political science and director of Latin American Studies at Central College, Pella, Iowa, is author of *Mexican Political Biographies, 1935-1975* (University of Arizona Press, 1976) and of articles in *Foro International, Latin American Research Review, Journal of Inter-American Studies and World Affairs, Journal of Developing Areas, The Americas, Revista Inter-Americana de Sociología,* and *Historia Mexicana.*

Kenneth F. Johnson, who received his doctorate at UCLA, has taught at the University of Southern California and is now at the University of Missouri in St. Louis. He is the author of *Mexican Democracy: A Critical View* (1971) and *Political Forces in Latin America: Dimensions in the Quest for Stability* (with Ben B. Burnett, 1970).

Donald B. Keesing is senior economist in the Development Economics Department of the World Bank. Trained at Harvard, he has taught economics at Columbia University, Stanford University, University of North Carolina at Chapel Hill, and Williams College. He has authored numerous articles in the fields of international trade and economic development published in *American Economic Review, Journal of Political Economy, Economic Journal, Journal of Development Economics, Review of Economics and Statistics, Journal of International Economics, Journal of Economic History, World Development,* and *Public Finance.*

Maj-Britt Nilsson, from Sweden, received her B.A. degree from UCLA in 1973. As part of her graduate research in Latin American Studies, she spent 1973 and 1974 in Bolivia, and earned her M.A. from UCLA in 1976.

Jorge F. Pérez-López, now economist in the Division of International Prices, U.S. Bureau of Labor Statistics, was formerly lecturer on economic policy, School of Business, State University of New York, Albany. His recent research with Edward E. Murphy on "Trends in U.S. Export Prices and OPEC Oil Prices," (*Monthly Labor Review,* 98:11 [November 1975], pp. 36-43) shows that OPEC import costs do not justify ever higher oil prices.

About the Editors

Kenneth Ruddle, former editor of the *Statistical Abstract of Latin America,* is now research associate in the Resource Systems Institute, East-West Center, Honolulu, Hawaii.

James W. Wilkie, who is also a contributor to this volume, is professor of Latin American History at the University of California, Los Angeles.